T0345132

Security and Organization within IoT and Smart Cities

Security and Organization within IoT and Smart Cities

Edited by
Kayhan Zrar Ghafoor, Kevin Curran, Linghe Kong
and Ali Safaa Sadiq

CRC Press
Taylor & Francis Group
Boca Raton London New York

CRC Press is an imprint of the
Taylor & Francis Group, an **informa** business

First edition published 2021
by CRC Press
6000 Broken Sound Parkway NW, Suite 300, Boca Raton, FL 33487-2742

and by CRC Press
2 Park Square, Milton Park, Abingdon, Oxon, OX14 4RN

© 2021 Taylor & Francis Group, LLC
CRC Press is an imprint of Taylor & Francis Group, LLC

ISBN: 9780367893330 (hbk)
ISBN: 9781003018636 (ebk)

Typeset in Times
by Deanta Global Publishing Services, Chennai, India

To our Families

Contents

Preface

The Internet of Things (IoT) has witnessed rapid progress in recent years. This technology provides Internet connectivity between objects and cyber space. Hardware manufacturing, software industry and networking capabilities are acting as game changers and promote the rapid deployment of IoT technologies. Smart Cities bring together the IoT technology and city infrastructure for better quality of life in areas such as energy usage, healthcare, environment, water and transportation. This can be done through IoT large scale deployment and sensing, data acquisition and heterogeneous networking. However, citizens in such smart environments are vulnerable with their private information and this will directly affect city services related to the daily life of people. The connectivity of billions of IoT devices opens many security vulnerabilities and threats that must be detected and mitigated. There is a significant interest to enable Artificial Intelligence (AI) techniques – that incorporate metaheuristics, machine learning and optimization algorithms for intelligent IoT communications and networking management. Specifically, machine learning algorithms and big data techniques open up indispensable opportunities to further analyze the characteristics of IoT networks.

AI has evolved as an important tool and an attractive research topic that constitutes a promising solution for IoT network optimization, intelligent attack analysis and detection, and providing quality of service (QoS) to deployed Smart Cities' networks. Thus, it is becoming necessary to develop intelligent techniques powered by AI to enable smart decisions, adaptation and modeling various technical problems in next-generation, massively connected IoT devices.

This book aims to provide the latest research developments and results in the domain of AI techniques for smart cyber ecosystems. It presents a holistic insight into AI-enabled theoretic approaches and methodology in IoT networking, security analytics using AI tools and network automation, which ultimately enable intelligent cyber space. This book will be a valuable resource for students, researchers, engineers and policy makers working in various areas related to cybersecurity and privacy for Smart Cities.

This book includes chapters entitled "An Overview of the Artificial Intelligence Evolution and Its Fundamental Concepts, and Their Relationship with IoT Security", "Smart City: Evolution and Fundamental Concepts", "Advances in AI-Based Security for Internet of Things in Wireless Virtualization Environment", "A Conceptual Model for Optimal Resource Sharing of Networked Microgrids Focusing Uncertainty: Paving the Path to Eco-friendly Smart Cities", "A Novel Framework for Cyber Secure Smart City", "Contemplating Security Challenges & Threats for Smart Cities", "Self-Monitoring Obfuscated IoT Network", "Introduction to Side Channel Attacks and Investigation of Power Analysis and Fault Injection Attack Techniques", "Collaborative Digital Forensic Investigations Model for Law Enforcement: Oman as a Case Study", "Understanding Security Requirements and Challenges in the Industrial Internet of Things: A Review", "5G Security and the Internet of Things",

"The Problem of Deepfake Videos and How to Counteract Them in Smart Cities", "The Rise of Ransomware Aided by Vulnerable IoT Devices", "Security Issues in Self-Driving Cars within Smart Cities", and "Trust-Aware Crowd Associated Network-Based Approach for Optimal Waste Management in Smart Cities".

This book provides state-of-the-art research results and discusses current issues, challenges, solutions and recent trends related to security and organization within IoT and Smart Cities. We expect this book to be of significant importance not only to researchers and practitioners in academia, government agencies and industries, but also for policy makers and system managers. We anticipate this book to be a valuable resource for all those working in this new and exciting area, and a "must have" for all university libraries.

Kayhan Zrar Ghafoor
Shanghai Jiao Tong University, China

Kevin Curran
Ulster University, UK

Linghe Kong
Shanghai Jiao Tong University, China

Ali Safaa Sadiq
University of Wolverhampton, UK

Acknowledgement

This book would not have been published without the contribution of several people. First and foremost, we would like to express our warm appreciation to the authors who worked hard to contribute the chapters and have chosen this book as a platform to publish their research findings. Special thanks go to the contributors' universities and organizations who allowed them the valuable time and resources towards the effort of writing the chapters. We would also like to express our warm appreciation to the reviewers who gave their valuable time to review chapters and help selecting the high-quality chapters.

Finally, we want to thank our families who supported and encouraged us despite all the time it took us away from them. Last and not least: we beg the forgiveness of all whose names we have failed to mention.

Kayhan Zrar Ghafoor
Shanghai Jiao Tong University, China
Kevin Curran
Ulster University, UK
Linghe Kong
Shanghai Jiao Tong University, China
Ali Safaa Sadiq
University of Wolverhampton, UK

About the Editors

Kayhan Zrar Ghafoor is currently working as an associate professor at the Salahaddin University-Erbil and visiting scholar at the University of Wolverhampton. Before that, he was a postdoctoral research fellow at Shanghai Jiao Tong University, where he contributed to two research projects funded by National Natural Science Foundation of China and National Key Research and Development Program. He is also served as a visiting researcher at University Technology Malaysia. He received a B.Sc. degree in electrical engineering, a M.Sc. degree in remote weather monitoring and a Ph.D. degree in wireless networks in 2003, 2006 and 2011, respectively. He is the author of two technical books, seven book chapters and 65 technical papers indexed in ISI/ Scopus. He is the recipient of the 2012 UTM Chancellor Award at the 48th UTM convocation.

Kevin Curran is a Professor of Cyber Security, Executive Co-Director of the Legal Innovation Centre and group leader of the Cyber Security and Web Technologies Research Group at Ulster University. He sits on the Advisory Group of the UK Cyber Security Council and the Northern Ireland Civil Service Cyber Leadership Board. His achievements include winning and managing UK & European Framework projects and Technology Transfer Schemes. Professor Curran has made significant contributions to advancing the knowledge and understanding of computer networks and security, evidenced by over 850 publications. Google Scholar lists his citations as 8012 with h-index of 36 and i10-index of 116. His expertise has been acknowledged by invitations to present his work at international conferences, overseas universities and research laboratories. He is a regular contributor to print, online, radio and TV news on computing and security issues. He was the recipient of an Engineering and Technology Board Visiting Lectureship for Exceptional Engineers and is an IEEE Public Visibility technical expert since 2008. He currently holds a Royal Academy of Engineering / Leverhulme Trust Senior Research Fellowship, awarded in 2016. Professor Curran's stature and authority in the international community is demonstrated by his influence, particularly in relation to the direction of research in computer science. He has chaired sessions and participated in the organising committees for many highly-respected international conferences and workshops. He was the founding Editor in Chief of the International Journal of Ambient Computing and Intelligence and is also a member of numerous Journal Editorial boards and international conference organising committees. He has authored a number of books and is the recipient of various patents. He is a senior member of the IEEE and a Fellow of the British Blockchain Association (FBBA). He has served as an advisor to the British Computer Society in regard to the computer industry standards and is a member of BCS and IEEE Technology Specialist Groups and various other professional bodies. He is one of the most interviewed technology experts in the UK with over 1500+ interviews in recent years https://kevincurran.org/interviews/.

Linghe Kong [S'09, M'13, SM'18] is currently a research professor at Shanghai Jiao Tong University. Before that, he was a postdoctoral fellow at Columbia University and McGill University. He received his Ph.D. degree from Shanghai Jiao Tong University in 2012, a Master's degree in TELECOM from SudParis in 2007, and the B.E. degree from Xidian University in 2005. His research interests include wireless communications, sensor networks and mobile computing.

Ali Safaa Sadiq is a senior IEEE member and currently a faculty member at Faculty of Science and Engineering, School of Mathematics and Computer Science, University of Wolverhampton, UK; he is also an adjunct staff at Monash University and Centre for Artificial Intelligence Research and Optimisation, Torrens University, Australia. Ali has served as a lecturer at the School of Information Technology, Monash University, Malaysia. Previously he has also served as a senior lecturer at the Department of Computer Systems & Networking Department, Faculty of Computer Systems & Software Engineering, University Malaysia Pahang, Malaysia. Ali has received his PhD, M.Sc, and B.Sc degrees in Computer Science in 2004, 2011, and 2014 respectively. Ali has been awarded the Pro-Chancellor Academic Award as the best student in his batch for both Masters and PhD. Ali has also been awarded the UTM International Doctoral Fellowship (IDF). He has published several scientific/research papers in well-known international journals and conferences. He was involved in conducting five research grants projects, three of which are in the area of network and security and the others in analyzing and forecasting floods in Malaysia. He has supervised more than five Ph.D. students and three Masters' students as well as some other undergraduate final year projects. He is currently involved in a research project named "CyberMind" that was funded by UK-Innovation. His current research interests include Wireless Communications, Network security and AI applications in networking.

Contributors

Ghufran Ahmed
Department of Computer Sciences
National University of Computer and
    Emerging Sciences
Islamabad, Pakistan

Younis Al-Husaini
Deakin University Centre for Cyber
    Security Research and Innovation
Deakin University
Geelong, Victoria, Australia

Haider Al-Khateeb
Wolverhampton Cyber Research
    Institute (WCRI)
Wolverhampton, University of
    Wolverhampton
Londonderry, UK

Rangel Arthur
Faculty of Technology
State University of Campinas
    (Unicamp)
Campinas, Brazil

Faisal Bashir
Cyber Reconnaissance and Combat
    (CRC) Lab
Bahria University
Islamabad, Pakistan

Ramesh Babu Battula
Department of Computer Science and
    Engineering
Malviya National Institute of
    Technology
Jaipur, India

Souvik Bhattacharyya
Department of Computer Science and
    Engineering
University of Burdwan
Barddhaman, India

Athan Biamis
School of Computing, Engineering &
    Intelligent Systems
Ulster University
Londonderry, UK

Ajay Biswas
Department of Computer Science and
    Engineering
University of Burdwan
Barddhaman, India

Kevin Curran
School of Computing, Engineering &
    Intelligent Systems
Ulster University
Londonderry, UK

Dipnarayan Das
Department of Computer Science and
    Engineering
University of Burdwan
Barddhaman, India

Gregory Epiphaniou
Wolverhampton Cyber Research
    Institute (WCRI)
University of Wolverhampton
Wolverhampton, UK

Reinaldo Padilha França
Faculty of Technology, Department of
    computing
State University of Campinas (Unicamp)
Campinas, Brazil

Kayhan Zrar Ghafoor
School of Mathematics and Computer
    Science
University of Wolverhampton
Wolverhampton, UK
and
Department of Software Engineering
Salahaddin University-Erbil
Erbil, Iraq

Hassan Jalil Hadi
Cyber Reconnaissance and Combat
    (CRC) Lab
Bahria University
Islamabad, Pakistan

Choy Kok Han
School of Information Technology
Monash University
Bandar Sunway, Malaysia
and
School of Computer Science
University of Nottingham
Nottingham, UK

Farhan Haroon
Cyber Reconnaissance and
    Combat (CRC) Lab
Bahria University
Islamabad, Pakistan

Yuzo Iano
Faculty of Technology, Department of
    computing
State University of Campinas
    (Unicamp)
Campinas, Brazil

Abeer Iftikhar
Department of Computer Science
Bahria University
Islamabad, Pakistan

Harsimranjit Kaur
Institute of Engineering and Technology
Chitkara University
Punjab, India

Shaminder Kaur
School of Engineering and Technology
Chitkara University
Himachal Pradesh, India

Suleman Khan
Department of Computer Sciences
Northumbria University
Newcastle, UK

Halgurd S. Maghdid
Department of Software Engineering
Koya University
Kurdistan Region-F.R.
Erbil, Iraq

Danish Mahmood
Department of Computing
Shaheed Zulfikar Ali Bhutto Institute of
    Science and Technology
Islamabad, Pakistan

Samuel McCammon
School of Computing, Engineering &
    Intelligent Systems
Ulster University
Londonderry, UK

David McElhinney
School of Computing, Engineering &
    Intelligent Systems
Ulster University
Londonderry, UK

Tariq Mehmood
Department of Computing
Shaheed Zulfikar Ali Bhutto Institute of
    Science and Technology
Islamabad, Pakistan

Seyedali Mirjalili
Center of Artificial Intelligence
    Research and Optimization
Torrens University Australia
Brisbane, Queensland, Australia

Ana Carolina Borges Monteiro
Faculty of Technology, Department of
    computing
State University of Campinas
    (Unicamp)
Campinas, Brazil

Aos Mulahuwaish
Department of Computer Science and
    Information Systems
Saginaw Valley State University
University Center, Michigan

Muhammad Najam Ul Islam
Cyber Reconnaissance and Combat
    (CRC) Lab
Bahria University
Islamabad, Pakistan

Lei Pan
Centre for Cyber Security Research and
    Innovation
Deakin University
Geelong, Victoria, Australia

Kashif Naseer Qureshi
Cyber Reconnaissance and Combat
    (CRC) Lab
Bahria University
Islamabad, Pakistan

Danda B. Rawat
Department of Electrical Engineering
    and Computer Science
Howard University
Washington, DC

Ali Safaa Sadiq
School of Information Technology
Monash University
Bandar Sunway, Malaysia
and
Wolverhampton Cyber Research
    Institute
School of Mathematics and Computer
    Science
University of Wolverhampton
Wolverhampton, UK

Naveen Naik Sapavath
Data Science and Cybersecurity Center
Howard University
Washington, DC

Arunima Sharma
Department of Computer Science and
    Engineering
Malviya National Institute of
    Technology
Jaipur, India

Balwinder Singh
Centre for Development of Advance
    Computing
Mohali, India

Mohammed Adam Taheir
Faculty of Technology Sciences
Zalingei University
Zalingei, Sudan

Claudia Tweedie
School of Computing, Engineering &
    Intelligent Systems
Ulster University
Londonderry, UK

Matthew Warren
Centre for Cyber Security Research and
    Innovation
Deakin University
Geelong, Victoria, Australia

Conor Woodrow
School of Computing, Engineering &
    Intelligent Systems
Ulster University
Londonderry, UK

1 An Overview of the Artificial Intelligence Evolution and Its Fundamental Concepts, and Their Relationship with IoT Security

Reinaldo Padilha França, Ana Carolina Borges Monteiro, Rangel Arthur and Yuzo Iano

CONTENTS

1.1 INTRODUCTION

Artificial Intelligence (AI) enables machines to learn from experiments, to adjust to new data inputs and to perform tasks as if they were human beings. It is a branch of computer science research that seeks, through computational symbols, to build mechanisms and/or devices that simulate the human being's ability to think and solve problems, that is, to be intelligent. Nowadays, technologies ranging from computers becoming chess masters to autonomous cars rely on deep learning and natural language processing. With these technologies, computers can be trained to perform specific tasks by processing large amounts of data and recognizing patterns in that data [1, 2].

Early AI research in the 1950s explored issues such as problem-solving and symbolic methods, arriving in the 1960s, when the US Department of Defense became

1

interested in this type of technology and began training computers to mimic basic human reasoning. Artificial Intelligence can be roughly defined as the ability of machines to think as human beings learn, perceive and decide which paths to follow rationally in certain situations [1, 2].

The desire to build machines capable of reproducing the human ability to think and act has existed for many years. This can be seen in the existence of autonomous machines. These early works paved the way for the automation and formal thinking that we see in today's computers, including decision support systems and intelligent research systems that can be designed to complement and expand human capabilities [3, 4].

With the computational evolution, Artificial Intelligence has gained more strength; considering that its development has enabled a great advance in computational analysis, and the machine can even analyze and synthesize the human voice. At first, studies on AI sought only one way to reproduce the human capacity for thinking, but it was no different to all research that evolves [3, 4].

Nowadays there are technologies like "Machine Learning" which, instead of programming rules for a machine and waiting for the result, are able to let the machine learn these rules on its own from the data, reaching the result autonomously. Where we speak of "Deep Learning", we are referring to a part of machine learning that uses complex algorithms to "mimic the neural network of the human brain" and learn an area of knowledge with little or no supervision. The system can learn how to defend against attacks on its own. There is also "Natural Language Processing," (NLP) which processing uses machine learning techniques to find patterns in large pure data sets and recognize the natural language. Thus, one example of applying NLP is sentiment analysis, where algorithms can look for patterns in social network posts to understand how customers feel about specific brands and products [5, 6].

AI automates repetitive learning and discovery from data, where it is different from hardware-driven robotic automation. Instead of automating manual tasks, AI performs frequent, bulky, computerized tasks reliably and without fatigue. For this type of automation, human interference is still essential in setting up the system and asking the right questions [7, 8].

AI adds intelligence to existing products, since in most cases Artificial Intelligence will not be sold as an individual application. Instead, the products people already use will be enhanced with AI functionality. Automation, chat platforms, robots and smart devices can be combined with large amounts of data to enhance many home and office technologies, from security intelligence to investment analysis [7, 8].

AI adapts through progressive learning algorithms to let data do the programming, finding structures and regularities in the data for the algorithm to acquire a capability: it becomes a classifier or a predictor. So just as the algorithm can teach itself how to play chess, it can teach itself which products to recommend next. And the models adapt when they receive more data. Retroactive propagation is an AI technique that allows the model to adjust through training and input of new data when the first response is not entirely correct [9, 10].

AI analyzes more data, and does so in greater depth, using neural networks that have many hidden layers; building a five-layer, hidden fraud detection system was almost impossible a few years ago. This has all changed with impressive computational power and big data, since it needs a lot of data to train deep learning models because they learn directly from the data. The more data that it is possible to put into them, the more accurate they become [9, 10].

AI achieves incredible accuracy through deep neural networks; examples ranging from interactions with Alexa to Google searches and Google Photos are all based on deep learning, where they keep getting more accurate as we use them. In the medical field, deep learning AI techniques, image classification and object recognition can now be used to find resonant cancers with the same precision as well-trained radiologists [9, 10].

AI gets the most out of data, when algorithms learn on their own, the data itself can become intellectual property. The answers are in the data; to be obtained is just need to apply AI to extract them. Since the role of data is more important than ever, it can create a competitive advantage. If these data already exist in a competitive industry, and yet everyone is putting similar techniques into practice, it is possible to get the one with the best data set [11, 12].

AI can be found today in healthcare providers, with Artificial Intelligence applications that result in medication and personalized x-ray readings. Personal assistants can act as coaches, reminding the user to take their medicine, to exercise or to eat healthy foods. In retail, AI provides features for online retailers, such as offering personalized recommendations and negotiating payments with consumers. Inventory management and site layout technologies are also enhanced with AI. In manufacturing, since AI can analyze IoT data from factories as it is transmitted from connected equipment to forecast load and demand using recurring networks, a specific type of deep learning network applied to sequential data. As in sports, where Artificial Intelligence is used to capture match images and provide coaches with reports on how to better organize the game, which includes position and strategy optimization on the pitch.

AI is a new wave of innovation, where economists call it the fourth industrial revolution, marked by the convergence of digital, physical and biological technologies, creating links between the boundaries of the three areas. Since AI is part of this next wave of innovation, it brings big changes in the way people and businesses relate to technology, share data and make decisions [11, 12].

The future of AI points to an increasingly transparent, ethically built technology that is part of everyday tasks, at work or in our personal lives, enhancing our cognitive abilities. AI can make humans more productive by releasing professionals from certain mechanical and repetitive tasks so that they can make the most of their ability to create and innovate in other industries [11, 12].

Therefore, this chapter aims to provide an updated review and overview of AI, addressing its evolution and fundamental concepts, showing its relationship as well as approaching its success, with a concise bibliographic background, categorizing and synthesizing the potential of technology.

1.2 ARTIFICIAL INTELLIGENCE FUNDAMENTAL CONCEPTS

Artificial Intelligence is a branch of computer science that aims to develop devices that simulate the human ability to reason, perceive, make decisions and solve problems, in short, the ability to be intelligent; it is the ability of electronic devices to function in a way that resembles human thought, implying perceiving variables, making decisions and solving problems, operating in a logic that refers to reasoning [1, 13].

According to the definition, intelligence is the "faculty of understanding, thinking, reasoning and interpreting", that is, the "set of mental functions that facilitate the understanding of things and facts", containing the ability to take advantage of the effectiveness of a situation and use it in the practice of another activity, as well as the ability to resolve new situations quickly and successfully, adapting to them through the acquired knowledge; as well as "artificial", it was "produced by man and not by natural causes" [3, 14].

Therefore, Artificial Intelligence is a field of science, whose purpose is the study, development and the use of machines to carry out human activities in an autonomous way. It is developed so that the devices created by man can perform certain functions without human interference [5, 15].

Through AI algorithms they learn differently from human beings, looking at things differently, being able to see relationships and patterns that escape us. With the computational evolution of AI, the development of algorithms is a central issue in it, which are a sequence of instructions that guide the operation of a software. In turn, it can result in movements of a hardware (a robot for example), as long as the logic of the algorithms it is used to create extremely complex rules. So that they (algorithms) can solve problems on their own, even when there are two or more paths to follow in a task, so for that, it is necessary to combine algorithms with data [7, 16].

Thus, AI made possible a great advance in computational analysis, and the machine can even analyze and synthesize the human voice, since it improves the performance of existing analytical technologies, such as computer vision and time series analysis, and includes language and translation barriers, expanding existing human capabilities and making them better. Machines perform tasks that are often more complex, solving problems with thousands of variables, but they will always work from the previous programming, a code that considers these variables, processes the data and determines what to do in each situation [9, 17, 18].

The main limitation of AI is that it learns from the data, since there is no other way to incorporate knowledge into it, meaning that any inaccuracy in the data will be reflected in the results, where any additional layer of forecasting or analysis needs to be added separately. Currently, Artificial Intelligence systems are trained to perform well-defined tasks, such as playing chess, or even those more advanced tasks such as driving a car. These systems are very specific, which focus on a single task and are still far from behaving like human beings [10, 19].

It is even a cliché to say that the volume of information produced by people has been growing exponentially, especially in recent years with social networks and other digital platforms with the rise of the Internet – but this is the central idea to understanding "Big Data", a massive set of data which serves as a basis for learning the most diverse AI techniques, such as machine learning, since this data revolution favored the AI scenario, where with more information available, researchers and companies are looking for intelligent and automated ways of processing, analyzing and using the data [10, 19].

The great advantage of Artificial Intelligence is that it allows people to perform tasks much faster, and with a degree of accuracy thousands of times greater than that of humans, where it improves decision making, helping to simplify analysis processes, able to organize and provide greater clarity to "fuzzy" or "confusing" data, being able to develop processes that involve correlations, regressions, structuring analyses of the data generated, among other things, serving as a basis for decision making; even more, if it is linked to a Big Data solution, which is capable of handling a huge volume of unstructured data, especially a company that values data-driven decision making [11, 19].

A virtual AI solution is capable of employing algorithms to perform more accurate segmentations, in order to suggest goods that are tuned to the analyzed consumer profiles, increasing the chances of developing good commercial strategies, considering its high level of process replicability, since the systems that compose it are able to perform the same analyses several times, ensuring that any workflow becomes scalable [11, 19].

AI contributes to the automation of logical, analytical and cognitive activities, generating greater speed in the treatment of information, serving as a complement to the automation of physical tasks, especially the production provided by robotic machines [1, 13].

An AI solution can be used to monitor machines and computational systems, which in the case of systems, their information comes from databases, reports, histories, among others. With respect to equipment, it can use data from sensors, cameras, records in monitoring software, among others. Thus, it has the ability to discover bottlenecks, failures and other weaknesses in the company's processes, reducing errors and increasing operational efficiency, reducing costs [1, 13].

Still considering its ability to make predictions about possible difficulties, so that the company takes action on time, through diagnoses of different sectors and processes, contributing to the mapping of risks and opportunities. In this sense, AI frequently checking key business performance indicators, contributing to a higher level of accuracy in the strategies defined by the managers [3, 14].

AI can optimize the service offered to the public in different aspects, in increasing agility in transactions, in delivering more efficient communication and with increased personalization, since AI can reduce the time needed to get responses and, at the same time, adapted to customer preferences; it can provide a "superior personalized personal experience", helping to eliminate the customer service dissatisfaction paradigm offered by companies [3, 14].

The use of AI can be fundamental to gaining competitive advantages, since the successful use of this technology can produce more and decrease its costs, gaining an immense competitive advantage. In the same way, self-learning systems are not autonomous systems, it is computers with the ability to examine complex data to learn and perfect specific tasks, which are becoming more popular nowadays [5, 15].

Artificial Intelligence basically consists of automated statistics from a base and variables. It consists of computational systems capable of making decisions based on standards analyzed in a large amount of data, instead of a pre-defined fixed logic, such as those used in conventional systems. That is, it makes it possible to understand the scenario, model and forecast demand, through an ideal cut and according to the type of activity or behavior being measured.

Still considering that the AI-based system is able to "learn" and increase its accuracy over time. Still pondering that AI technology when integrated the Internet of Things (IoT), uses the information collected by equipment and devices for the learning.

The IoT opens up a world of possibilities to promote greater integration between systems and equipment, in addition to feeding a database for AI. Artificial Intelligence applied to IoT should work as a blank canvas for the development of new products and services. In other words, the former's ability to efficiently debug a high volume of data, coupled with the latter's possibilities of interacting with users, represents virtually infinite options.

Common devices, when connected to the Internet, expand their data collection capacity and expand their view on the environment in which they are installed and located and possible trends. As a result, better services will be provided, from the registration and tracking of data to regularly monitor the determined state of a desired characteristic in the analyzed environment.

The large volume of data that can be captured by IoT sensors requires analysis and interpretation in order to actually be used. AI acts as a key role in IoT applications, where AI to gain insights from data more quickly and efficiently by identifying patterns and anomalies.

Together, these two technologies present a new paradigm, as they complement each other. Therefore, Artificial Intelligence comes in with the capture and processing of data. The Internet of Things with its property to deliver, in real time, the product or service to users.

1.3   AI TECHNOLOGIES AND EVOLUTION

An AI solution involves a grouping of various technologies, such as artificial neural networks, algorithms, learning systems, among others, that can simulate human capabilities linked to intelligence, such as reasoning, perception of the environment and the ability to analyze for making a decision. Where it is possible to highlight that the concept of AI is related to the ability of technological solutions to perform activities in a way considered intelligent, "learning for themselves" due to learning systems that analyze large volumes of data, enabling them to expand their knowledge [1, 3, 13, 14].

Generally, AI technologies are divided into two distinct approaches: Symbolic AI, where the mechanisms effect transformations using symbols, letters, numbers or words, thus simulating the logical reasoning behind the languages with which human beings communicate with each other; and connectionist AI, inspired by the functioning of human neurons, thus simulating the mechanisms of the human brain, such as Deep Learning, where the ability of a machine to acquire Deep Learning, imitating the brain's neural network. It is still possible to highlight a third approach, evolutionary AI, which uses algorithms inspired by natural evolution, that is, the simulation of concepts such as environment, phenotype, genotype, perpetuation, selection and death in artificial environments [3, 5, 14, 15].

"Machine Learning" involves a method of data evaluation that automates the development of analytical standards, involving computers using data to learn with just the minimum of programming, based on the conception that technological systems can learn using data, in order to discover patterns, make decisions and improve with little human interference, improving the performance of an activity over time [1, 13, 29].

Instead of programming rules for a machine and waiting for the result, it is possible to let the machine learn these rules on its own from the data that it is fed, arriving at the result autonomously, as the personalized recommendations on the current digital streaming platforms. However, machine learning is only a part of Artificial Intelligence, in which a program accesses a large volume of data and learns from it automatically, without human intervention [9, 18, 30].

"Deep Learning" is a special type of machine learning that involves artificial neural networks with several layers of abstraction; these artificial neural networks are discrete layers and connections that propagate data in the same way as it happens in the chain of human thought, being applied to pattern recognition and classification applications supported by data sets, referring to the part of machine learning that uses complex algorithms to mimic the brain's neural network and learn an area of knowledge with little or no supervision [3, 14, 32].

Thus, Deep Learning algorithms have the intelligence to recognize the voice and natural language, images and learning processes on their own, where the learning process takes place between their layers of mathematical neurons, in which information is transmitted through each layer, since in this scheme, the output of the previous layer is the input of the posterior layer. In this way, Deep Learning "trains" machines to perform activities as if they were human, processing data, as in the identification of images and speech recognition [5, 15, 33].

"Natural Language Processing" aims to study and attempt to reproduce development processes linked to the functioning of human language, using machine learning techniques to find patterns in large sets of pure data and to recognize natural language; where machines can understand better the texts, which involves context recognition, information extraction and development of summaries, among others, it is also possible to compose texts based on data obtained by computers, used in areas such as customer service and in the production of corporate reports. As in sentiment analysis, where algorithms can look for patterns in social media posts to understand how customers feel about specific brands and products [11, 19, 34].

In order for AI to be implemented, it needs a lot of data, and it is also important for the process of integrating the AI platform with business workflows and software, as well as to increase the accuracy of the information generated by it, a solution Big Data Analytics is important to generate insights and information from unstructured data, which will be used by the AI solution; it is still possible to use IoT to capture information from the equipment that feeds the AI, which will be grouped with the data generated by the solutions that manage them [11, 19, 28, 34].

AI is applied in various segments of the economy, such as Industry, having been a keynote of the industry for many decades in relation to automation, where machines keep getting smarter, since there is already equipment that manufactures and check products without needing to be operated by a human [1, 13, 29].

In the GPS (Global Positioning System), the routes are suggested by the application indicating the best path, where AI is used to interpret data provided automatically by other users about the traffic on the roads. Regarding autonomous cars in development, it does not need a driver to guide them, due to a combination of various technologies and sensors that provide data for the algorithms to guide the movement of automobiles [1, 3, 13, 14, 29, 32].

Customer service with respect to chatbots and systems with natural language processing increasingly intelligent to replace human attendants and be available to users with questions 24 hours a day. Also, technology is present in the same online commerce and retail environment, online store algorithms recognize user purchasing patterns to present them with offers according to their preferences [10, 19, 31].

In financial institutions, algorithms are used to analyze market data, manage finances and relate to their customers. Still, in law firms and legal departments, they already consider and rely on robots to perform, in a faster, more accurate, direct and economically accessible way, much of the processing work with reading and data processing that a professional does today. Nourishing these professionals with refined information for decision making and establishing the best applicable legal strategy [5, 7, 15, 16, 33].

AI represents a set of software, logic, computing and disciplines that aim to make computers perform functions that were thought to be exclusively human, such as perceiving the meaning in written or spoken language, learning, recognizing facial expressions and so on [10, 19, 31].

It is already present in the human routine, with increasingly modern smartphones, which rely on AI performing increasingly personalized tasks, since, behind every personalized recommendation and relevant research results, there is a combination of technologies that makes intelligence artificial work [10, 19, 31].

AI is an attractive concept for many parties involved in the business, science and government, since in economic terms, there is much advantage in having machines that perform tasks that used to need human beings, considering that an efficient AI solution can "think" more and process more information than any human brain, yet considering the potential to take human skills to places where people have a hard time reaching, such as remote locations on earth or outer space, where human expertise can be useful [9, 10, 18, 19, 30, 31].

In this sense, to be successful with AI, it is invariably necessary to bring enough computing power to support a reasoning task of the machine.

1.4   AI TECHNOLOGIES AND IOT

IoT is a technology capable of connecting electronic devices that are used daily connected to the internet, that is, it is a technological (re) evolution that allows the mutual connection between things, and the connection between things and users through applications, websites, among others. This range of possibilities and devices created and connected, makes the relationship between people and technology richer and thus changes the way they interact with the world around them [49, 50].

Data protection and cybersecurity are issues discussed in decision making at all companies since data is the new "money" in business.

Concerning IoT, it is necessary to have other cybersecurity technologies that provide layers of protection. Without them, an attacker can have access to devices for use such as locks, refrigerators, smart toys, smart TVs, cars, machines, among the most diverse types, since they are connected via the Internet. The major concern is regarding the vulnerability of these systems; preventing sensitive data from being exposed. When having a digitally invaded device, it is possible to have access to images, sounds, personal data and to have the life of a user monitored [49, 51].

With respect cybersecurity attacks caused by the disappearance of IT (Information Technology) perimeters and the scarcity of security qualifications, artificial intelligence is seen as a key tool to eliminate IoT cybersecurity gaps and win the battle against stealth threats in your IT infrastructures [50, 51].

A practical example of the union of AI and IoT in the virtual world is related to those IoT security systems that incorporate machine learning and other technologies based on Artificial Intelligence that are essential to detect and stop attacks directed at user devices and IoT and protect data and other high-value assets [49, 52].

A practical example of this union between AI and IoT, in the physical world, which impacts within the context of Smart Cities, is in the monitoring systems for cameras, since they are more traditional equipment of surveillance systems, still pondering that the cameras can also be operated through the IoT. In this model, the devices capture the images and transmit them to a central intelligence via the Internet [52, 53].

And with the use of Artificial Intelligence including natural language processing, facial recognition and augmented reality, it is possible to save significantly unnecessary complex infrastructures. Since this tool makes it much easier to deploy or even expand existing monitoring systems [52, 53].

Another example is in the case of motion sensors, in which these features are also optimized with the use of IoT. This tool allows chips to be allocated to internal and external areas of a property and to send motion detections to the heads of the security centre [49, 52].

What can be integrated with AI strategies for modeling a mechanism to control the image analysis process? This process would be carried out at a high level controlled by one or more instances of AI, which control or "program" mechanisms for processing and recognizing these signals, integrating intelligent processes with them. That is, digital knowledge-based for the interpretation of typical scenes and the recognition of positioned objects [49, 52].

In this way, it is easier to monitor warehouses, commercial complexes and homes more easily. When the sensor issues the alert, a team can be sent to the location to check the occurrence. If this is not possible, users can reposition the cameras and check the occurrence remotely. For these characteristics, places that offer restricted access to a small number of people, such as laboratories and centres with a large amount of intellectual property, benefit from this type of tool [49, 52].

With Artificial Intelligence, it is still possible to use sensors in digital cameras, it is common for video cameras to use three sensors (3CCD system – charge-coupled device), each sensor with a filter or a triple of trichrome filters on it, as safety devices and prevention, since it is possible to insert strategic motion sensors directly on office doors and to harness the warning system. In this way, attempts at data theft, fraud in logins, misuse of passwords by unauthorized individuals and embezzlement of money are filmed in real-time, collecting evidence [49, 52, 53].

In this sense, technological advances will continue to drive IoT applications, enabling significant improvements in terms of performance, energy consumption, connectivity, security and Artificial Intelligence, through image recognition, voice interaction and learning capacity.

1.5 DISCUSSION

Among the emerging technologies of this century, two deserve to be highlighted, which are the Internet of Things and Artificial Intelligence, because even with all the potential they have when operating in isolation, they can be combined to guarantee even greater optimization of processes, considering that AI is an area that studies how to make computers more like humans: autonomous and capable of making relevant decisions in the face of unknown contexts, with the main objective of Artificial Intelligence being to make a machine capable of imitating cognitive functions of a human being, so that it can make decisions based on past experience or even respond to actions completely unknown up to that moment [5, 7, 15, 16, 33].

The Internet of Things, on the other hand, is a branch of modern computing characterized by the use of wireless sensors, coupled with common everyday objects and connected to the great world network; this technology will lead the new Internet era, which connects elements of the real world, computers and people, which talks about a network that will connect everything in a large database, bringing various benefits to everyday life, such as preventing crime and accidents, allowing high productivity in industries through preventive maintenance on machinery and, of course, creating truly smart homes with connected devices, considering the possibilities of this technology are endless [24, 25].

With a connection to a processing centre, the sensors transmit information about the state of the objects, while another device, the actuator, is responsible for performing specific actions, and with that, it is possible to monitor these "things" and prevent certain incidental situations, or that is, favoring management with more control, since the philosophy of this technology concerns everyday objects being connected to the Internet, sharing a common database. Given that this is seen in practice with physical devices such as electronic devices, vehicles and buildings, sensors and others, capable of communicating with each other over a network, according to the IoT concept [24, 26].

IoT concerns the network of computers and devices, so it is concerned with issues of connectivity, competition, protocols, among other aspects, which is in contrast to AI, as a branch of cognitive computing that cares about philosophical issues, principles of analysis data, linguistics, statistics and neuroscience, among others [25, 27].

In fact, IoT does not exist without AI, for a very simple reason, IoT requires that several devices are connected and interacting with each other, taking into account that when using a human being to analyze and filter all the data generated between these interactions, thousands of data would be generated, so analyzing all of them manually would be almost impossible [20, 24].

Both technologies are easy to implement: IoT applications can be deployed in an agile manner bringing results in a short time; likewise, AI can be configured in a simple way, with specific functions in existing software, since it is increasingly common for the appearance of means of transport, door handles and household items connected to the Internet and consequently to computers and cell phones. Likewise, cars are joining the list of technological products, seeing an increasing tendency for vehicles to be connected and to be able to communicate with the user through applications on their smartphone [21, 26].

In the business sector, the Internet of Things allows a new form of interactivity with customers, reflecting on Industry 4.0 which brings several technologies to the factories, among which the main ones are precisely AI and IoT. Through IoT, it is possible to capture data in almost any situation, which generates a huge amount of information for companies, and with AI, it uses data to predict behaviors and make decisions [22, 27].

This is where AI comes in with a fundamental role of carrying out an analysis and obtaining results automatically, thus preventing a situation where a specific person has to analyze data manually. In addition, as AI has the ability to respond to various actions and behaviors, even unexpected, its use is indispensable with the IoT [23, 25].

The idea is to create systems that use the potential of these two innovations (AI and IoT) to have more efficient operations, to improve the interaction between man and machine and gain more robustness in data analysis, combining the need for data and IoT analysis with the optimization and treatment of AI, creating solutions that are able to offer customization and learning at the same time. Dealing with connected systems, which analyze habits, patterns and preferences of almost anything and make quick and assertive decisions. Since there is a large volume of data generated by IoT sensors, it is possible to create an intelligent system to make decisions based on this information [21, 22, 26, 27].

For this reason, both technologies complement each other in general; the data that the Internet of Things generates can be processed by Artificial Intelligence software, which will optimize decision-making and contribute to increasing the agility of the processes [20, 24].

In a monitoring context, the sensors and actuators connected by the IoT architecture collect an immense amount of information in real-time, which is practically impossible for a human being to process. In this sense, an AI is activated to explore and analyze this data, in order to make the best possible decision [21, 22, 26, 27].

Artificial Intelligence is present in the human daily life in things, where sometimes it is not even perceived, such as the AI applied present in our social networks, since some mechanisms evaluate the user's search patterns, what is more viewed, and so the content displayed on this user's timeline is optimized and, as a consequence, it becomes more relevant to him or her [20, 24].

Another example is customer service, which is also in the process of being initiated by AI practices, which are systems that reproduce human actions, such as making decisions. In the same sense, that contact with the customer happens via chat, and instructions and information was passed on to him without his realizing that the attendant is not a person [20, 24, 25].

The spell checkers of text editors and smartphones are also the result of AI; to identify that there is a term misspelled, a system is needed that points out the problem and presents the right spelling [1, 13, 20, 25].

Most of these applications use predictive analytics, which makes it possible to forecast a given situation in the future based on information from the past and on probability. From this, it is possible to get an AI to do a certain action whenever a sensor in the IoT network indicates a predetermined state; this would dispense with the need for human work and optimize this activity with increased accuracy [14, 23, 25, 32].

In the corporate world, within the industrial sector, the aid of both technologies (AI and IoT) on the machines is an important factor in the drastic reduction of errors, cost reduction and, thus, better results for the company. Since, over the years, there was a movement known as "factory robotization", where, through Artificial Intelligence machines, they are able to operate without the need to be programmed by humans, that is, they are totally autonomous [3, 23, 25, 29].

Automobile companies in the recent past have installed sensors in the car capable of recognizing dangerous movements and activating safety mechanisms to prevent accidents or more serious damage to drivers. In logistics, systems with AI and IoT are also found to be capable of managing all inventory, both in the location and validation of each item (IoT), as well as in the decisions about which products will be shipped, in what order and at what time (AI) [3, 23, 25, 29].

There are also examples in marketing (with analysis of consumer behavior), health (such as surgeries performed remotely), agriculture (with sensors that perform various measurements and make decisions based on them) and in many other areas [9, 17, 18, 22].

The effective relationship between Artificial Intelligence and the Internet of Things is mainly dealing with the market, since it will enable companies to innovate their management systems and optimize the development of their products. They are directly linked from the moment that the AI determines the data generated by the system and allows them to be used in an optimized way by the IoT [14, 19, 31].

AI and IoT are already part of the current and modern world, and it is important to be concerned with them to ensure a competitive advantage, since the use of these tools drives business, with the possibility of generating automated and more agile services, which, as a consequence, impacts the final consumer [11, 19, 28, 34].

In other words, it is useless to capture this huge volume of data if they are not interpreted and used correctly; the AI takes on the role of assuming more and more human actions, with more and more sophisticated software, which these actions will be applied to devices via the IoT.

So we can conclude that there is no conflict between AI and IoT, but a similarity, since IoT depends on AI to work well.

1.6   FUTURE TRENDS

For Artificial Intelligence to have a positive impact, it must be integrated with other technologies, considering cybersecurity becoming increasingly important for companies and therefore it must be a primary theme. With the help of AI, it is possible to implement the intelligence in antivirus systems and the development of security tools. In this way, it is possible to identify phishing threats, dangerous links and other threats more quickly. Likewise, Blockchain can work together with Artificial Intelligence to solve security, scalability and trust issues [47, 48].

It is also worth considering that autonomous cars do not make much sense without the Internet of Things (IoT) working with AI, since the IoT activates and regulates the sensors of the car, which collects data in real-time, while the AI models act in the vehicle decision-making part [45, 46].

Cyber attacks are increasing rather quickly, overcoming existing defensive measures, since, by limitation, humans are no match for today's cybercrime tricks. As such, AI systems will continue to play a significant role in controlling these attacks, with the use of Machine Learning, organizations are able to detect these security breaches with ease [43, 44].

Still it is worth considering that most real-time marketing activities are limited to automatic responses only. However, driven by AI, chatbots are a great example of how AI can contribute to corporate communication, increasingly being used by companies. Which are undergoing evolution, becoming even more intelligent, it has been possible to create optimized forms communication between machines, allowing companies to maintain a more agile and constant contact with their customers. With the help of this technology, organizations will manage interactions with customers in real-time across all channels, and they can also use AI marketing to improve customer retention [41, 42].

AI can also help marketers to find new audiences on social media and other platforms.

There will be an even greater rise in virtual assistants, developed through AI, which can facilitate people's routines by automating customer service and sales tasks, considering that in the coming years we will see a growth in the number of virtual assistants and chatbots, trends that are already used by banks and insurance companies [39, 40].

Facial recognition is one of the main features of biometric authentication; however, there are still reports on its imprecision and due to the large investment and in-depth research in this field, specialists are increasingly improving these tools; therefore, facial recognition is improving significantly with regard to accuracy and readability [37, 38].

With regard to security and privacy, the implementation of laws such as the GDPR (General Data Protection Regulation) and the LGPD (General Law for the Protection of Personal Data) oblige companies worldwide to be more concerned with the privacy of third party data, since many people do not know how organizations use their information, and in some cases, are not even informed about its use. For this reason, many people are raising concerns about AI security policies. In this sense, efforts are increasingly present to protect individual data using AI as a basis [35, 36].

And in the same sense, the extent the society more and more will depend on AI for some tasks, the more it will become familiar as many other technologies with which it will interact every day. Which leads to this growing dependence on AI will cause the that "artificial" intelligence becomes increasingly "natural" to human eyes.

1.7 CONCLUSIONS

The definition of AI is related to the ability of machines to think like human beings, to have the power to learn, reason, perceive, deliberate and decide in a rational and intelligent way, since it is the most powerful technological change in the area of computing, making smarter choices, as well as integrating predictive analytics into the applications we use every day.

It is through it and other technologies in development that devices connect to each other, modifying and simplifying the way people perform routine tasks.

Regardless of the fact that theoretical models about AI have existed for a long time, computers still needed three things to evolve, in fact, from simple computing to real AI:, which basically were access to a large amount of raw data to feed the data models, so that they continue to improve; there must be excellent data models for classifying, processing and analyzing data intelligently; as well as high power computing at an affordable cost so that fast and efficient processing is possible.

Thus, based on it (AI) the devices are able to adapt according to the data they receive, which this process differs directly from the system of common computers, which always follow the same logical commands. Making the advancement of this concept allows for routine applications, such as facial and voice recognition and word processing, which are increasingly simplified as possible.

IoT is the term created to explain the fact that several objects used in daily life are connected through the Internet, generating data and facilitating daily tasks, which allows obtaining data on human tendencies that, before, it was hard to imagine would be possible; the technology operating in this general information about behaviors that make up the volume of data is known as Big Data.

It is difficult to translate all this accumulation of data with traditional methods, because, in addition to the large amount, it is difficult to guess what information will be found, and that is where the technological process of natural language comes in, for example. Considering, through the combination of these strands AI, the computer shapes itself according to the information it finds, then, throughout the process, it changes with the results delivered, through machine learning.

Connecting diverse environments of life such as work, leisure, home, travel and others, in a single experience, AI will not only help people when we ask, but will also accompany them, anticipating needs and remembering important tasks.

In the same sense that, the technology present in social networks use image recognition to recommend photo markings; people use voice processing through personal assistants; online sales platforms make personalized product recommendations using machine learning algorithms; traffic apps predicts the best routes from your location with just one click, while autopilot cars use AI techniques to avoid traffic jams and collisions. In the same sense that the main online search engines are able to automatically fill in searches using AI resources and also predict what users want to search with great precision.

In this sense, it is possible to say and highlight that AI is already used in several sectors to analyze consumer trends, aiming to improve corporate processes and attract customers.

REFERENCES

1. Russell, S. J., & P. Norvig. 2016. *Artificial intelligence: A modern approach*. Malaysia: Pearson Education Limited.
2. Nilsson, N. J. 2014. *Principles of artificial intelligence*. Morgan Kaufmann.
3. Barr, A., & E. A. Feigenbaum, (Eds.). 2014. *The handbook of artificial intelligence* (Vol. 2). Butterworth-Heinemann.
4. Nilsson, N. J., & N. J. Nilsson. 1998. *Artificial intelligence: A new synthesis*. Morgan Kaufmann.
5. Mitchell, R. S., J. G. Michalski, & T. M. Carbonell. 2013. *An artificial intelligence approach*. Berlin: Springer.
6. Rahwan, I., & G. R. Simari, (Eds.). 2009. *Argumentation in artificial intelligence* (Vol. 47). Heidelberg: Springer.
7. Genesereth, M. R., & N. J. Nilsson. 2012. *Logical foundations of artificial intelligence*. Burlington: Morgan Kaufmann.
8. Steels, L. 1993. The artificial life roots of artificial intelligence. *Artificial Life*, 1(1_2), pp. 75–110.
9. Haugeland, J. 1989. *Artificial intelligence: The very idea*. MIT Press.
10. Poole, D. L., & A. K. Mackworth. 2010. *Artificial intelligence: Foundations of computational agents*. Cambridge University Press.
11. Cohen, P. R., & E. A. Feigenbaum, (Eds.). 2014. *The handbook of artificial intelligence* (Vol. 3). Butterworth-Heinemann.
12. Huhns, M. N. 2012. *Distributed artificial intelligence* (Vol. 1). Elsevier.
13. Jackson, P. C. 2019. *Introduction to artificial intelligence*. Courier Dover Publications.
14. Szolovits, P. (Ed.). 2019. *Artificial intelligence in medicine*. Routledge.
15. Hudson, V. M. 2019. *Artificial intelligence and international politics*. Routledge.
16. Steels, L., & R. Brooks. 2018. *The artificial life route to artificial intelligence: Building embodied, situated agents*. Routledge.
17. Krishnamoorthy, C. S., & S. Rajeev. 2018. *Artificial intelligence and expert systems for engineers*. CRC Press.
18. Agrawal, A., J. Gans, & A. Goldfarb. 2018. *Prediction machines: The simple economics of artificial intelligence*. Harvard Business Press.
19. Konar, A. 2018. *Artificial intelligence and soft computing: behavioral and cognitive modeling of the human brain*. CRC Press.
20. Allam, Z., & Z. A. Dhunny. 2019. On big data, artificial intelligence and smart cities. *Cities*, 89, 80–91.
21. Pramanik, P. K. D., S. Pal, & P. Choudhury. 2018. Beyond automation: The cognitive IoT. Artificial intelligence brings sense to the Internet of Things. In *Cognitive computing for big data systems over IoT* (pp. 1–37). Springer.
22. Vermesan, O., A. Bröring, E. Tragos, M. Serrano, D. Bacciu, S. Chessa, … & P. Simoens. 2017. *Internet of robotic things: converging sensing/actuating, hypoconnectivity, artificial intelligence and IoT Platforms*. River Publishers.
23. Poniszewska-Maranda, A., & D. Kaczmarek. 2015. Selected methods of artificial intelligence for Internet of Things conception. In *2015 Federated Conference on Computer Science and Information Systems (FedCSIS)* (pp. 1343–1348). IEEE.
24. Mittal, M., S. Tanwar, B. Agarwal, & L. M. Goyal. (Eds.). 2019. *Energy conservation for IoT devices: Concepts, paradigms and solutions* (Vol. 206). Springer.
25. Siozios, K., D. Anagnostos, D. Soudris, & E. Kosmatopoulos. 2019. *IoT for smart grids*. Springer.
26. Al-Turjman, F. (Ed.). 2019. *Artificial intelligence in IoT*. Springer.
27. Solanki, V. K., V. G. Díaz, & J. P. Davim. 2019. *Handbook of IoT and big data*. CRC Press.

28. Davenport, T. H., P. Barth, & R. Bean. 2012. *How 'bigdata' is different*. MIT Sloan Management Review.
29. Alpaydin, E. 2020. *Introduction to machine learning*. MIT Press.
30. Raschka, S., & V. Mirjalili. 2019. *Python machine learning: Machine learning and deep learning with Python, scikit-learn, and TensorFlow 2*. Packt Publishing Ltd.
31. Molnar, C. 2019. *Interpretable machine learning*. Lulu.com.
32. Ramsundar, B., P. Eastman, P. Walters, & V. Pande. 2019. *Deep learning for the life sciences: Applying deep learning to genomics, microscopy, drug discovery, and more.* O'Reilly Media, Inc.
33. Charniak, E. 2019. *Introduction to deep learning*. MIT Press.
34. Eisenstein, J. 2019. *Introduction to natural language processing*. MIT Press.
35. Forcier, M. B., H. Gallois, S. Mullan, & Y. Joly. 2019. Integrating artificial intelligence into health care through data access: can the GDPR act as a beacon for policymakers? *Journal of Law and the Biosciences*, 6(1), p. 317.
36. Franklin, J. 2019. *GDPR has kept AI ethical despite concerns*. International Financial Law Review.
37. Tang, J., X. Zhou, & J. Zheng. 2019. Design of Intelligent classroom facial recognition based on Deep Learning. *Journal of Physics: Conference Series*, 1168(2), p. 022043. IOP Publishing.
38. Chen, K., S. M. Lu, R. Cheng, M. Fisher, B. H. Zhang, M. Di Maggio, & J. P. Bradley. 2020. Facial recognition neural networks confirm success of facial feminization surgery. *Plastic and Reconstructive Surgery*, 145(1), pp. 203–209.
39. Guzman, A. L. 2019. Voices in and of the machine: Source orientation toward mobile virtual assistants. *Computers in Human Behavior*, 90, pp. 343–350.
40. Bernard, D., & A. Arnold. 2019. Cognitive interaction with virtual assistants: From philosophical foundations to illustrative examples in aeronautics. *Computers in Industry*, 107, pp. 33–49.
41. Davenport, T., A. Guha, D. Grewal, & T. Bressgott. 2020. How artificial intelligence will change the future of marketing. *Journal of the Academy of Marketing Science*, 48(1), pp. 24–42.
42. Kumar, V., B. Rajan, R. Venkatesan, & J. Lecinski 2019. Understanding the role of artificial intelligence in personalized engagement marketing. *California Management Review*, 61(4), pp. 135–155.
43. Yampolskiy, R. V., & M. S. Spellchecker. 2016. Artificial intelligence safety and cybersecurity: A timeline of AI failures. arXiv preprint arXiv:1610.07997.
44. Darraj, E., C. Sample, & C. Justice. 2019. Artificial intelligence cybersecurity framework: Preparing for the here and now with AI. In ECCWS 2019 18th European Conference on Cyber Warfare and Security (p. 132). Academic Conferences and Publishing Limited.
45. Lin, P., K. Abney, & R. Jenkins, (Eds.). 2017. *Robot ethics 2.0: From autonomous cars to artificial intelligence*. Oxford University Press.
46. Nathani, B., & R. Vijayvergia. 2017. The Internet of intelligent things: An overview. In 2017 International Conference on Intelligent Communication and Computational Techniques (ICCT) (pp. 119–122). IEEE.
47. Salah, K., et al. 2019. Blockchain for AI: Review and open research challenges. *IEEE Access*, 7, pp. 10127–10149.
48. Mamoshina, P., L. Ojomoko, Y. Yanovich, A. Ostrovski, A. Botezatu, P. Prikhodko, … & I. O. Ogu. 2018. Converging blockchain and next-generation artificial intelligence technologies to decentralize and accelerate biomedical research and healthcare. *Oncotarget*, 9(5), p. 5665.

49. Xiao, L., X. Wan, X. Lu, Y. Zhang, & D. Wu. 2018. IoT security techniques based on machine learning: How do IoT devices use AI to enhance security? *IEEE Signal Processing Magazine*, 35(5), pp. 41–49.
50. Ali, B., & A. I. Awad. 2018. Cyber and physical security vulnerability assessment for IoT-based smart homes. *Sensors*, 18(3), p. 817.
51. Li, J., Z. Zhao, R. Li, & H. Zhang. 2018. Ai-based two-stage intrusion detection for software defined iot networks. *IEEE Internet of Things Journal*, 6(2), pp. 2093–2102.
52. Fang, H., A. Qi, & X. Wang. 2019. Fast authentication and progressive authorization in large-scale IoT: How to leverage AI for security enhancement. *IEEE Network*, 34(3), 24–29.
53. Szychter, A., H. Ameur, A. Kung, & H. Daussin. 2018. *The impact of artificial intelligence on security: A dual perspective.*

2 Smart City
Evolution and Fundamental Concepts

Arunima Sharma and Ramesh Babu Battula

CONTENTS

2.1 SMART CITY

The city is considered to be an area surrounded by human habitats, including services like transportation, education, communication and others. These services are getting more effective and easier to manage with the help of the Internet of Things. The Internet of Thing (IoT) [1] gathers all of the data from the surrounding environment with the help of sensors in different formats. Data gathered from different sources help to monitor, manage and control the services within a city. The development of "Smart Cities" with the integration of IoT leads analytic technology and wireless IoT protocols in the context of smart usage of resources. IoT will enhance the impact of services, improve quality, increase performance, reduce cost and utilize resources efficiently. The proclamations on Smart City initiatives and investments are also hastening. Among the major IoT projects, Smart City projects are prominent. At initial level, Smart City initiatives get a positive response, and these programs are initially driven by government and private stakeholders. Many countries, are trying to improve their living standards by adopting Smart City concepts.

2.2 CHARACTERISTICS OF A SMART CITY

Smart City, is a city that is enriched with the resources required to maintain all services without any interruption and delay. Some features required to develop a city into smart city are energy, mobility, data, infrastructure and devices. The United Nations suggested 17 sustainable development goals for a better future, in the Sustainable Development Agenda 2030 [2] (Figure 2.1). These goals help to achieve the basic requirements around the globe.

2.2.1 SMART ENERGY

Devices require a source of energy to perform any operation. With the expectation of an increase in the number of devices with time it becomes impossible to provide

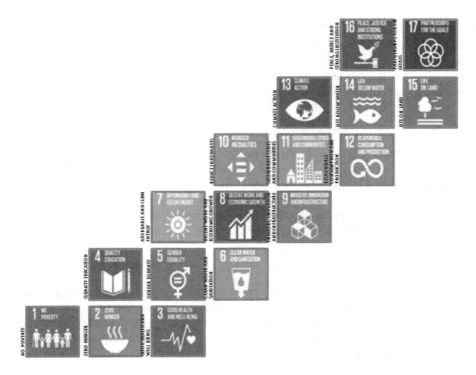

FIGURE 2.1 17 Sustainable Development Goals [2]

energy to all devices. Renewable energy [10] sources are the best way to overcome the issue of carbon consumption and to obtain an efficient amount of energy required without harming the environment.

2.2.2 SMART DATA

In a Smart City every digital device is going to be get connected with each other by the help of high speed Internet. Heterogeneous data is going to get generated in large volume with high speed. This type of data is termed "Big Data" [3]. Different factors like data volume, velocity with which data is going to be getting generated, variety of data in different formats, and much more critics making it a sensitive aspect.

2.2.3 SMART TRANSPORT

Smart City needs a smart way to manage the traffic without any interruption. In case of emergency an immediate response is required by services like ambulance, fire trucks and others. Transportation needs to be responsive with respect to the nearby environment. It will help to reduce the occurrence of accidents on the road. Currently different automated vehicles are being developing to make future of transportation [11] efficient and effective.

2.2.4 SMART INFRASTRUCTURE

Data [6] require a better way to manage and interpret situations. They require architecture to connect all the entities together. The whole structure needs to be strong to manage all of the services effectively within the city. The responsiveness has to be high to manage and control all things.

2.2.5 CONNECTED DEVICES

Different devices developed by different developers and used by different users generate complexity and a lack easiness to be used together. To decrease the complexity and accessibility it is necessary to connect all devices from a single platform so that their maintenance and management will become easy. The developer usually does not create software versions that are compatible with others, which require regular software updating to maintain the Integrity among devices.

2.2.6 CONNECTED MOBILITY

All of the devices connected to each other play an important role to maintain the consistency between each other and control on the nearby environment. They communicate with each other and perform in real time operations. The effect of mobile nodes has to be setup in such a way that there will remain independency among nodes in the mobile network. In place of the fixed connected network [5] Smart Cities required a dynamic control system that can also work efficiently in the dense area. With the help of 5G wireless communication, the mobility of a device does not affect its performance.

2.3 COMPONENTS OF SMART CITY

Several entities [7] are there which affects smartest city in different manners which are categorized among six categories (Figure 2.2). They are needed to be compatible for an effective application in the smart city frame. These components are as follows -

2.3.1 ECONOMY

The Smart City needs devices and techniques which are not costly in terms of manufacturing and maintenance. The cost factor plays the most important role in terms of getting accepted by users. It has to be in a range of different holders of the city. By using IoT devices the Smart City will become capable of reducing the cost of management and it will make it easy to maintain any services.

2.3.2 GOVERNANCE

Administration plays an important role in establishing a framework around the city. This frame has several different components of IoT which work in parallel together

FIGURE 2.2   Components of Smart City [15]

and maintain a consistency. The acceptance and implementation is governed by them.

2.3.3 ENVIRONMENT

The Smart City is not only concerned about the citizens, but also about the nearby environment and living beings. Pollution control, the irrigation system and others are the main concerns of the Smart City. It supports renewable sources to reduce carbon consumption and tries to use natural resources smartly.

2.3.4 LIVING

The lifestyle of people will get affected in smart city in different manner whenever a new solution is get introduced to make daily life better and efficient. Different parts of Smart city are helping to make living standard not only better but safe also.

2.3.5 PEOPLE

People are the main entities in the Smart City. They are the users of the whole service, which is designed to make their life safe, easy and social. IoT is helping to make people connected.

2.3.6 MOBILITY

Mobility with constant services are must expected quality by devices. But the management of services with mobility becomes challenging with increasing population and number of devices respectively. The services get affected by this dense area and the restriction of the network. 6G the new upcoming communication mobile generation will be helpful with the IoT framework to establish uninterrupted services in Smart City.

2.4 ROADMAP

Any strategy for Smart City is get established when it fulfil some conditions or standards which are considered as a roadmap for Smart City. These standards are developed on the basis of Community, Policy and support of citizens.

1. *Community*: In Smart City community is a group of people or users for which any process needs to be getting developed which can help them in some way by resolving issues and challenges of daily life.

In Community it is necessary to gather data related to users within with respect to the present framework. The main objective for the operation in system needs to fulfil initial requirements. It helps to utilize available resources efficiently and develop community in a better way.

2. *Policy:* Every new initiative needs to come under certain limits to complete its role safely. These policies will help to set the responsibilities, goal, plan, phases and steps of the process to be followed in certain time.
3. *Citizen Support:* Any plan of government or administration is not going to be fruitful without the support of citizens and acceptance from them. In Smart City it is one of the biggest challenges to make citizens adjustable and agree for any new plan or management. The inputs and outputs initiated by management help to modify the strategies which takes time to make them suitable for citizens.

2.5 APPLICATION OF SMART CITIES

2.5.1 HEALTH MANAGEMENT

Healthcare is counted as the main essential facility, and a city which has fit, healthy citizens is stable in every province. Smart Health Management is a combination of

Smart IoT Technology in the health sector. At the present time, several initiatives have been aimed at reassuring a wide view of health and wellbeing. Smart Health technology communicates and is involved in various tasks which produce health related data with the help of IoT devices. These data are shared among doctors, researchers and professionals for better diagnosis and resolutions of health issues in real-time. These Electronic Health Data are easy to maintain, which saves costs and the time of both patients and hospital staff.

IoT in healthcare simplifies the connection between heterogeneous data collected from different smart devices and sensors to extract valuable information. Recent advanced technologies based on AI (Artificial Intelligence), image analysis and others play the leading role after in identification and observation with the help of data. It helps in early diagnosis and prevention regarding any health issues which are present or can arise in the future. IoT helps in integrating the test results, real time monitoring, past health data and other important information. This improves the system effectiveness. AI is used for data analysis of different laboratory tests, X-Rays, CT scans and past data records. AI-based apps make data easy to access any time, any where. Recent technologies like Blockchain provide secure methods for sharing and maintaining Electronic Health Records with additional services like payments, transactions and insurance [12].

2.5.2 SMART TRANSPORTATION

Smart Cities use transportation [8] and mobility as an important parameter in the development of cities. As cities are turning "smart", smart transportation is a key element in understanding their visualization of the future. There are many cities which are facing issues of high population. These cities are having a large population residing required an organized public transportation system. Technical gap in the city transportation system required to be the bridged in their voyage to turn smart. Smart transportation is one of the major areas evolving in the life of "Smart Citizens". It includes distributed systems that collect data regarding traffic, vehicles, and related services like tolls, nearby places, vehicle system information, etc. These data help to increase system efficiency and accessibility, and to optimize the model.

Modified system updates help to upgrades existing modes of transport by applying software update or introducing new ones (hardware update). Connected automated cars, "Smart" cars, mobile apps, vehicle rental services, bicycle sharing, electronic vehicles, etc., are some examples of the Smart Transportation system.

One of the main aim of Smart Transport systems [15] is to reduce the use of private transportation with respect to public transportation. It helps to preserve fuel and the environment. The selection of a green energy based transportation system and clean fuel are beneficial for the future. In Smart Transportation systems there will be sufficient number of assets to provide services to the growing urban population. But for better living standards, cities need to look beyond conventional solutions, like the interlinking of roads, construction upgrades and electric vehicles. Smart Cities are facing several challenges: traffic congestion, insufficient parking areas, lack of connectivity, road safety and environmental pollution. Smart transportation is capable of handling these challenges by suggesting an incorporated mechanism that is easy to use, multi-modal and intelligently integrates automated traffic control, tolls and fare collection. These Smart services provide services like smart parking, vehicle location identification and route diversion updates. A central control system can combine smart transportation with real-time response, auto data updating, collecting user information, emergency services management and vehicle system monitoring.

2.5.3 WASTE MANAGEMENT

The present technologies in the field of smart waste management include the use of IoT sensors that measure levels of the waste in Smart bins. The real time data of Smart bins are sent over Cloud for further management and data analysis. By manipulating this data, several decisions are taken "smartly" like decisions of waste collection, the optimized path to collect waste and much more. They are having the flexibility and notification required, but Smart waste management [14] has several drawbacks and challenges. Fault tolerance, physical security, data sharing and privacy are some of the issues present in the waste management system. RFID tags, weight sensor, ultrasonic sensor and controller are some devices that are used in bins nowadays.

The "smart bins" have several advantages, including as follows

- The use of solar energy gives a continuous power supply to IoT devices and sensors. The green energy decreases the cost and power consumption. This also increases the capacity of the system and reduces waste collection.
- The smart bin uses wireless media for communication of information on different levels and ensures data get processed in real time. 5G-based communication is the best for areas having high mobile density.
- Path optimization for waste collection visits reduces congestion on the roads and creates less interruption in traffic flow, resulting in quick collection in busy areas to overcome overloaded bins.
- A reduction in the number of waste collection visits helps to save fuel, power and money. It also helps the environment by reducing carbon dioxide emission.
- The "smart bins" are easy to use and handle. Some bins support waste classification.

User feedback regarding Smart Bins improve performance and make it better from both economic and environmental perspective. It helps to raise public awareness to move towards renewable energy sources. Environmental cleanliness, recycling, better planning, etc., are some common benefits of Smart Waste Management.

2.5.4 SURVEILLANCE

At present, the cities we are living in are considered to be living entities. These Smart Cities are developing, growing and becoming more and more complex with time. Nevertheless, many of their most persistent issues, such as the requirement for service modification and monitoring misconduct, remain complicated like before. On the other hand, city bureaucrats now have the abilities to implement and modify analytics technology according to requirements. These abilities help to make surveillance effective for Smart Cities.

With the escalation in surveillance technology [13, 16] and analytical approaches, Smart Cities work more smartly and effectively to increase performance efficiency. ne of the major challenge is to resolve connectivity issues. It is never guaranteed that strong connection is available within each and every corner of city premises. Therefore, the most necessary task is to manage the data gathered, irrespective of data inter relation and data correctness, to make sure the system can take real-time decisions. An adequate amount of data (local) storage is essential for the system to differentiate the most sensitive data at the point of computation. This requires edge computing technology with embedded data storage.

The rapid progress of digital data in real time demands edge analysis in less time with digital storage for different correlated applications. Fast, data access and management are becoming ever more critical. According to a recent study, "The Digitization of the World from Edge to Core", it is estimated that in an upcoming area, we have zeta-bytes of data per day till 2025, which is the multidimensional variety of data generated with high velocity in high volume within Smart cities must set up a smart way to develop techniques to use data for good. In different ways, cities are already doing these operations by using intelligent street lights, optimizing traffic, emergency response, advanced surveillance and enhanced security operations, leading to a drop in the crime rate.

In future, a true smart city needs an "edge computation" approach to the collection, classification and management of data closer to the devices or sensors. Therefore, data can be stored and analyzed for a longer duration of time in the edge or cloud or backend storage. Edge computing collects data on network video recorders (NVRs) in real-time. With the integration of AI and image analysis technologies, it is easy to find, locate and update user regarding the nearby environment to send warnings.

2.5.5 WATER MANAGEMENT

One of a Smart City's most significant pieces of infrastructure is its water management system. As populations grow, it is expected that consumption of all resources as well as of water is going to increase. "Smart water management" signifies moving towards smart use of water bodies and treatment of wastewater to ensure the best use of the precious resource of water. Water is the basis of life and is used in different applications such as energy production, industry, agriculture, etc. A smart water system is designed to gather significant and useful data about the faults in the system, water flow, water pressure and distribution across the city. Further, it is challenging to estimate consumption and use of water accurately.

Water distribution and management must be rigorous and feasible. It should be prepared with the required capacity to be supervised and communicate with other systems to achieve more refined and accurate information. Additional proficiencies are expanded when systems are able to share information.

"Smart Water Management" is one of six main module that helps a city to be a smart city, with smart energy, mobility, smart infrastructure, public services and amalgamation. The goal is to make cities more sustainable and efficient. In Smart City water management we generally talk about general approaches regarding handling this priceless resource, and the substructure systems surrounding its source, treatment and distribution. Modification of water management systems with Internet connection, and big data management become Complicated. This also allows measurement of useful valuse such as reservoir and groundwater, and quick updates, which improve efficiencies. The capabilities of flood prediction in real-time mapping and weather prediction help to save the lives of many.

The identification of irregularities in water consumption patterns is beneficial to both the providers and end users. Smart cities can optimize and reduce water wastage and the cost of supply. Demand of high-energy request for water management and delivery systems are often take too lightly. It significance that improving working efficiency through useful data will decrease greenhouse gas emissions and reduce costs at the same time.

Spontaneously arranging repair tasks will help avoid major disasters. Globally, as the water demand propagates and climate change generates a question mark in the future regarding water, it is to be expected that water loss is mitigated. Maybe as a solution water treatment plants with real time communication can detect and maintain water smartly to prevent or mitigate any damage.

Instigating smart solutions comes with essential challenges and limitations. Updating city infrastructure with recent IoT technologies is the best solution. Small scale solar can be used in some areas as a source of power for sensors, but issues of privacy and security need to be resolved.

2.5.6 SMART PARKING

Smart Parking has been converting the parking experience and cumulative profits for an enormous range of customers. Techniques that depend on variation through practice, innovation, and significance services, with an exceptional manner incorporate different advantages.

Among several available mobile applications through smartphones and other devices, AI based solutions provides the fastest route and lowest prices, and points out attractions along the way. Data-backed capabilities give us significant status on daily activity and help refine driving routine for best benefits.

The rapid growth in the number of vehicles on the road, along with the maladministration of accessible parking spaces, leads to parking-related complications; smart parking systems offer ways out of this issue.

With the upsurge of Smart Cities, AI will be a big part of our daily lives. It could even help resolve one of the complicated problems most drivers face daily: the search for a place to park their vehicle.

Daily parking issues arise due to:

- Unviability of sufficient parking spaces in a highly populated area.
- Inefficient use of available space.

- Dynamic search of available nearest parking spaces.
- Difficulty in locating vehicles in crowded parking lots.
- Traffic congestion.
- Parking spaces are taken by others.
- Inconvenient and improper parking.
- High parking cost.
- Absence of handicapped spaces.
- Unclear policies and rules.

Merging innovation and technology in smart parking help Smart Cities to increase efficiency and tackle several issues. Smart parking will decrease fuel consumption because the parking space can be searched easily. Drivers will also save costs and time. Smart parking makes the most use of smartphones and other sensing devices to determine vacant parking slot. It is done through the use of surveillance cameras, and sensors embedded at individual parking spaces.

Taffic jamming being an extensive issue in many urban areas, smart parking offers a fractional but major solution. Most of the traffic is caused by routine activity. The everyday search for vacant parking spaces consumes lots of fuel. If the search time gets reduced or eliminated, congestion in traffic can be decreased by a lot. Artificial Intelligence carries on developing and advancing, better solutions that can be used to expand our communities' development. More cities are analysing and adopting smart parking. Innovative wireless technologies are prominent for efficient management and development of smart cities, with the help of Internet of Things (IoT). Updations like services for observing parking data, dynamic notifications and sensors are being discovered to aid in city policy.

Exploring real-time parking data and analysing it to quickly and easily search for nearby available parking will lessen many problems produced in urban areas. With the continuous growth of urban spaces, in the future, smart parking will be an emerging solution that is necessary for the success of any Smart City. Smart parking will provide several solutions to support cities in helping their citizens. This will also help to manage traffic efficiently.

2.5.7 DATA MONITORING

A Smart City, cities must require one thing, reliable (sensor) data to take decisions on. For the reason that in the digital era, data is the new gold for a Smart City. By injecting sensors across city substructures and generating new data sources, including mobile devices, Smart City management [4] can carry out Big Data analysis. Big data has vast potential to enhance and make efficient use of available services. It basically consists of large multidimensional data that can be analysed to take appropriate decisions. Big data analysis reveals data patterns and extracts useful information.

Information and communications technology play an important part by making data collection easy. This technology is also known as Internet of Things (IoT). IoT helps to establish communication between connected devices to exchange data via the Internet. Smart city IoT sensors and connected devices gather data from various gateways mounted in a city premises and then analyse them for better decisions.

Other technologies like cloud and analytic approaches offer a cost-effective means of handling data and solutions, creating efficient systems that already exist. Machine learning applications that fetch data from IoT devices can provide real-time updates through mobile applications.

2.5.7.1 Three Layers of Data

- The first layer is the technology, which comprises a critical frame of devices and sensors connected by high-speed 5G communication networks.
- The second layer is applications specific, which converts raw data into notifications, perception and action required.
- The third layer is application usage by different entities in cities. Many applications get updated and managed according to the requirements of users.

2.5.7.2 Issues for the City Management

Smart Cities applications and their service providers cannot utilize the data if it is present in dissimilar form and databases have limited access. There is already a wide variety of data, though much of it is in storage to serve specific requirements. It includes government figures, maps and details on public proposals.

Improved parking, efficient lighting, upgraded traffic flow, smarter security, enriched waste management and disaster planning are all zones where technology can make a change. However, there is a lot of disimilarity in how to connect all of these diverse standards and take along them in a mutual, incorporated manner.

Forming a Smart City may be determined by how well administrations can share and analyse the data being produced. Without the facility to share key statistics in real time, industries functioning both in the private and public sector cannot improve the applications that support automation, nor the software resolutions that form the "smart" abilities of a city and its groundwork.

Additionally, each new sensor type frequently requires a new database, which is a time consuming task and again gives focus to process. These systems often do not exchange data with each other through means that are valuable or spontaneous, making it difficult to extract insights from the data.

A major challenge in Smart City is the upfront cost of inhabiting the town with enough sensors to be significant, and recognitions of sensor data. In evolving cities, the reality is that processes are uncoordinated and data capture is still manually processed.

Huge groups of folks mean tons of data are produced. Big data is being used to appreciate when, how and why crowds gather, and to forecast their activities and actions. There are zillions of sensors in City area already, observing various things. In the future, these sensors will proliferate until they can observe the whole nearby environment from streetlights and trashcans to road circumstances and energy intake.

2.5.7.3 Data Challenges

Administration of information is not constrained to information catch and capacity. It incorporate information that is shared and joined, dissected and utilized across divisions, among associations, and even with the network on the loose.

In each significant city in the United States, and beyond, there are a large number of sensors delivering a stunning measure of information every millisecond, second, moment, hour and day. That information is caught, put away and pretty much overlooked after that. Information sharing speaks to both a prerequisite and an open door for Smart City organizations. Obviously information sharing across citywide offices and stages is a basic component of any Smart City's plan. My forecast is that most urban areas will execute information sharing as a major aspect of a developmental excursion from information joining to information trades, and afterward to information commercial centres.

Sharing information opens productivity and open APIs are the most ideal approach to do it. A simple trade of information by means of APIs as well as information commercial centres, alongside the capacity to effectively improve the basic system, of any Smart City.

There is likewise a developing pattern for city specialists to discharge APIs to support designers and network associations to utilize open information.

Any information sharing should empower cloud-based information sharing. It will improve protection, interoperability, security and secure information sharing, deft application advancement and testing.

The stage should bolster both open and private sharing. During intermix of information, administration, security and utilization checking turns out to be increasingly critical to get control.

In the end, it should offer the capacity to comprehend and control information into data that individuals from a wide range of jobs can comprehend and use to make different arrangements. Large data remains at the cutting edge of this undertaking to give unavoidable availability at a citywide scale.

2.5.8 SELF-DRIVING CARS

The mechanization of routine assignments is currently an idea that intrigues numerous enterprises. Among its most progressive examples are self-governing vehicles. The innovative application they all offer are self-driving autos and shared portability. Those are set to alter the way in which we explore urban communities.

These ideas will make our entire urban communities better, with the goal that it's adjusted to self-sufficient vehicles [15]. This will give much more secure streets. Automated driving would not require individuals' choices, which could frequently be hazardous and nonsensical to take you from direct A toward point B. It results in a huge diminishing in mishaps and a huge number of spared lives.

Major mechanical advancement currently gives the likelihood to have favorable circumstances in urban communities of things to come, together with independent driving and the new foundation. When advantages of 5G, joined with the Internet of Things, each one of those rising developments cooperating will change the customary look of urban areas and they will get better also.

2.5.9 SMART STREET LIGHTNING

The "Smart" lighting arrangements [13] brings a change in urban communities and structures compared to the previous years. It can be happen due to advancement by IoT arrangements turning in most Smart City systems around the world.

Urban areas can seize with the establishment of shrewd lighting arrangements through vitality (cost) and support investment funds (which are immense thinking about that as much as 40 percent of a city's road lighting and new productive lighting can set aside up to half of these expenses) or the improvement of the ecological effect.

Smart lighting arrangements can assume a key job in a Smart City system, wherein road and other outside lighting establishments fill in as spine of a system. Today, most urban communities that put in new shrewd lighting or retrofit existing apparatuses pick frameworks that as of now are furnished with sensor innovation or that can be overhauled effectively to use the benefits of IoT applications. Present Smart lighting systems can help urban areas in observing the earth, to build open and traffic-wellbeing, to redesign networks as WiFi hotspots or to convey area based administrations like shrewd stopping and best route.

2.5.9.1 Key Takeaways for Considering Smart Lighting

Smart lighting solutions open door for urban communities that can be better in terms of power and cost. The key advantages are:

- Tremendous decrease of vitality and support cost;
- Expanded open security from improved lighting;
- More secure traffic because of expanded perceivability of risks;
- Quantifiable natural effect because of diminished energy utilization.

Smart lightning will enhance capacity of a Smart city by incorporating with:

- Mobile broadband connectivity;
- Traffic light controls;
- Smart parking;
- Traffic management;
- Electric vehicle (ev) charging stations;
- Environmental monitoring (emissions, noise);
- Public safety through video cameras.

Smart lighting can be a spine for a brilliant city arrangement. In any case, urban communities ought to know about various existing frameworks and advances. Similarity, information security, and system excess issues ought to be considered right off the bat. Its adaptability as far as the general system size just as far as overhauls of future applications/usefulness ought to be considered.

2.5.10 EMERGENCY SERVICES

Smart citizens are very conscious and interest in the smooth operative emergency [14] response services, even although they would apparently hope under no circumstances to have to put such facilities to the test. Postponements in response times could mean the difference between life and death. Subsequently, emergency response is fairly high on the schedule for forward-thinking cities considering implementing Smart inventiveness.

Smart Cities are trying to make it easy for people to utilize the services on their own through digital services. Instead of being restricted to voice calls, numerous global cities are conducting tests for improvement of capacity to receive text, images, and position data, enabling services to collect enhanced visuals and information on an event more rapidly than was previously possible.

It is only the commencement of the possible catalyst for revolution and effectiveness gains in Smart infrastructure could signify for emergency services. The speedy development of IoT technology could mean that in the future, call centres, CCTV cameras and data centres will all be associated and equally communicating in real time. Advantage of the interconnected environment of the Smart City visualization is the direct collaboration with Smart Traffic management systems, which could substitute greater proficiency. Emergency vehicles can have their routes selected using Intelligent Traffic Systems (ITS) which regulate the ways traffic lights are phased, aiming to diminish red light interruptions. This could be controlled by tracking adjacent traffic, foot walkers and avoiding or reducing red light periods, when not required. Local GPS systems would also preference the most suitable route for emergency vehicles, setting speed limits and overall traffic management to the highest convenience and meaningfully reducing drive times. In emergency situations it can save time and the lives of many people.

2.5.11 SMART ENERGY MANAGEMENT

Energy administration can be defined as the science involved in the development, guiding and monitoring of energy supply and consumption to maximise efficiency and comfort, and to reduce energy expenditures and pollution through sensible, cautious and well-organized use of energy. In modest terms, energy management includes energy savings. In terms of energy savings, energy organization involves the process of monitoring, controlling and preserving energy in many ways. It includes enhanced energy use, administration of resources and active energy utilization.

With the growth in urbanization, managing the energy footprint is one of the issues that Smart Cities are facing. With the expansion of present cities and their evolution to Smart Cities, energy management has become an essential factor of urban revolution. A Smart City is an ecological and well-organized urban centre whose objectives are to provide its citizens with a high living standards. Smart Cities are anticipated to become more self-governing and manage their energy smartly, considering local resources and the requirements of numerous stakeholders. In this context, Smart energy management involves understanding the prospective of energy management as a basic structure for Smart Cities.

Smart energy management is a module of Smart City expansion that takes aim at a site-specific constant evolution towards sustainability, self-sufficiency and resilience of energy organisations, while guaranteeing availability, affordability and ability of energy services, through improved incorporation of energy preservation, energy productivity and local renewable energy sources. It is categorized by an amalgamation of technologies with statistics and communication technologies that permits the combination of multiple areas and enforces cooperation of multiple participants, while ensuring sustainability of its actions.

The mainstreaming of Smart energy management mainly includes the merging of technology with energy, enabling strategies, official changes, awareness, training and capability construction programs, energy conservation, energy audits, etc.

2.5.12 SMART AGRICULTURE

Smart agriculture signifies the collaboration of IoT solutions in the field of agriculture. Likewise, Smart Farming is a farming administration concept using contemporary technologies that enhance the quantity and quality of agricultural harvests.

Nowadays, farmers have access to GPS tools, soil analysis, water, light, moisture, temperature controlling, spontaneous water sprinkling, precision agriculture, data managing and IoT technologies.

With smart agriculture, farmers can observe the field environments from everywhere using their mobile devices. IoT-based smart farming is extremely efficient. It makes farming specific and cost-effective when compared with the traditional method.

2.5.12.1 IoT Applications for Smart Farming

The rise of well-organized industries, connected cars and Smarter Cities are all vital modules of the IoT domain. However, the application of expertise in fields such as IoT in agriculture has an extreme global influence. Smart farming established on IoT technologies will support farmers to reduce waste and boost productivity. This can range from the amount of fertilizer used in the soil to the number of voyages the farm vehicles have to make to the arena.

According to research, smart farming can be organized in seven categories as follows:

- Farm vehicles management;
- Large and small field farming;
- Livestock observing;
- Indoor farming;
- Fish farming;
- Forestry;
- Storage monitoring (resources).

Intelligent connectivity permits amplified crop harvests, crop quality and livestock management through improved noticing of soil conditions, better use of insecticides and fertilizers, and more precise forecast of weather conditions. Big data, supported by Artificial Intelligence (AI) use numerous real-time data values to make more up-to-date food production decisions. Coupled drones are used for crop spurting, land administration and in-flight surveillance.

Through machine learning and data investigation, AI-assisted agricultural applications will endure to allow long-term developments with improved understanding of the entire agricultural method. Management of transportation vehicles can enable crops to be transported in better circumstances resulting in longer lives.. Through optimum routing and intensive care of temperature, everything can be under remote control when in transport.

The innovative prospective of a smart web of sensors, actuators, cameras, robots, drones and other connected devices brings an extraordinary level of control and automatic decision-making. In the upcoming time, pesticide and fertilizer use will drop. Overall productivity will also be enhanced. IoT technologies support better traceability of food which leads to better food safety.

2.5.13 WEARABLE DEVICES

Fitness tracker or fitness bands and even health assessment mobile apps are applications of Smart wearable devices which are popular nowadays. These devices are considered smart because they do not only sense but also monitor real time health related data.This collected information helps to keep a track of health and provide quick solutions at the right time.

Administrations that can easily depict the requirements of their citizens help them to move towards a healthy lifestyle. It helps to ensure a creative and satisfied public, and keep down healthcare expenses. With trade in wearable devices anticipated to increase, governments will have new occasions to endorse healthy lifestyles. Hospitals will be able to observe at-risk patients 24x7. Fitness trackers and apps can be delivered to residents free of cost. Such applications are mainly efficient for countries with openly sponsored health management systems.

2.5.14 SMART EDUCATION

Smart education is an ideal way of learning and teaching new generations in the digital era. In contrast to conventional classroom teaching styles, smart education is a communicating, cooperative and visual model, designed to enhance student involvement and permit teachers to familiarize themselves with students' abilities, interests and learning fondness.

Students were restricted within the bounds of the classroom and smart education makes it more interactive and effective way of learning with social interacting abilities. Still, the acceptance and success of educational technologies lies behind other social trends such as users' fast acceptance of digital devices and facilities. Now, the progressively digital and technological based behaviours of students, teachers and parents are monitored. It is assumed that digital education at school makes a positive difference to students' knowledge.

Conventional classroom skill in schools and other educational institutions is often old-fashioned and does not deal the functionality that up-to-date digital and media-rich teaching should contain to increase student involvement and learning output. Smart Cities require education institutes and schooling systems which guarantee that students acquire skills, including digital mastery, creative thinking, effective communication, cooperation and the skill to create high-quality developments. In order to reach this better goals of development, educators need to concentrate on the basic building blocks of student accomplishment.

In spite of daily use, there is space for growth in expertise with new implementation. A benefit of smart education is that it should permit teachers to meet the requirements of students with precise modes of learning, such as those who are typically visual students. It is important to clarify to students query, especially when the content lacks fundamental.

Smart classroom creates the professionalization of the education process, supporting teachers to improve, organize and enhance their lectures based on requirements of students and circumstances. Most important it increased efficiency and teaching performance. In this student-centric framework, the teacher is no longer a controlling entity, but a guide and companion, in what is successfully a bi-directional development.

2.5.15 UNDERGROUND TUNNELLING

Available space in cities is an always-increasing issue. With expanding cities from the perspective of population, underground substructures such as railways, roads and services are in high demand. Cities have a deficiency of surface space but there is space available underground which can be used for tunnelling. And it is usually an inexpensive way to construct below ground level instead of increasing the length of the streets.

Creating substructure below ground has strong impact. First, it decreases pressure on prized surface property, releasing space for constructions and open areas. Underground land is less costly because there is no need to make payments to owners for land found underneath the surface.

In addition, tunnelling is less troublesome than construction at ground level. Most tunnelling nowadays is created by using tunnel boring machines. It is engineering corresponding of keyhole operation once right to use channels have been done it is put to work, nobody knows they are around. That means trade as normal at street level, with no noise trouble, dust or traffic congestion.

2.5.15.1 Tunnelling Renaissance

Smart Cities all over the globe are considering space below ground level to build high-capacity metro arrangements. Underground railway networks play a significant role in battling congestion and stimulating economic expansion, all accomplished with negligible land revenue.

The Middle East is one area where tunnelling is in high demand. Previously there were no railways at all in that area.. The Dubai Metro in the UAE is a good illustration, the world's first extended fully-automated railway, including tunnels. Atkins provided a comprehensive tunnelling scheme for the development, as well as geotechnical and site research, crossings, bridges and expert services. The Middle East is seeing a major development in its underground services and it is a very significant market. The escalation of metro systems in this region is extraordinary because there are so many in limited spaces.

2.6 FUTURE OF SMART CITIES

Cities are facing countless challenges [17]. Smart Cities are essentially relying on social and political entities. Therefore it requires the establishment of the right environment for a successful economy, one that generates and defends jobs, and promotes equality in the new digital era. Smart Cities must provide working structures at reasonable prices. Most essential here is mobility in the system, but extra significant factors must be included like safety and disaster management, suitable education, healthcare and reasonably priced housing; in other words, a city where people want to live.

As citizens are flourishing, cities are obligated to keep their assets in order and ensure the low cost power, heating, and cooling based on renewable energy sources. They must also include recycling and waste-management facilities, fresh air and water, and innovative businesses, students and the scientific community.

This all indicates that cities require solutions that not only make them safe, well-organized, and liveable with high mobile infrastructure, but also they need innovation and economic evolution, such as data-based applications like car-pooling or neighbourhood-level logistics facilities. The more complications a Smart City platform can resolve, the more it is expected to be adopted.

2.6.1 INNOVATIVE TECHNOLOGIES FOR SMART CITY

1. *Hybrid energy systems* – It includes manufacture, storage and consumption of renewable energy that can drift spontaneously between structures, power grids [9] and customers. If possible this takes commercial encouragement schemes, such as renter electricity, which allow consumers to be both customers and producers.
2. *Multimodal transport systems* – It is based mainly on power from renewables. These have need of not only predictable communal transport systems, electric vehicles and charging equipment, but also engagement, routing and statistics systems that make communal mobility more interesting to consumers thus making the private vehicle out-dated for travel.
3. *Interoperable software platforms* – In this, all varieties of data are combined, scrutinized and managed with the aim of refining services or the initiation of new ones.

2.6.2 BETTER QUALITY OF LIFE

Smart Cities offer improved use of available space, a reduced amount of traffic, cleaner air and more well-organized public facilities, all of which enhance quality of life. Smart Cities offer more new occupation and financial opportunities as well as robust links with the communal entities.

City specialists must be vigorous at many diverse levels both through interactions and participation through their digital media. This includes improving their procedures, infrastructure and services.

Therefore we can say the Smart City of the future is appealing, connected and sustainable.

2.7 TECHNOLOGIES EVOLVING SMART CITIES

Smart Cities utilise the data captured by several different Internet of Things (IoT) devices and deal with them with the help of Artificial Intelligence (AI). Organizers hype the benefits of these data-driven techniques, but from the perspective of urban cities "is it useful?" In the earlier days, urban inventions highlighted visions and results, but they did not include the environmental and social factors. Smart Cities are typically considered to be safer, healthier and economically strong, but how much has been reached? What are its real impacts? Evolution of Smart Cities are classified in three categories as follows:

2.7.1 SMART CITIES 1.0: SURVEILLANCE, DIGITAL AND ECO-FRIENDLY CITIES

Today's Smart Cities were born to face any tragic situation which can be environmental or man-made. After some major attacks, cities installed 24x7 surveillance systems which include cameras and AI to make public areas safe and secure. Usually it includes public-private partnerships (PPP) managed by city administration and private organizations. Smart Cities daily generate large amounts of data in a top-down manner without any proper view or format. In China, social profiling is used to maintain a view of political and social topics of a citizen to take decisions regarding travel, education and housing. In Toronto, Google advertises its Sidewalk Lab as a way to refresh the waterfront, but users are divided over rising issues about the data privacy and transparency.

Smart Cities projects face financial issues after time duration. Many cities depend on smart digital meters, smart parking and online tickets that face connectivity issues. Most of them support digital cash transaction becomes a major innovative profits sources. However, in terms of sustainability smart metering increases pollution by supporting gas-powered vehicles. To be truthfully smart, cities need to decrease their carbon footprint by endorsing "smart mobility" like walking, biking, transit and electric vehicles (EVs).

2.7.2 SMART CITIES 2.0: SUSTAINABLE, AND RESILIENT CITIES

Ever since the Paris Agreement, many cities are adding sustainability strategies to their data-driven projects with the aim: "What we can measure gets managed in proper format." IoT sensors and AI are being organised to manage and decrease data traffic, energy required and carbon releases. Some of these programs have been effective in enumerating and monetizing climate strategies.

With the recent increase in incidents like hurricanes, forest fires and other natural tragedies, cities are adding flexible effective planning to their smart cities projects.

AI-driven weather and destruction predicting tools are being required by insurers, financiers and administrators wanting to save many lives. As global warming rapidly increasing, cities are moving towards smart technologies to forecast and cope; fire, police, medical, water and other essential services for the duration of and after disasters.

Smart Cities [18] are also emerging as ground-breaking business models. Instead of conventional source of power Smart Cities are supporting renewable energy from solar grid, speed up the shift towards clean energy while saving time and money. Smart Cities are also discovering how to dynamically involve citizens and corporations using mobile apps managed by AI systems, such as San Francisco's pioneering Civic Bridge Day. Smart Cities are learning to apply technologies while ensuring user participation, transparency, authority and responsibility among city organizations, citizens, companies and visitors. Their vital goal is development and improvement in city services.

2.7.3 SMART CITIES 3.0: GREEN, RIGHTFUL CITIES

The perfect model for all city bureaucrats, residents and businesses is the green city that is open, non-discriminatory, non-violent and equitable which is difficult to achieve due to urban renewal, overcrowding, homelessness and increasing income differences. To achieve these goals [19] we require high-quality education and employment, reasonably priced housing, appropriate transport and rich cultural life, while reducing bad energy use and carbon emissions. These goals are mandatory to avoid global warming and create cities worth living in. They can only be accomplished if cities invest in their social arrangements, which have been abandoned for years. VR/AR, IoT, AI, blockchain and other new technologies are dominant apparatuses with the potential for cultivating and accelerating better change. Developed dense reasonably priced housing near transport hubs in walkable societies, greenery to decrease carbon, attractive public places that inspire art, music, sports and other activities, innovative education that bridges generation gaps, and changed civic self-importance in working organised to improve cities. As a social being it can be achieved through collaboration only. Truly Smart Cities will cultivate smart citizens.

REFERENCES

1. An, J., et al. 2019. Towards global IoT-enabled smart cities interworking using adaptive semantic adapter. *IEEE Internet of Things Journal*, 6(3), pp. 5753–5765.
2. Anthopoulos, L. G. 2015. Understanding the smart city domain: A literature review. In *Transforming city governments for successful smart cities* (pp. 9–21). Cham: Springer.
3. Cui, Q., et al. 2018. Big data analytics and network calculus enabling intelligent management of autonomous vehicles in a smart city. *IEEE Internet of Things Journal*, 6(2), pp. 2021–2034.
4. Du, R., et al. 2018. The sensible city: A survey on the deployment and management for smart city monitoring. *IEEE Communications Surveys & Tutorials*, 21(2), pp. 1533–1560.

5. Herrera-Quintero, L. F., et al. 2019. ITS for smart parking systems, towards the creation of smart city services using IoT and cloud approaches. In 2019 Smart City Symposium Prague (SCSP). IEEE.

6. Kolozali, Ş., et al. 2018. Observing the pulse of city: A smart city framework for real-time discovery, federation, and aggregation of data streams. *IEEE Internet of Things Journal*, 6(2), pp. 2651–2668.

7. Kong, X., et al. 2019. Mobile crowdsourcing in smart cities: Technologies, applications, and future challenges. *IEEE Internet of Things Journal*, 6(5), pp. 8095–8113.

8. Li, Z., et al. 2017. A hierarchical framework for intelligent traffic management in smart cities. *IEEE Transactions on Smart Grid*, 10(1), pp. 691–701.

9. Liu, Y., et al. 2019. Intelligent edge computing for IoT-based energy management in smart cities. *IEEE Network*, 33(2), pp. 111–117.

10. Moudrá, K., et al. 2019. Potential of a travel mode change in smart cities: A review. In 2019 Smart City Symposium Prague (SCSP). IEEE.

11. Nam, T., and T. A. Pardo. 2011. Conceptualizing smart city with dimensions of technology, people, and institutions. In Proceedings of the 12th annual international digital government research conference: digital government innovation in challenging times. ACM.

12. Nelson, A., et al. 2019. Replication of smart-city, internet of things assets in a municipal deployment. *IEEE Internet of Things Journal*, 6(4), pp. 6715–6724.

13. Pradhan, M. 2019. Interoperability for disaster relief operations in smart city environments.In 2019 IEEE 5th World Forum on Internet of Things (WF-IoT). IEEE.

14. Sharma, A., & Battula, R. B. (2019, October). Architecture for Waste Management in Indian Smart Cities (AWMINS). In 2019 International Conference on Information and Communication Technology Convergence (ICTC) (pp. 76–83). IEEE.

15. Sharma, A., & Battula, R. B. (2020, January). FOOTREST: Safety on Roads Through Intelligent Transportation System. In 2020 International Conference on Information Networking (ICOIN) (pp. 818–820). IEEE.

16. Sharma, A., Khandelwal, S., Singh, B., Sharma, A., & Battula, R. B. (2020, July). Honour: VeHicle tO INfrastructure COmmUnication for Indian SmaRt Cities. In 2020 43rd International Conference on Telecommunications and Signal Processing (TSP) (pp. 601–608). IEEE.

17. Sookhak, M., et al. 2018. Security and privacy of smart cities: A survey, research issues and challenges. *IEEE Communications Surveys & Tutorials*, 21(2), pp. 1718–1743.

18. Xie, J., et al. 2019. A survey of blockchain technology applied to smart cities: Research issues and challenges. *IEEE Communications Surveys & Tutorials*, 21(3), pp. 2794–2830.

19. Zhang, Y., et al. 2020. Information trading in internet of things for smart cities: A market-oriented analysis. *IEEE Network*, 34(1), pp. 122–129.

3 Advances in AI-Based Security for Internet of Things in Wireless Virtualization Environment

Naveen Naik Sapavath, Danda B. Rawat and Kayhan Zrar Ghafoor

CONTENTS

3.1   INTRODUCTION

IoT devices are vulnerable to personal data breach. As a large number of IoT devices are being produced and being used by many users, the data is also increasing tremendously. This data collected by IoT devices is the very sensitive data of a user. To keep track of such large chunks of users' personal data becomes very hard. So, to protect the users' personal data and to improve the privacy of users, we investigate learning models to keep track of the personal data and the type of attacks to secure the sensitive data. We have studied AI-based techniques to improve the privacy of the IoT devices based on neural networks and deep learning. AI-based secure data transmission between IoT devices, authentication of the user, policies on access control and AI models to detect malicious users are the focus of this chapter. We have studied various

ML-based learning techniques for wireless virtualization to enhance the network capacity and RF slicing and security for wireless Internet of Things [8, 10, 11, 14, 15]. AI techniques are being used in every technology as it has the capability to address the solutions to many security problems raised in transportation systems (V2V networks), IoT devices in smart homes and hospitals, manufacturing industries, space technologies, etc. [3, 12, 16, 17]. AI/ML algorithms are very helpful to maximize the capacity of wireless networks by increasing the privacy of the user data in virtualized environments. IoT devices must be more robust to defend and detect attacks such as intrusions, spoofing, jamming, DoS attacks and network layer attacks such as routing attacks. All of these vulnerabilities should be addressed by means of AI and machine learning algorithms to protect the private data of the user. In recent times, there was an attack using IoT botnets targeting giant companies like PayPal, Netflix, CNN, etc. These IoT botnets are evolved by the malware called Mirai, which is used to retrieve personal data such as the login information of the legitimate user [1, 5]. The attack is based on not maintaining the uniqueness in the passwords and usernames. Beside the fact that the IoT has lots of advantages but it is lacking in security aspects. Since every device in the network can communicate with the other IoT devices anywhere in the world through the Internet, this enables unauthorized users or malicious users to access the personal data without the knowledge of the legitimate user or the IoT device [6, 7]. Such device to device (D2D) communication increases the threat of data leakage. We investigate AI/ML techniques to improve security for IoT devices in the wireless virtualized environment so that it minimizes the attack affect, secures the IoT devices and protects the private data of IoT devices.

In other words, the IoT devices need be proactive against security attacks with the help of AI models as shown in Figure 3.1. The challenging part is securing the different IoT devices, which have different requirements and objectives, which makes the developing of AI models complex in that scenario. In the next few points, we emphasize future generation secure IoT related system keywords. We discuss briefly each key word.

- *IoT design with Security*: Due to different attacks in the world of the Internet, it is time to come up with AI enabled IoT devices and make them more robust to defend attacks, tighten IoT security. To achieve an attack-free IoT device, it must be tested continuously, authenticating the user at both access ends to the device. These techniques make the IoT device free of vulnerabilities. Continuous testing makes the system more robust and it can avoid patching security issues every time there is a vulnerability. And patching may fix the security issue or not and may not be effective when compared to a system which is designed to be more robust and secure right from scratch or at the initial stage of design. In fact, designing IoT devices in the beginning phase with security models decreases many attack issues and avoids personal data leakage. Of course, the costs go up for in-built AI models for IoT security.
- *Intelligence & Learning Techniques*: As the abnormality is dynamic and the malicious activity changes every time, the general approaches and models to measure the security attacks may not be sufficient to protect IoT devices. These

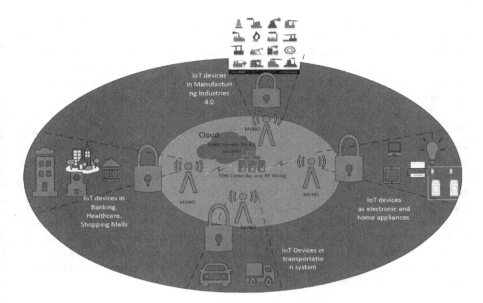

FIGURE 3.1 AI/ML based Secured IoT Devices for different segments in wireless virtualized environments

old approaches and models are used to measure or detect very common and specific attacks. As the malicious act behaves dynamically, IoT devices fail to predict or be proactive before the attack. One such scenario is attacks such as cross layer; the cross layer attack can attack anywhere on the network protocol stack [13]. The target of the attack is undefined. It could attack any layer and make abrupt changes to the system which could lead to massive damage to the system; such attacks are not predicted with traditional approaches. So, there must be some learning models, which can predict the attack and make the IoT device alert, and combat the attack beforehand [2]. AI and Deep Learning models are promising learning models in such scenarios which can detect and mitigate the attacks which lead to securing the IoT device effectively.

- *Polymorphic Hardware System*: In future generation communication, the IoT devices should be integrated with security models in both hardware and software. To generate context aware attacks and polymorphic measures, software defined networks (SDNs) can be assembled with IoT networks to avoid the attacks on different layers on the network protocol stack. The IoT should be assembled with polymorphic bolted-on security mechanisms that will be able to withstand dynamic attacks at multiple levels of the network stack. With all these features the IoT system will be able to predict and sense the attacks beforehand.

Traditional detection models like misuse detection models are designed to detect familiar attacks. But in the world of Internet and information technology there are several attacks which are novel in nature and unique and whose identity is nowhere found. So, the traditional detection models may not be efficient to deal with novel attacks. Misuse detection is highly effective in detecting known attacks. However, it is insufficient against unknown or novel attacks because their signatures are not yet known. In addition to that, any changes to the known signatures of the attacker will increase the false alarm rate rapidly and it will affect the reliability and accuracy of the IoT device. Some of the detection models are applicable for specific behavior of the attack while can not be applied on other type of attacks. If any of the specifications are denied or violated, then the system will infer the suspicious activity and abnormality. These types of models are effective when there are unknown attacks which are a threat to the IoT device security. Moreover, assigning specifications to the system is a complex procedure for every unique IoT security problem. Anomaly based detection is based on sudden changes in normal activity. This type of detection uses learning models based on four approaches: Biological neural network models, based on rule techniques, advanced statistical models, cognitive learning models. Using these learning models, we can detect the misuse detection attacks, and the security risk factors using these models are almost zero with a high possible detection rate of unknown attacks.

3.2   IOT DATA CHARACTERISTICS

IoT data is different from general big data. To better understand the requirements for IoT data analytic, we need to explore the properties of IoT data and how they are different from those of general big data. IoT data exhibits the following characteristics [6]:

- *Large-Scale Live Streaming Data*: Various data retrieving devices are employed and distributed for IoT applications, and these devices are helpful to produce live streams of IoT data. This will assist in capturing large IoT data.
- *Data Heterogeneity*: Due to the wide variety of IoT devices which produce different varieties of information about the user which results in data heterogeneity.
- *Correlation between Time and Space*: Due to the large number of IoT applications, each of the IoT devices is equipped with sensors to a given location, which gives the relation between location and time of each generated data set.
- *Noisy Data*: During acquisition and retrieval of the large number of small data in all the IoT applications, such tiny data will eventually be subject to errors and effected by noise.

Obtaining sensitive information and the knowledge from the big data will be useful to improve the quality of one's life, which is not easy work and not a straightforward process. To accomplish such tough and complex processes, the traditional approaches of learning models are not helpful, so there is a need for new approaches and new techniques, new learning algorithms and decent infrastructure. Fortunately, tremendous growth in advanced computing and deep learning models and machine learning techniques make them the suitable choice to do advanced analytic and data analytic and classification of data to extract sensitive information from IoT applications. Due to live and fast streaming of large data there is scope for a new data analytic other than big data analytic which supports high speed data streams which requires time sensitive actions. Many data scientists and researchers have described many machine learning approaches and architectures to speed up the data analytic that uses data cloud services and infrastructures. But to do all these time sensitive applications and their related AI/ML algorithms requires smaller platforms; something like system edge platforms and ensembles in the IoT device itself. Suppose there is a scenario of a self-driving car which needs to take quick decisions such as lane changing and speed change. Quick data analytic of various data streaming from different sources such as vehicle to vehicle, multiple vehicle sensor communications can be supportive to such kinds of quick decisive applications. Using data streaming from cameras, signals, RADARS, speedometers and these device learn from traffic signs [4, 9]. In such a scenario, data analytic at cloud will be affected by latency. Moving the data to cloud would delay the data analytic process that could possibly cause car accidents and traffic violations in the case of autonomous cars. A more dangerous scenario would be predicting and detecting pedestrians by autonomous vehicles. Pinpoint prediction is supposed to perform in real time scenarios to avoid some serious accidents. All these examples recommend that fast and quick data analytic for IoT devices has to be nearer to the source of the data to avoid latency issues and communication delays.

Big data generates from various IoT data because it continuously streams the data. So IoT data is one of the main sources of big data. Live streaming of big data implies that the data produced or retrieved from the small intervals of time which need to be accurately analyzed to infer the information to make quick decisions. In general the big data implies large chunks of data sets which commonly use the software and hardware platforms but they are not able to maintain (analysis, storage, processing) such large numbers of big data sets. The two approaches discussed earlier should be considered differently because their data analytic response times are different from each other. The informative data is delivered after many days. Data fusion is useful to add the necessary data from multiple data sources and provides accurate information. This fusion process plays a big role in improving the IoT data environment. Such kinds of roles where the data has to be integrated from all small sources of data together provide action insights and accuracy of the information for time sensitive IoT applications. These data analytic techniques are suggested by many researchers in the area of IoT applications because their processing speed is fast [17]. After doing parallelism of data, large data points are broken down into many smaller and tinier data sets, such kinds of data sets are easier to perform data analytics parallel and simultaneously. Small number of data to be processed faster in a task pipeline of computation capability. Even though these techniques are helpful to decrease the latency time to get back a response from the live streaming IoT data analytic structure, they are not a good fit or best method to solve time-sensitive IoT applications. After bringing the data sources closer to the IoT devices there is no point in doing data parallelism because streaming data analytics is faster when the data sources are available closer to the IoT devices which decreases the latency. Big data analytics on IoT devices lead to their own aspects such as computation limits, limited storage and the source of power at the IoT devices. IoT data is a popular source of big data, because all the IoT devices are connected through the Internet where it generates lots of data from the different environments. Determining the look-a-like patterns in the data and extracting them from the input plain data is the main task of the IoT big data analytics to make a fair decision and seek insights from the raw input data so that one can make the predictions. In that scenario, inferring these type of information and knowledge from the big data is very helpful to many business sectors. Extraction and classification of sensitive information which is private will be very useful to individuals and business organizations.

3.3   DIFFERENT TYPES OF SECURITY ATTACKS IN THE IOT NETWORK

All the IoT devices and humans are interconnected through the Internet to serve and function each other at any time and location. In IoT, all the devices and people are connected with each other to provide services at any time and at any place. Most of the devices connected to the Internet are not equipped with efficient security mechanisms and are vulnerable to various privacy and security issues, e.g., confidentiality, integrity and authenticity, etc. For the IoT, some security requirements must be fulfilled to prevent the network from malicious attacks. Here, some of the most required capabilities of a secure network are briefly discussed.

- *Resilience to attacks*: The system should be capable enough to recover itself in case it crashes during data transmission. For example, a server working in a multiuser environment must be intelligent and strong enough to protect itself from intruders or an eavesdropper. In such a case, if it is down it should recover itself without intimating to the users of its down status.
- *Data Authentication*: The data and the associated information must be authenticated. An authentication mechanism is used to allow data transmission only from authentic devices.
- *Access control*: Only the persons who have authorization must have the access control. The managing of passwords and usernames of respective users must be controlled by the system administrator. The system administrator should define individual access rights so that users will access only the data which is relevant to them so that the privacy of the data will be controlled through access control.

Nowadays, the lifestyle of each individual has changed because of IoT device evaluation. Even though IoT devices are very beneficial to everyone they are vulnerable to security attacks and threats in everyday life. Most of the security issues and threats relate to loss of information and data privacy leakage and loss of information as shown in Figure 3.2. In IoT networks, the physical layer network is mostly affected by the

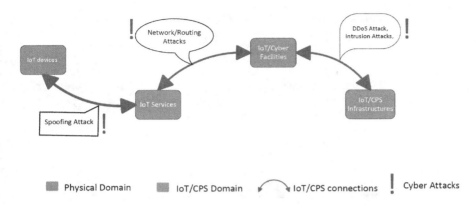

FIGURE 3.2 Different types of attacks in the IoT system

security threats and physical security risks. The IoT contains various hardware devices and software platforms with various user data credentials, where every IoT device needs its own security requirements and its device characteristics. The privacy of each user is very important because on the IoT platform the user's private data is shared across all devices. The smart home threats are described as follows in Figure 3.3. Hence the AI/ML learning models are necessary to secure the privacy of the IoT user and user's personal information. However, all the IoT devices in the network undergo various types of machine-to-machine communication (M2M), which means there are several security attacks and malicious user attacks on different layers of communication protocol: for example, physical layer, application layer, network layer, transportation layer, etc. The sensitive information such as user's private data will be covered from others using AI/ML encryption algorithms, which are as follows.

1) *Life cycle protection of E2E Data*: To ensure privacy of the data in the IoT network, device to device protection is provided with end to end (E2E) data protection from sender to receiver through the communication channel in the entire network. The data which is retrieved from various connected IoT devices will be shared with others, such that it demands the data privacy architecture to ensure the privacy and security. So, the entire full cycle of data will be secured and confidential, and the privacy easy to manage.

2) *Planning of security*: The dynamic change in the connections and communication among the IoT devices according to situation. Because of the dynamics, the devices must ensure the security and there is a need for planning. For instance, the external device communication and internal communication security policies of the IoT devices in smart home applications should follow the same policies.

3) *Visualization of security and privacy*: Almost every attack is based on reconfiguration of various users' databases. It is impossible and unnatural to compile such vast security and privacy mechanisms using traditional models. So, researchers are more focusing on the AI/Ml algorithms.

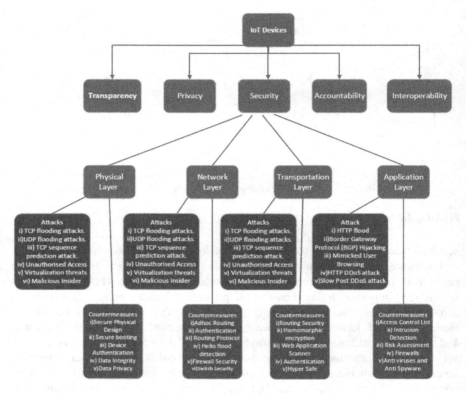

FIGURE 3.3 Different types of IoT attacks and countermeasures

It is highly recommended to derive some security and privacy models and counter measures which will be deployed automatically based on the type of attacks as shown in Figure 3.3.

3.4 SMART HOME SECURITY THREATS

Due to lack of security models in the security of smart homes they are easily exposed to attacks from malicious users to steal the private information of the user at very early stages. Most of the smart home providers will not consider the security parameters at the initial step of the process. The potential threats and attacks in smart homes are because of stealing the information by eavesdropping and distributed denial of service attacks and sensitive data leakage, and the abnormality of the data. Most of the attacks in smart homes are done by unauthorized data access. The potential security issues in smart homes are discussed below.

1) *Malicious trespassing*: Whenever there is an attack on a door pass code and altering the pass code and entering the correct code using a brute force technique which leads to access by the unauthorized users. In such cases, the

malicious user can trespass on smart doors in smart homes without breaking the doorways, which results in loss of valuable property and threat to life, and the affect will be in various forms. To avoid such attacks the pass codes will be changed periodically and should be very complex to crack. The password should contain more than ten characteristics at least. So that the attackers will take a longer time to break the long passwords and they are almost impossible to predict for the unauthorized user. In the same way access control and the authorization mechanisms will be deployed to combat the malicious attacks.

2) *Personnel data monitoring and leakage of the data*: Privacy and safety are the main parameters in smart homes. Because there are many sensors which work simultaneously, these sensors are used for bay monitoring systems, door braking systems, fire alarm sensors, video surveillance cameras, etc. If all these monitoring systems are hacked by the attacker or intruder then the unauthorized users will steal all this personal information without knowledge of the authenticated user. To protect such data and combat the attacks, AI/ ML based data encryption techniques should be applied between IoT device sensor devices and gateway of the network to detect unauthorized users.

3) *Denial of service attacks (DoS)*: If an attacker gets a chance to attack the smart home network, they will send many numbers of unknown messages and overwhelm the network with req/ack signals. Attackers are also capable of doing targeted IoT device attacks by using some unique abnormal codes so that there could be a potential case of denial of service to that particular device, which is interconnected with other IoT devices in the smart home. In this scenario, IoT devices are not able to perform the basic tasks because of scarcity of resources caused by such attacks. To protect from all these attacks, it is essential to apply one authentication protocol to block and iden-tify unauthorized malicious access.

4) *Data falsification*: Whenever the IoT devices in a smart home communicate with other IoT devices within the server the malicious attacker may retrieve the data pockets by altering the TCP routing table in the network gateway. This is generally described as data falsification so to avoid such attacks the ML/AI algorithms need to be applied to learn and detect such attacks.

Even though security measures such as SSL (secure socket layer) techniques are applied, a malicious user or attacker can find a way and surpass the duplicate certifi-cate. In a way the malicious user can misunderstand the data content, or confiden-tiality data leakage may occur. To ensure the security and privacy of a smart home from all these attacks, not only SSL but also the SSL with authentication will mini-mize the severity of the attack and protect the privacy of the data. Such mechanisms should be applied. It is also necessary to avoid and block malicious users and devices in the network, which damage the smart home network with unauthorized access. For instance, as shown in Figure 3.3 there will be a denial of service attack by over-whelming the network. IoT devices are the future of technology where all hardware devices connect to the global Internet and communicate with each other IoT device. The IoT devices include many handheld devices such as smartphones, laptops, and many other intelligent devices. All these systems have the feature of RFID and QR code scanning which is quick response code. And all these work with wireless communication among various devices. The IoT technology serves many sectors and organizations across the globe, it helps in establishing connection between human to human and physical devices to human, device to device and also vehicle to vehicle in the transportation system.

3.5 DIFFERENT AI/ML MODELS TO COMBAT IOT SECURITY ATTACKS

Computer science has various learning models; one of them is machine learning, which is a sub-field of computer science. Without any programming an Artificial Intelligence is deployed on the machines which are capable of learning without external programming, and learn their environments and actions, so that the devices will be able to make a win-win decision to protect the devices from the security attacks and threats. AI, machine learning methods originated from two theories of computation learning and pattern recognition models. To do intelligent data analysis necessary concepts of machine learning and AI models are discussed and popular machine learning algorithms are applied as shown in the taxonomy of the models in Figure 3.4.

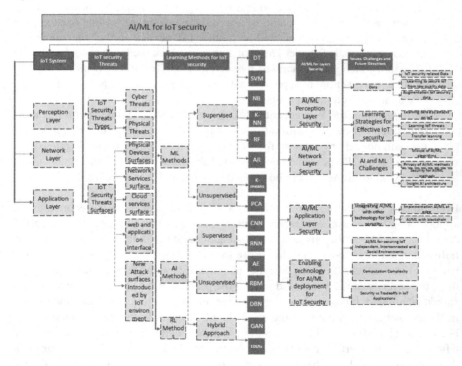

FIGURE 3.4   Different types of AI/ML algorithms to countermeasures IoT attacks

In each learning algorithm in the paradigm of AI and machine learning there will be a set of input data which are used as training data or training set. Overall learning models are categorized into three types: reinforcement, unsupervised and supervised. For instance, with reference to supervised learning, the training data contains the set of input data with targeted corresponding vectors known as labels. When it comes to unsupervised learning, there will not be any labels for the training set. On the other hand, reinforcement learning is different from supervised and unsupervised learning. Its main focus is learning problems; accordingly, it determines what are the appropriate actions it has to take in order to maximize the reward function to a particular situation. It takes a sequence of actions which eventually lead to payoff maximization. With respect to this chapter we focused on supervised and unsupervised learning because most of the IoT data analyses are eligible to deploy these algorithms. The main aim of the supervised learning is to acquire the knowledge of how to estimate the appropriate corresponding output for a given input using the predetermined function. The classificationis done by using some applications which use labeling the data, so that the classification task is simpler. Certain cases, which have the requirement of continuous variable, can be categorized as regression tasks. The aim of the unsupervised learning is a bit difficult because it has the advantage of separating the identical data as clusters within the input data.

The process of classifying the data based on similarity is called clustering. However, unsupervised learning is helpful to optimize the data by discovering the similarity and clustering the large input data using preprocessing. Using preprocessing, the original data is labeled and it will be shifted to the new domain of the optimized data. The idea of preprocessing data will be very useful in assisting the machine learning and artificial learning model and improves the results in terms of accuracy of the model by doing feature extractions quickly. There are a number of efficient machine learning and AI models to train smart devices but choosing the right learning model is a challenging task to improve the accuracy of the given model for a IoT device. In subsequent subsections, we consider the training data given for a model is defined as $\{(f_i, g_i)\}^{K_{i=1}}$ which is basically K training samples denoted with f_i input vector of the model and g_i is the respective output vector of a model. In this scenario, the large number of input data can be collected in a matrix dimension that can be written as $F=(f_1,....f_K)^T$ and we also acquire its respective vectors of the output which is also represented in matrix as $G=(g_1, ,g_k)^T$. In later sections we do not consider these assumptions, these assumptions are limited to the first three subsections. Based on our studies with respect to accuracy prediction in AI, ML and reinforcement models, we have figured out that the accuracy for AI models is better compared to the latter two models which are ML and reinforcement models as shown in Figure 3.5.

3.5.1 CLASSIFICATION

3.5.1.1 KNN (K-nearestneighbors)

In this method, the aim of the classification algorithm is to cluster the new input data which is not seen before based on the similarity. This algorithm works based

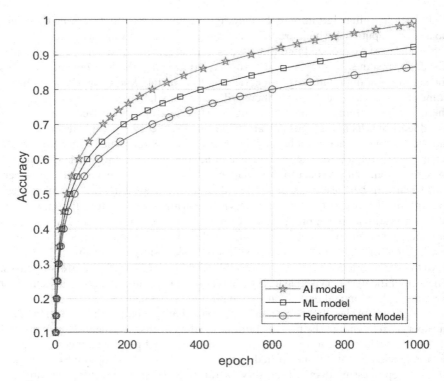

FIGURE 3.5 Comparison of different AI/ML techniques using accuracy levels

on choosing the nearer data to the k-data points in the training input data set. Those data which are closed to the set K in the sample data space are classified. To find the neighbor data set nearer to the k data set, there is a need of calculating Euclidean distance or angle between them or norm or hamming distance which ever is easy to calculate based on the data points. To develop the algorithm for a problem, we consider data input vector as f and by predicting the label classes of data one can determine the K nearest neighbor using f x g using the random variable x which is discrete in nature. Moreover, it acts as indicator function, which is

$$I(s) = 1 \quad \text{if the distance is close}$$

$$= 0 \quad \text{otherwise} \tag{2}$$

KNN has storage problem, Every time it has to store large number of training set. storage is the main limitation for KNN. Otherwise the classification form of KNN is defined as

$$p(x = b \setminus b, K) = \frac{1}{K} \sum_{i \in N_{\text{nk}(f)}} I(8_{i=b}) \tag{3}$$

So, the problem of storage in KNN will lead to unscalable data sets. The researchers' main focus is to address this kind of problem in KNN by modeling based on tree search with less computation. However, the authors have addressed this issue by constructing a tree-based search with a one-off computation. Moreover, there are online KNN classifications.

3.5.1.2 Classification based on naïve Bayes

For a given data, which is new and never existed before as input vector j, given to classifier, which is naive Bayes, this is one of the most promising families of classifier, because of its accuracy. Bayes classification works on Bayes' theorem the approach of naive, so it is named as naive Bayes, which is a probabilistic approach. So, the naive Bayes classifiers work based on Bayes theorem. By considering the independence among the features of the given distribution of a random variable which are a family of probabilistic classifiers.

3.5.1.3 Support Vector Machine (SVM)

Support vector machine (SVM) is used for classification and by extending certain features it can be used for regression, which is support vector regression (SVR). Both the models are similar in nature except for some regression features. SVR models depend on training points and the subset of them. Many SVR approaches exist which includes epsilon, nu, based support vector regression. All these approaches will optimize the IoT data and are used as training data points to train the SVR models.

3.6 SUMMARY

The IoT network consists of a large number of devices which are connected and communicating with each other and the data transmission is very rapid. The data generated by IoT devices is very large and transmits the data using sensors consisting of a vast number of different devices that relate to each other and transmit huge amounts of data. Smart home and smart city, smart industries and smart vehicles are the best examples of the IoT, which serves the needs of different domains such as urban planning, cloud services, energy, mobility, etc. All these services can be vulnerable without proper security algorithms. Using AI/ML models, the IoT data can be optimized and encrypted to analyze the security attacks and data privacy from the IoT data. To sense the prior knowledge and system learning, many big data analytic algorithms can be applied. The challenge of IoT application is choosing the right AI/ML/reinforcement algorithm for a specific application. In this chapter, we have studied many algorithms related to AI/ML to address the security problems and data privacy. We consider various factors about IoT data in wireless virtualization environments such as IoT data collection, IoT data optimization using AI/ML algorithms. Different IoT applications have different types of IoT data, so we discuss the classification of data using various classification techniques. On the other hand, in this chapter, the data generated by the IoT devices will have various features which are similar in nature, so we have considered the similarity in the IoT data. The important aspects of this material are the various AI/ML algorithms for different types of IoT security attacks and applications to analyze the IoT data. And also, we discuss the various attacks that IoT devices could suffer. Based on the type of attack our chapter recommends which type of AI/ML algorithm is supposed to be applied in wireless virtualization environments based on the advantages and accuracy levels of the AI/ML/reinforcement learning algorithms applied to different IoT applications and environments.

REFERENCES

1. Alam, S., M. M. R. Chowdhury, and J. Noll. 2010. Senaas: An event-driven sensor virtualization approach for internet of things cloud. In *2010 IEEE International Conference on Networked Embedded Systems for Enterprise Applications* (pp. 1–6). IEEE.
2. Chandra, R. and P. Bahl. 2004. Multinet: Connecting to multiple IEEE 802.11 networks using a single wireless card. In *ieeeinfocom 2004* (Vol. 2, pp. 882–893). IEEE.
3. Letaief, K. B., et al. 2019. The roadmap to 6g: Ai empowered wireless networks. *IEEE Communications Magazine*, 57(8), pp. 84–90.
4. Mahdavinejad, M. S., M. Rezvan, M. Barekatain, P. Adibi, P. Barnaghi, and A. P. Sheth. 2018. Machine learning for internet of things data analysis: A survey. *Digital Communications and Networks*, 4(3), pp. 161–175.
5. Milton, R., D. Hay, S. Gray, B. Buyuklieva, and A. Hudson-Smith. 2018. *Smart IoT and soft AI*. IET.
6. Monostori, L. 2003. Ai and machine learning techniques for managing complexity, changes and uncertainties in manufacturing. *Engineering Applications of Artificial Intelligence*, 16(4), pp. 277–291.
7. Parvez, I., A. Rahmati, I. Guvenc, A. I. Sarwat, and H. Dai. 2018. A survey on low latency towards 5g: Ran, core network and caching solutions. *IEEE Communications Surveys & Tutorials*, 20(4), pp. 3098–3130.
8. Rawat, D. B., N. Sapavath, and M. Song. 2019. Performance evaluation of deception system for deceiving cyber adversaries in adaptive virtualized wireless networks. In Proceedings of the 4th ACM/IEEE Symposium on Edge Computing (pp. 401–406). ACM.
9. Sapavath, N. N., D. S. Alorini, D. B. Rawat , and M. Garuba. 2019. Maximizing secrecy rate and payoff through wireless virtualization in heterogeneous wireless networks. In 2019 International Conference on Computing, Networking and Communications (ICNC) (pp. 131–135). IEEE.
10. Sapavath, N. N. and D. B. Rawat. 2020. Wireless virtualization architecture: Wireless networking for internet of things. *IEEE Internet of Things Journal*, 7(7), pp. 5946–5953. doi: 10.1109/JIOT.2019.2942542.
11. Sapavath, N. N., S. Safavat, and D. B. Rawat. 2019. On the machine learning–based smart beamforming for wireless virtualization with large-scale MIMO system. *Transactions on Emerging Telecommunications Technologies*, 30(9), p. e3713.
12. Wen, H., P. K. Tiwary, and T. Le-Ngoc. 2013. Wireless virtualization. In *Wireless Virtualization* (pp. 41–81). Springer.
13. Yao, M., M. Sohul, V. Marojevic, and J. H. Reed. 2019. Artificial intelligence defined 5gradio access networks. *IEEE Communications Magazine*, 57(3), pp. 14–20.
14. Rawat, D. B. 2019. Fusion of software defined networking, edge computing, and blockchain technology for wireless network virtualization. *IEEE Communications Magazine*, 57(10), pp. 50–55.
15. Rawat, D. B., A. Alshaikhi, A. Alshammari, C. Bajracharya, and M. Song. 2019. Payoff optimization through wireless network virtualization for IoT applications: A three layer game approach. *IEEE Internet of Things Journal*, 6(2), pp. 2797–2805.

16. Rawat, D. B., R. Doku, and M. Garuba. 2019. Cybersecurity in big data era: From securing big data to data-driven security. *IEEE Transactions on Services Computing*, 2019.

17. Ghafoor, K. Z., L. Kong, D. B. Rawat, E. Hosseini, and A. Sadiq. 2019. Quality of service aware routing protocol in software-defined internet of vehicles. *IEEE Internet of Things Journal*, 6(2), pp. 2817–2828.

4 A Conceptual Model for Optimal Resource Sharing of Networked Microgrids Focusing Uncertainty
Paving the Path to Eco-Friendly Smart Cities

*Danish Mahmood, Tariq Mehmood,
Ghufran Ahmed and Suleman Khan*

CONTENTS

4.1 INTRODUCTION

The advent of the smart grid creates the opportunities to improve the utility and performance of the power system [1]. The advancement in computational techniques and information and communication technologies (ICT) unfolded optimum ways of solutions to address the challenges of the traditional power system. The centralized traditional power system is prone to disastrous one-point failure. On the other hand, major generation sources of traditional power systems are fossil fuel-based power plants. These generation sources are depletive in nature and emit carbon and nitrogen [2]. The contribution of fossil fuel-based power plants in pollution and global warming demands constraint of the operations of such plants. Whereas the explosive growth in population and electric devices exponentially increased the power demand and the reliability of the power system [3]. Hence the escalation call for power generation with higher levels of reliability and stability. This state of affairs in the power sector is demanding the imposition of systematic controls on and monitoring of conventional power systems and aggressive work on alternate power resources to attain the balance in supply and demand with reliability and scalability of the power system. The advancement in computational technologies makes possible the optimal scheduling of power resources. The developments in communication technologies enable the effective and efficient monitoring and control of power generation and distribution.

The traditional power engineer cannot deal with the emerging challenge of power balancing without the adoption of advanced computing methodologies. The computer aided techniques and methodologies, such as advancement in data mining techniques, make possible the identification of the most frequent patterns of RES power generation, normal and uncertain behavior of consumers regarding energy consumption. The advanced statistical methodologies are capable of learning from identified historic data patterns and predicting the future trends of power generation and consumption. The accuracy of this prediction resultantly helps in optimal resources scheduling with minimal change in scheduling decisions.

Such advancements in integrating communication and computing technologies with traditional power grid systems enable the smart grids to offer effective and efficient communication between power supplier (the utility) and the end user, paving the path to a power aware Smart City. This communication feature of smart grids ensures effective and efficient power supply side management (SSM) and demand side management (DSM) at the same time [4]. The SSM refers to the monitoring and control of power generation, while DSM deals with the monitoring and control of power consumption behavior of consumers by exploiting the numerous tariff related schemes.

Distributed energy resources (DERs) in smart grids contain renewable energy sources (RESs) like photovoltaic, solar, wind, small hydro turbine, etc. The RESs offer environment friendly power generation with lower maintenance cost and long-term cost saving. Consequently, the RESs become the most suitable choice for a modern day power solution. The transitional process from fossil-based and non-renewable fuels to renewable and sustainable energy is in progress around the world and global capacity of 23,50,755 MW was installed by the end of 2018 [5].

The MG emerged as the most favorable choice to effectively utilize the DER and connect them with distribution networks [6]. The consortium for electric reliability technology solution (CERTS) for the first time introduced the concept of MGs [7]. MGs are capable of organizing and coordinating the operation of distributed RES and potentially reducing the cost of energy as well and facilitating the consumer to attain the self-sufficiency, reliability and resilience of energy. Normally, MGs have identical basic structures; however, there is no such standardized structure that the world follows [8]. Moreover, MGs have decisive potentials to facilitate the necessitated integration of RES in the modern power system [9]. MG comprises of controllable distributed generators (CDG) to supply the stable energy, energy storage system (ESS) to store excessive power along with non-controllable and controllable loads [10]. MGs can be operated in both islanded as well as grid connected modes. In each mode, there are certain benefits can be achieved subjected to different variables like geographical location, availability of grid line etc.

Networking of multiple self-governed microgrids (MGs) situated at nearby locations emerged as suitable alternatives to improve resiliency and reliability of power system networks. The network of MG provides the effective and efficient power infrastructure to exploit the cost effective and environmental-friendly DER [10]. The design of MG makes possible the integration of renewable and non-renewable distributed generations (DGs) to supply loads within a clearly defined electrical boundary. Advanced control and communication technologies enable the operation of multiple MGs in coordination with the distribution system to supply day by day increasing power requirements efficiently. Networking of multiple MGs enables more reliable and economic power supply to the consumers [11]. In case of emergency, the coordinated operation of the MG network ensures the power supply to the critical loads for longer periods and helps the traditional power stations in restoration of the power supply [12]. Regardless of the advantages, the interconnection of MGs triggers the challenge of energy management [13]. The energy management system (EMS) emerged to address the rising challenge of energy management (EM) [14] within MG and the network of MG. An EMS is a comprehensive automated and real-time system used for optimal scheduling and management of DER and controllable loads. The EMS provides the supervision and control of DER, ESS and controllable loads through scheduling. The optimal scheduling of surplus power within a networked grid depends upon , adopting correct decision variables which are further dependent on accurate forecasting [15, 16] .

The uncertainty directly affects the supply-demand balance, i.e., it is the core objective of MG resource scheduling. The intermittency of RESs in MGs and fluctuation in power demand are the major sources of uncertainty. From literature, it is observed that mostly studies manage the uncertainty at network level which increases the computational overhead and time complexity. However, it is proved from literature that if the uncertainty of MG is mitigated at MG level it will improve the performance of MG in network. In this chapter we provide a conceptual model regarding mitigation of uncertainty at MG level.

The overall model of a power aware Smart City that has multiple MGs is illustrated in Figure 4.1. All MGs are interconnected and have direct links with the utility grid which enables the power and information sharing. The uncertain decision variables of networked MGs are supposed to be forecasted for the short term, based on time series data of 30-day historic data of load and generation output.

The rest of the chapter is organized as follows: Section II provides a comprehensive review of related work, considering techniques and methodologies. Section III outlines the conceptual system model for optimal resource sharing and scheduling networked MG. Major emphasis of this model is to provide an abstraction leading to a power aware Smart City, and Section IV concludes the chapter.

4.2 RELATED WORK

An energy management system (EMS) enables MG to optimally schedule power resources and the energy storage system (ESS) in a way to achieve the balance of supply and load [18]. Numerous studies have been carried out to investigate optimal

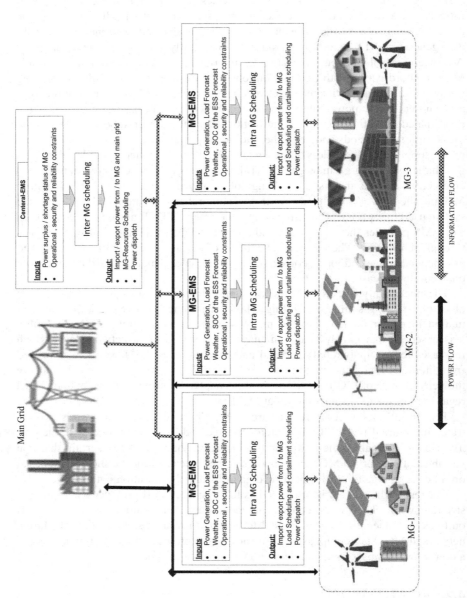

FIGURE 4.1 Conceptual diagram – power aware Smart City

scheduling and energy management of interconnected MGs. The strategies suggested in literature for optimal EMS are either centralized or decentralized. A centralized strategy offers better control; however, there is lack in scalability and they have one point of failure. Decentralized mechanisms offer the scalability but are compromised on control. For example, Zhao et al. [9] proposed a centralized EMS, based on system of system architecture for interconnected MGs, which used column and constraint generation (C&CG) algorithm for problem formulation and MILP for optimization. A centralized EMS for the unified operation of interconnected MGs in a distribution system is proposed to minimize the operation cost in grid-connected operation mode and preserve a reliable power supply in the islanded operation mode in Ref. [16]. Bazmohammadi [1] proposed a hierarchical approach to optimally develop the power scheduling to manage power trading, storage and distribution in a smart grid composed of a macro grid and cooperative MGs. Although, numerous studies have proposed optimal scheduling of MGs however, uncertainity problem persists. Wang et al. [10] addressed the aforementioned issues comprehensively and developed a two-stage layered approach equipped with hybrid control strategy and achieved better results. In the proposed model the uncertainties are broadcasted from MG-EMS to CEMS, which creates computational overload and time complexity that exponentially increases with the growth of MGs in the system. On the other hand, the presence of uncertainties in the local operation of MG affects its capability to cooperate with other MGs in the network [1]. In this study we mitigate the uncertainties of MG locally and consider the demand associated uncertainty at the level of CEMS. Additionally, a power sharing mechanism based on sharing economy concept is introduced, i.e., no profit and no loss-based power sharing model. The novel feature of this study will be an effective and efficient hybrid-control layered EMS model with less computational overhead and time complexity. Table 4.1 explicitly demonstrates state of the art work regarding management of networked micro grids for a power aware Smart City.

4.3 CONCEPTUAL SYSTEM MODEL

The problem focused in this study is NP-hard and needs to be addressed in hierarchal fashion. At the lower level the resources have to be optimized at individual MG-level, and at network level the resources of all participating MGs need to be optimized. However, a major focus should be on optimization of individual MG resources locally. Forecasting accuracy of generation-output and consumer's power demand is crucial for the optimality of EMS. The generation-output of RES and consumer's power demand is dependent on weather and placement. To ensure the accuracy of generation-output and consumer's power demand forecasting there is a vital need to consider weather forecasted data in order to estimate power generation out-put and power demand. The accurate generation-output and consumer's power demand forecasting at individual MG-level enables the EMS to optimally schedule the operations of RES and ESS and assure the stability of the grid through scheduled power exchange. The accuracy of prediction is limited to the characteristics of methodology used for particular modules. Larger prediction horizons and time intervals

TABLE 4.1

Comprehensive literature review of state of the art work regarding networked MG management

Ref.	Focused Area	Main Feature	Techniques Applied	Limitations	Tool(s)	Uncertainty Handling
[9]	Energy management system in order to manage the intermittence and volatility of renewable energy resources.	Two level optimization model proposed in this study. Uncertainty of RES considered in first level optimization at each MG level. The issue of spatial unbalancing in demand and generation addresses at 2nd level optimization at MMG Level.	• Column & Constraint Generation C&CG Algorithm (For decomposition of problem into master & slave problem) • MILP for optimization	• Optimal strategy for BESS sharing at MMG level is not considered.	MATLAB	Yes
[10]	Energy management for networked MGs	A temporally-coordinated optimal operation method for MGs is proposed. Diverse uncertainties are modelled and integrated into the system operation model. A multi-stage stochastic operation method is proposed to handle the uncertainties. Network constraints are fully modelled to guarantee the operating security. The nonlinear problem is linearized and efficiently solved by commercial solvers.	• MILP • Mean-variance Markowitz Theory	CBESS is an overhead of system which leads to enhancement in capital cost and operational cost as well.	MATLAB CPLEX	Yes

(Continued)

TABLE 4.1 (CONTINUED)
Comprehensive literature review of state of the art work regarding networked MG management

Ref.	Focused Area	Main Feature	Techniques Applied	Limitations	Tool(s)	Uncertainty Handling
[18]	Energy management in network of smart grids	The economic and stability requirement of MGs is ensured by developing multi-market driven power scheduling.	Stackelberg game theory	In simulation of proposed model, the load is assumed as 25% for each MG. This assumption leads to artificial or manipulated results.	MATLAB	No
[19]	Energy management problem in multi MGs	The MILP is most favorably used in EMS. The convergence rate of MILP decreased with the increase of problem size. This particular limitation becomes problematic in on-line large-scale multi-MG optimization Problem. This study addresses this issue and proposed linear and quadratic problem formulation to effectively solve the large-scale multi-MG optimization in real-time.	Multi-objective optimization problem solved by Utopia point method and compromise programming method is used in this work. Convex energy optimization problem formulated.	Uncertainty of net-demand is ignored in proposed model.	IBM ILOG CPLEX (used to solve the MILP Problem MATLAB	No

(Continued)

TABLE 4.1 (CONTINUED)
Comprehensive literature review of state of the art work regarding networked MG management

Ref.	Focused Area	Main Feature	Techniques Applied	Limitations	Tool(s)	Uncertainty Handling
[20]	Energy management in fully decentralized controlling environment through multi-agent.	Centralized energy management and control system face limitation while communicating the state information of distributed system and loads to the central controller. The failure of central controller is also a major challenge to the reliability of the system. This study introduced the Q-learning method to address the state and action. The problem of central failure is countered through decentralized MAS.	Optimal policy learning is achieved by use of reinforcement learning technique. Fuzzy Q-Learning technique applied to deal with the continuous state-action space. The limitation (i.e. inefficient for large state-action space) is countered by discretization of state-action space.	According to independent learning approach each agent acts with autonomy. In this approach the environment is no longer stationery and convergence cannot be assumed, because the agents consider their state and ignore the actions of others agents.	MATLAB	No
[21, 23]	Uncertainties' associated with distributed generation and demand of islanded and interconnected operation of MGs are addressed	Numerous studies are available on multi energy coordination based on deterministic and periodic operation but the power load, transactional prices and uncertainties of RES are ignored. This study addressed this gap in literature.	MILP	For problem formulation same power factor for all DGs are considered and ignore the Power Losses	12 Core Simulator OP5600	Yes

(Continued)

TABLE 4.1 (CONTINUED)
Comprehensive literature review of state of the art work regarding networked MG management

Ref.	Focused Area	Main Feature	Techniques Applied	Limitations	Tool(s)	Uncertainty Handling
[16]	The area of study is the problem of cooperation among MGs and macrogrid	A hierarchical power scheduling approach to optimally manage the power trading, storage and distribution in smart grids by considering macro grids and cooperative MGs are investigated.	Convex Optimization	Storage capacities and generation cost of MGs are assumed in problem formulation which leads to some compromising results	MATLAB	Yes
[1]	Energy management system while considering the uncertainties in interconnected MGs is proposed in this study	To mitigate the uncertainty from RES generation and load are managed at MG Level	CCMPC Receding Horizon Control	Operating cost increased by considering uncertainties in proposed model.	CIGRE Based benchmark Distribution network simulated	Yes
[22]	Optimization of periodic scheduling of MGs	Short term scheduling of MGs by considering uncertain parameters of Wind and solar generation, load profile and market price	Second order cone programming MILP	Consideration of only worst-case scenario of uncertain parameters	Gourbi CONOPT GAMS	Yes

(Continued)

TABLE 4.1 (CONTINUED)

Comprehensive literature review of state of the art work regarding networked MG management

Ref.	Focused Area	Main Feature	Techniques Applied	Limitations	Tool(s)	Uncertainty Handling
[23]	Energy management strategy is developed by providing additional information of adjustable power and demand response.	EMS proposed in literature consider the surplus power or shortage power to maintain the power balancing. In this study adjustable power is considered to attain the equilibrium of demand and supply.	Mixed Integer Linear Programming MILP (for optimization Modified Contract net protocol (MCNP for communication b/w agents. Bi-level EMS applied (MG-EMS, CEMS)	Uncertainties of RES, demand and supply are not considered in any context.	JADE with IBM ILOG CPLEX MCNP	No
[24]	Energy management in multi energy MGs by considering the uncertainties	Temporally-coordinated optimal operation method for MGs is proposed Diverse uncertainties are modelled and integrated into the system operation model A multi-stage stochastic operation method is proposed to handle the uncertainties	DROOP algorithm DAPI algorithm	The study doesn't meet any numerical solution	OPAL-RT simulator	No

(Continued)

TABLE 4.1 (CONTINUED)
Comprehensive literature review of state of the art work regarding networked MG management

Ref.	Focused Area	Main Feature	Techniques Applied	Limitations	Tool(s)	Uncertainty Handling
[25]	Scheduling of generation and storage in MGs	Optimal scheduling of energy storage and generation in presence of RES with the objective of generation cost reduction and reliability enhancement is proposed in this study	Artificial Fish Swarm Algorithm (AFSA)	Result of AFSA didn't compare with any previous algorithm or GA. Cost of generation is the function of power generated, whereas the wind generation is assumed rather than calculation.	MATLAB	Yes
[14]	Optimal scheduling on interconnected MGs and resilience enhancement under uncertainty	Optimal scheduling of networked MGs while considering the adjustable loads for resilience assessment and minimization of operation cost	Probabilistic model development for input data Resilience modeling for networked MGs GAMS BARON	During disruption event MG is not permissible to change its sell or buy state, load curtailment of MG for hourly demand is assumed.	MATLAB	Yes

(Continued)

TABLE 4.1 (CONTINUED)

Comprehensive literature review of state of the art work regarding networked MG management

Ref.	Focused Area	Main Feature	Techniques Applied	Limitations	Tool(s)	Uncertainty Handling
[26]	Optimal energy management of interconnected MGs	Development of local and global cost function for optimal power sharing in MGs. The proposed Algorithm composed by three main parts: Optimization of MG Improvement in economic benefits of each MG Evaluation of all possible combination of MG Pairs.	MILP	Uncertainties have an important impact on Operational cost which are not considered in any context	TOMLAB / CPLEX	Yes
[27]	Energy management system of multi MGs	Hour a-head scheduling is proposed while considering the uncertainties of RES. Two-stage energy optimization model is proposed in this study.	MIP Rolling method Stackelberg Game Theory	Uncertainties of load demand and power generation are neglected in model	MATLAB / CPLEX	Yes
[28]	Intelligent energy management system	Smart governance of power flow among hybrid MGs, ESS, grid and satisfaction of technical constraints in order to ensure the economical, reliable and sustainable power supply	GHI	Participation optimality is considered but ignored the optimal scheduling of ESS and other components of the system.	MATLAB	No

are error prone due to an increase in decision variables [29, 30]. Therefore, it is suggested to use short term prediction horizons and time intervals in order to improve the prediction accuracy. ARIMA is a hybrid methodology which gives better results for short term prediction made on the basis of time-series data [17]. We suggest the use of ARIMA for the forecast of generation-output and demand forecasting for short-term prediction (e.g., three hours).

The EM optimization problem is solved by using a number of methodologies. MILP is most favorably used in the literature due to its easy reproduction in commercial language. However, the computation time required to solve the EM problem is highly influenced by the size of the problem. It is evident from recent literature that the EM problem is solved through robust, stochastic and metaheuristic techniques. The results of metaheuristic techniques are more efficient as compared to other available techniques such as linear or nonlinear programing techniques. The change in optimization level can improve the results. Therefore, we suggest the use of PSO/ GA or any heuristic optimization technique for the solution of the EM problem. For the time being, proposed conceptual model PSO is under consideration.

Algorithm 1-1 is designed to solve the optimization problem at individual MG level. The algorithm is further divided into fourparts. Algorithm 1-1 part (a) performs the short-term forecasting of generation output based on 30-day historic generation-output and forecasted weather data using ARIMA. ARIMA gives better result for time series data when the forecasting horizon is short (i.e. three hours). Algorithm 1-1 part (b) provides the short-term forecast of power demand on the basis of historic consumer's demand and respective weather parameters of last 30 days.

ALGORITHM 1-1:

1) *Part (a): Real Time Forecasting of RES's Generation Output of MG.*
   1. Take the power generation data of the previous 30 days.
   2. Collect the periodic data of the weather forecast.
   3. Use the prediction model to predict the periodic RES generation output on the basis of steps 1 & 2.

2) *Part (b): Short-term Forecast of Power Demand of MG.*
   1. Prepare the power demand data of the previous 30 days.
   2. Determine the controllable and non-controllable loads.
   3. Use the prediction model to predict the periodic power demand for controllable and non-controllable loads.

3) *Part (c): Power Calculation: Surplus or Shortage*
   1. Consider the forecasted power generation output from Part (a).
   2. Consider the forecasted power demand from part (b) (for controllable and non-controllable loads).
   3. Collect the power available in BESS.

4. Compute the power balance state.
5. Schedule loads in accordance with available power in case of Power Shortage.
   a. Reduce the controllable loads in case of power shortage.
   b. Compute the power balance after reduction of controllable loads.
   c. Inform MG-CMS about power balance state.
6. In case of power surplus execute Part (d).
7. Inform the CEMS about the final state of power balance.

4) Part (d): BESS Modeling.
   1. In case of power surplus check battery storage state.
   2. Charge the battery in accordance with charge limits.
   3. Keep the lowest limit as 20% of maximum capacity for power consumption.

Algorithm 1-1 part (b) also determines the controllable and non-controllable load using the concept of direct load control (DLC). Part (c) of algoritim 1-1 calculates the power balance states on the basis of forecasted generation output, available energy in BESS and forecasted consumer's power demand. In case power shortage state is rendered, the loads of MG will be curtailed or scheduled in accordance with DLC listing. After implementing this mitigation strategy, power supply and demand balance state are re-evaluated and the final state will be communicated with central EMS. The same procedure will be executed in case any change in scheduling decisions appeared before communication with central EMS.

The BESS initially considered with zero energy, and the problem of BESS is formulated in part (d) by considering the lower and upper state of charge (SOC) bounds (i.e., 20% and 80%, respectively). The algorithm collectively is comprised of four parts, as can be seen in Figure 4.2.

4.4 CONCLUSION

In this study, optimal resource allocation and scheduling of grid connected MGs are critically reviewed. Different resource allocation methodologies are analyzed. In some studies, the power demand uncertainty is ignored and in others the generation associated uncertainty gets missed. However, few studies considered both RES generation associated uncertainty at community level. Management of uncertainty at upper or community level resulted in increased computation overheads and time complexity with the increase of MGs in network. This study proposed the management of uncertainty at MG-level in order to avoid the computational overhead and time complexity. The increase in the number of MGs in network and power sharing through market model is creating a threat to business model of utilities. In a future study we intend to work on a "power sharing economy" concept (i.e., no profit no loss) to avoid such types of expected conflict and promote the social benefit in society.

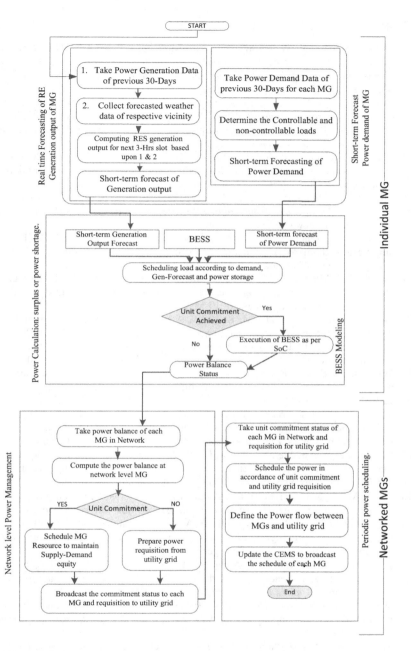

FIGURE 4.2   Conceptual model: Uncertainty aware networked micro grid for a Smart City.

REFERENCES

1. Bazmohammadi, N., A. Tahsiri, A. Anvari-Moghaddam, and J. M. Guerrero. 2019. A hierarchical energy management strategy for interconnected microgrids considering uncertainty. *International Journal of Electrical Power & Energy Systems*, 109, pp. 597–608.
2. Hou, J., C. Ji, J. Wang, and M. Ke. 2019. A review on optimization dispatching and control for microgrid. *Journal of Physics: Conference Series*, 1176 (4), p. 042046.
3. Liao, Y. 2013. Transformation of electric power grid into smart grid. *International Journal of Advance Innovations, Thoughts & Ideas*, 02(04), pp. 76–81. doi=10.1.1.913.2399
4. Marzal, S., R. Salas, R. González-Medina, G. Garcerá, and E. Figueres. 2018. Current challenges and future trends in the field of communication architectures for microgrids. *Renewable and Sustainable Energy Reviews*, 82, pp. 3610–3622.
5. International Renewable Energy Agency. 2018. *Renewable capacity statistics 2018 Statistiques de capacité renouvelable 2018 Estadísticas de capacidad renovable 2018*. International Renewable Energy Agency.
6. Yoldaş, Y., A. Önen, S. M. Muyeen, A. V. Vasilakos, and İ. Alan. 2017. Enhancing smart grid with microgrids: Challenges and opportunities. *Renewable and Sustainable Energy Reviews*, 72 (January), pp. 205–214.
7. The CERTS Microgrid Concept, as Demonstrated at the CERTS/AEP Microgrid Test Bed CERTS. [Online]. Available: https://certs.lbl.gov/publications/certs-microgrid-concept-demonstrated. [Accessed: 10-May-2019].
8. Hou, J., C. Ji, J. Wang, and M. Ke. 2019. A review on optimization dispatching and control for microgrid. Journal of Physics: Conference Series, 1176(4), p. 042046.
9. Zhao, B. et al. 2018. Energy management of multiple microgrids based on a system of systems architecture. *IEEE Transactions on Power Systems*, 33(6), pp. 6410–6421.
10. Wang, D., J. Qiu, L. Reedman, K. Meng, and L. Lei. 2018. Two-stage energy management for networked microgrids with high renewable penetration. *Applied Energy*, 226(May), pp. 39–48.
11. Bashir, A. A., M. Pourakbari-Kasmaei, J. Contreras, and M. Lehtonen. 2019. A novel energy scheduling framework for reliable and economic operation of islanded and grid-connected microgrids. *Electric Power Systems Research*, 171, pp. 85–96.
12. Liu, Y., H. Gooi, S. Member, and Y. Li. 2019. A secure distributed transactive energy management scheme for multiple interconnected microgrids considering misbehaviors. *IEEE Transactions on Smart Grid*, 10(6), pp. 5975–5986.
13. Alam, M. N., S. Chakrabarti, and A. Ghosh. 2018. Networked microgrids : State-of-the-art and future. *IEEE Transactions on Industrial Informatics*, 15(3), pp. 1238–1250.
14. Salyani, P., S. Najafi Ravadanegh, and N. Mahdavi Tabatabaei. 2019. Optimal scheduling of networked-microgrids to resiliency enhancement under uncertainty. In *Power Systems* (pp. 139–161). Cham: Springer.
15. Javidsharifi, M., T. Niknam, J. Aghaei, and G. Mokryani. 2018. Multi-objective short-term scheduling of a renewable-based microgrid in the presence of tidal resources and storage devices. *Applied Energy*, 216(July), pp. 367–381.
16. Wang, Y., S. Mao, and R. M. Nelms. 2015. On hierarchical power scheduling for the macrogrid and cooperative microgrids. *IEEE Transactions on Industrial Informatics*, 11(6), pp. 1574–1584.
17. Wen, L., K. Zhou, S. Yang, and X. Lu. 2019. Optimal load dispatch of community microgrid with deep learning based solar power and load forecasting. *Energy*, 171, pp. 1053–1065.
18. Yue, J. et al. 2019. A multi-market-driven approach to energy scheduling of smart microgrids in distribution networks. *Sustainability*, 11(2), p. 301.

19. Sandgani, M. R., and S. Sirouspour. 2018. Priority-based microgrid energy management in a network environment. *IEEE Transactions on Sustainable Energy*, 9(2), pp. 980–990.
20. Bui, V.-H., A. Hussain, and H.-M. Kim. 2018. A multiagent-based hierarchical energy management strategy for multi-microgrids considering adjustable power and demand response. *IEEE Transactions on Smart Grid*, 9(2), pp. 1323–1333.
21. Rafiee Sandgani, M., and S. Sirouspour. 2018. Energy management in a network of grid-connected microgrids/nanogrids using compromise programming. *IEEE Transactions on Smart Grid*, 9(3), pp. 2180–2191.
22. Kofinas, P., A. I. Dounis, and G. A. Vouros. 2018. Fuzzy Q-learning for multi-agent decentralized energy management in microgrids. *Applied Energy*, 219, pp. 53–67.
23. Li, Z., and Y. Xu. 2019. Temporally-coordinated optimal operation of a multi-energy microgrid under diverse uncertainties. *Applied Energy*, 240, pp. 719–729.
24. Ren, L. et al. 2018. Enabling resilient distributed power sharing in networked microgrids through software defined networking. *Applied Energy*, 210, pp. 1251–1265.
25. Kumar, K. P., and B. Saravanan. 2019. Day ahead scheduling of generation and storage in a microgrid considering demand Side management. *Journal of Energy Storage*, 21, pp. 78–86.
26. Garcia-Torres, F., C. Bordons, and M. A. Ridao. 2019. Optimal economic schedule for a network of microgrids with hybrid energy storage system using distributed model predictive control. *IEEE Transactions on Industrial Electronics*, 66(3), pp. 1919–1929.
27. Rui, T., G. Li, Q. Wang, C. Hu, W. Shen, and B. Xu. 2019. Hierarchical optimization method for energy scheduling of multiple microgrids. *Applied Sciences*, 9(4), p. 624.
28. Ebrahimi, M. R., and N. Amjady. 2019. Adaptive robust optimization framework for day-ahead microgrid scheduling. *International Journal of Electrical Power & Energy Systems*, 107, pp. 213–223.
29. Nayak, C. K., K. Kasturi, and M. R. Nayak. 2019. Economical management of microgrid for optimal participation in electricity market. *Journal of Energy Storage*, 21, pp. 657–664.
30. Vergara, P. P., J. C. López, J. M. Rey, L. C. P. Silva, and M. J. Rider. 2019. Energy management in microgrids. In *Microgrids design and implementation* (pp. 195–216). Springer.

5 A Novel Framework for a Cyber Secure Smart City

Kashif Naseer Qureshi, Hassan Jalil Hadi,
Farhan Haroon, Abeer Iftikhar, Faisal Bashir
and Muhammad Najam Ul Islam

CONTENTS

5.1 INTRODUCTION

The concept of Smart City is one of the remarkable vision with new and smart integrated technologies offer a wide range of services. In a Smart City, the individual is monitored and a map of their foundations, executives, administration, networks, well-being, instruction and indigenous habitat through data and correspondence advance Information and Communication Technologies (ICT). The Smart City is structured by Artificial Intelligence, and incorporated through sensors, hardware and systems that relate to modern frameworks involved databases, following dynamic calculations [1, 2]. The idea of Smart Cities is to play its vital role in good governance and tackle monetary rebuilding, natural, administration, management and open part issues with smart methodology. Problems are multiplying in recent urban life due to a shortage of resources and a lack of effective management. In such cases, the need of smart city communities are highly appreciated. The urban life requires extraordinarily smart services by suing advance technologies and the Internet.

The term "worldwide village" is deeply linked with the IoT based Smart City as a development relying on the latest research in the field of technology and global Internet. The Smart City concept is also attractive for manufacturers and sponsors for trading their items like iPads, smartphones, GPS and numerous other such technologies [3]. The automated city based on IoT provides smarter evolution in the lifestyle and enhance living standards. It is said that Smart Cities through advanced self-aware mechanisms could also boost the financial systems [4].

There are already numerous developed cities thought of as actual pioneers of the (IoT) based Smart Cities concept such as Singapore, Masder, Amsterdam, Barcelona and Paris [4]. The main components of the Smart City are illustrated in Figure 5.1. The latest information and communication technologies (i.e., RFID, IoT, AI, cloud computing, etc.) are utilized in Smart Cities to include the latest trends in their systems.

IoT is the network of physical objects that are interconnected to share information. The basic concept of IoT is to use the latest technology and integrate it into daily life

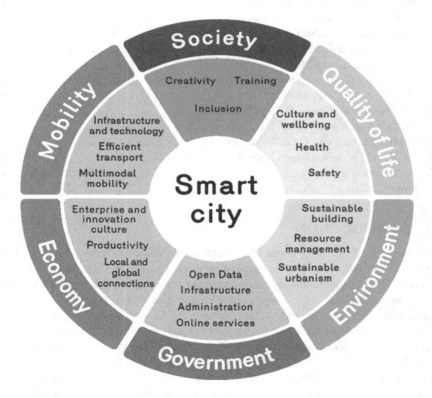

FIGURE 5.1   Main component of Smart Cities

in the simplest way. It is believed that the future of smart devices will define new standards of living and advanced services. However, it is very important to exchange data with the maker, worker and other linked devices. Every component in IoT is mostly self-sufficient in its working and it has clearly defined goals; it might have intra or inter network working mechanisms. IoT contributes an important part in the development of Smart City because it is highly dependent on the level of efficient and advanced technology that is being used on it. The IoT is considered as a top-notch research domain these days and it is believed that researching in this field can create a lot of new opportunities. The proper focus and development in this idea leads to in-depth exposure and creation of very user-friendly services. IoT works by integrating physical and virtual systems with an enormous spread in the domain of electronics systems [5].

The idea of Smart Cities is exclusively reliant on smart portable systems, efficient user-friendly technologies and the IoT based customized solutions. In short, it is concluded that Smart City is heavily dependent upon information technology and the portable advance system that can make human life better.

It can also not be ignored that like every other system, Smart Cities do face some hurdles along the way as well. Most of the issues are related to development, socio-economic and political problems. However, the biggest problem is technical issues. In all discussed problems, the security and privacy are the important and main concern in Smart Cities [6]. Manufacturers are more focused on making these products more portable and efficient at the same time, and while achieving this goal the factor of cybersecurity is not the priority. The field of information security handles all the problems related to making the data more confidential and integral. Cybersecurity aims to defend the data from cyber-attacks, which include numerous threats like worms, scams and many other vicious activities. These cyber-threats may exploit and compromise Smart Cities. Security is a crucial part of smart cities and requires special measures to protect Smart Cities from multiple cyber-attacks [7]. Developing ideas of Smart Cities need to classify the central provisions of information security high skills.

Defenseless Smart Cities are highly vulnerable to security attacks and need immediate measures to protect themselves. In nutshell, Smart City would not be marginalized without proper security mechanism [8].

5.2 CYBERSECURITY IN SMART CITY

The cybersecurity of Smart City has been a passion for experts. The motivation is to ensure the soundness of fundamental organizations like human administrations, organization and imperativeness in a Smart City. These all components of Smart City are considered to reorganize and address the issues of security to improve the organizations social and financial factors and all monetary variables [9]. These issues are clarified in Figure 5.2. The investigators perceive, uncover and suggest answers for the information security matters by considering the referenced issues. Furthermore, the authors in [10] discussed about the security and its related assurance concerns.

The IoT requires important attention from the investigators because it is the essential technology which transforms the idea of Smart City [11]. Security is one of

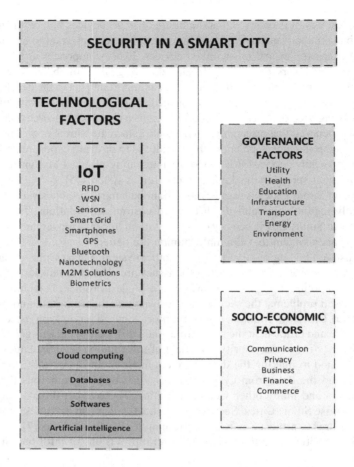

FIGURE 5.2 Manipulating factors on Cybersecurity in a Smart City

the important issue and need to design the more advance and smart security models. Machine to Machine (M2M) concept is one the valuable execution in IoT networks and in Smart City. Security is one of the critical factor for working up a Smart City The manufacture of gigantic data in the Smart City is unavoidable, counting national interests, government records and other information about the residents [12]. From such data, the Smart City networks can isolate noteworthy information helping to ensure consistent examination and all-inclusive enrolling. The author in Ref. [12] explains that big data gives numerous opportunities of an increasingly smart life and brings various challenges of security and assurance. These challenges are non-appearance of gadgets with huge data, untouchable data sharing, threats in creating open databases, data spillage and stresses on automated security.

In Ref. [14], computerized security challenges are discussed. Author discussed on the basis of two standard security and assurance. Here, authors presented a logical model that is among the people, IoT, and servers that are vulnerable against information security threats. Although the logical and graphical model of the IoT is based on security and privacy assurance or the way of detection, prevention and recovery. Additionally, Ref. [15] proposes a flowed structure for Internet of Thing applications, which ensures privacy, authentication, trust and assurance in information transport.

A distinctive evidence is observed that all security matters in Smart City is still not clear in terms of its complete implementation and policies. . At the present time, all the concerned accomplices for the security and insurance information perceived in using immaculate strategy. The makers prescribed separating by and large accomplices, the security necessities and matters are perceived in a predominant method. They also suggest a sweeping structure to contract with these subjects.

Right now [16], the activity of sharp script computer programs is inspected in the setting of information security. There is need to inspected the programming script implemented in automated city in terms of security matters. Authors also discussed about security issues and tried to identifying the security requirements in Smart City. In Ref. [17], the authors recommend an encryption intended to deal with the issues of data trustworthiness and security.

Canny structure is one of the significant area in automated city as it offers the kind of incredibly novel and capable system and its association with information systems [18]. The author in Ref. [19] talks about IS issues in an adroit system. The necessities of information security are recognized by the author, and various models are discussed and differentiated concerning the issues and systems. This paper [20] analyzes the association between secrecy and security issues and highlights its requirement. The maker by then suggests another idea for arranging the Internet with the end goal that security issues are overseen in a prevalent way. The reconstructing of the Internet systems and fascinating the idea the systems need to refreshing the systems and fulfill all the requirements.

The paper [21] depicts guidelines for application systems for an automated city and address the issues to build a Smart City. Even though the makers have analyzed various deterrents for Smart City because still the information systems issues have not been deliberated specifically.

Suciu et al. [22] proposed portraying the establishment of dispersed processing and IoT fittingly for an automated city with better security measures. For that, they have planned a framework for the information that can be directed by the appropriate registered organization. The security is still a stress for users of inan automated city. In Ref. [23] the authors discussed the security issues of occupants of an automated city. This consolidates five estimations according to the makers: character insurance, request security, region security, impression security and owner security. They propose a 5D model that watches out these five issues. The model designers insure that this model will reach the Smart City goals.

The legitimacy of a Smart City is considered by Gemma [24] particularly related with utilization of security assurance for individuals its similar to foundations and government policies They portray the sharp game plans and clarify the issues concerning the utilization of such game plans. The issue of security is analyzed in Ref. [25], where authors discussed the security issues to follow the assessment for the

Smart City. Authors explained that data mining is another key activity in smart urban networks because it need to recollecting the security concerns and data usage.

5.3 SECURITY IN GOVERNANCE, SOCIAL AND ECONOMIC PERSPECTIVE

It is essential to recognize the internal necessities in a Smart City in the setting of information security, as this will help with working up a predominant perception security measures. . Additionally, it will perceiving the privilege and feasible responses for security issues. As it was analyzed in section II, information security in a Smart City is generally dependent upon three parts: organization factors, monetary components and the inventive components. These components affect and recognize the information security issues in Smart City [26]. The ICT and security mechanisms are in progress for Smart City, but still not fully execute in systems especially in . These implementations also trigger new security concerns and issues systems confirmation and quality. Need to link the financial factors of organizations and its relationship with information security. Here it is said that the organizational factors and money related factors are dependent on the creative factors as these are executed in a Smart City through development. These factors join to affect the information security issues in a Smart City, which can again be managed through more advancements because it is a fundamental concern at the present time. In this way, the all the security requirements are fulfill need for critical centers. . In any case, to recognize the middle information security necessities, there is a need to think about the organization, social and money related factors as well [27].

5.3.1 ADMINISTRATION FACTORS

As seen in Figure 5.2, the organizational issues that affect and trigger the security issues fuse utility, prosperity division, system, guidance, transport, etc. The main concern of investigators for Smart City, that how to deal with whole system and the main issues, yet the systems poor execution lead to various security threats and attacks. These anonymous attacks and cheats can be amazingly perilous, which is a significant inspiration driving Smart City networks.

5.3.2 NEED FOR SECURITY TESTING

Security experts and professionals need to hired and appointed to tackle the critical security issues and provide more feasible and smart security solutions to customers [28]. There is need to handle the processes related to security testing. It is pressing need for security professionals to overcome the existing security issues in organizations.

5.3.3 DANGERS TO BASIC FOUNDATIONS

The most significant and essential zone is the basic framework where changing a solitary procedure in a basic framework can cause deferral or loss of basic administrations [29].

TABLE 5.1

Security Concerns in Smart Cities

IoT Technologies	Governess Factors	Socioeconomic Factors
RFID	**Utility**	**Smart Communication**
• Abuse of tags Tag killing	• Misuse of data	• Cybersecurity
• Threats to readers DoS		• Data integrity
• Spoofing Eavesdropping		
• Signal Interference		
• Jamming		
WSN	**Smart mobility**	**Individual Privacy**
• Tag killing	• Location privacy	• Issues in social networking
• Threats to data	Individual privacy	• Use of smartphones
confidentiality, integrity		• Location privacy
• Threats to readers DoS		
• Misuse of resources		
• Bandwidth degradation		
• Battery exhaustion		
Smartphones	**Management**	
• Threats through GPS	• Election Security testing	
• Bluetooth		
• Wi-Fi		

The fundamental basic foundations incorporate social insurance, industry and media transmission. The usage of basic foundations in Smart Cities is primarily on the IoT and smart grids. So, the dangers presenting to these two advancements ought to be thought about. Also, the big data also leads to enormous issues related to information respectability and versatility as it should be appropriately deal and ensured. This is the obligation of a Smart City's basic framework to keep up its security, flexibility and information respectability [30]. Therefore, there is a need for proper foundation to insure and tackle the noxious assaults which are harmful for Smart City communities and administrations. The wellbeing segment is one of the most significant factor for basic foundation, its purpose is just not protect the systems but also protect the other worries of a patient in healthcare systems [31]. Still there is a serious security threats in healthcare systems where the threat on pateint life where the basic medical record and data can be changed by the aggressor. So, the wellbeing data frameworks in a Smart City ought to have secure encryption frameworks.

5.3.4 SMART MOBILITY SECURITY AND PROTECTION NECESSITIES

An automated city need proposed security and data protection mechanism where the information related to people medical record, transportations services, social and financial affairs data exist. Here, limitation methodologies fuse RFID, Bluetooth, WIFI, GSM and GPS, in light of the fact that determined servers do not need to know device IDs. [30] Some of the PDA applications that offer versatile data services and used the data mining techniques. Additionally, the information sent and received from devices used in the smart transportability structure may be open to malignant attacks causing inaccurate traffic reports in satellite course systems [32]. Accordingly, it is clear by examining the issues in a savvy city that this space requires upgraded usage of ICT systems and need to propels recollecting for security.

5.3.5   VITALITY AND UTILITY IMPROVEMENT

Distributed computing provide smart features that are fitting for smart urban communities and systems programming stages [33]. Information security and its assurance is remain top factor for utilities and for the customers that are playing fundamental role in savvy city structures [34]. Likewise, the issues need to address before new system implementations. . For the additional imperativeness and utilities from fakes and threatening attacks, a fitting strategy should be made. This report by Semantic [35] recommends that open key establishment (PKI) or administered PKI can be used to deal with security issues in smart structures. The security issues and their answers in a smart system will be deliberated upon.

5.3.6   SOCIAL AND MONETARY COMPONENTS

In an automated city, society's have been facing social issues, which are regulated through advance systems development especially for emergency systems thereby need to change the Smart City into a one-stop organization structure [36]. Likewise, the advance city ensures the progress towards the automated systems which offers to improve the banking, cash and business practices with more capabilities . The social and money related factors in a Smart City join correspondence, solitary character, banking, and reserve. These are a fundamental part of a Smart City and need defense mechanism against security and its assurance issues.

5.3.7   CHALLENGES IN SMART CITY COMMUNICATION

The media transmission portion is part of the establishment of a Smart City which are defenseless against various security attacks. As various financial organization practices are also brought out through media transmission and remote frameworks, where the requirement for security and affirmation increases. Furthermore, machine to machine (M2M) trades offer great services for inhabitants in smart city [37]. In this way, the security risks relating to M2M communication should in like manner be considered. The use of mobile phones and tablets have new framework and better services for correspondence among the inhabitants of a Smart City. Furthermore, it has similarly incited new risks and assurance for information security. The comprehensive development is required for continuously tackle the new attacks and threats. As the PDAs are adopted late but these are the sharp objects for the software engineers [38]. Remote frameworks in organization by using IoT standards and advance ICT systems have positive impact in sagacious correspondence and for the security systems for smart arrangements.

5.3.8 SINGULAR PRIVACY

The safety of individuals is a basic right that should be guaranteed in a smart city. The users of a savvy city from various organizations develop heterogeneous frameworks and structures, and also consider one of the goal for software engineers who need to hinder their security rights for their benefit. Here the activity of long-ago relational correspondence should similarly be considered concerning insurance and information security. The assurance concerns need for long-extended relational correspondence and also depend upon the level of unmistakable confirmation of given information by the individual.. The all correspondence among service providers and users should be protect and user profile should need confidentiality in all manners.

5.4 PRIVACY PROTECTION IN SMART CITIES

For any advancement, the benefits of occupants should be guaranteed wherever and at whatever point. In spite of the upsides of Smart City organizations, security bursts are getting worst especially when the new setting for splendid smart city required. Most organizations of a Smart City rely upon ICT [39]. On occasion, customers (especially young people and the more established) are interested about security issues, and they become perfect concentrations for aggressors when they help through their mobile phones, tablets, and PCs, revealing individual data, for instance, sexual orientation, age and territory. Along these lines, this section focuses on insuring the Smart City. We at first describe security issues; then, we present and consider different insurance models. Finally, we rapidly inspect current security rules in different countries.

5.4.1 PRIVACY MODELS

In an information system, there are three principal forms: information move, stockpiling and preparing. Privacy concerns can occur during any of these procedures, which can influence the client's conduct. Services might be linked with the client's position, which can raise secrecy concerns. The writers in Ref. [40] proposed a Where, Who, What (W3) security model for location-based service (LBS). In Ref. [17], a three-layer model of client security was proposed to provide protection frameworks. Figure 5.3 shows the cybersecurity challenges in automated cities. Improperly, privacy safeguarding techniques do not discuss restrictions, for example, the normal difference in individuals and untrusted outsiders (cloud suppliers). Henceforth, for the further assessments need for more classification mechanism and significant tests.

5.5 CYBER THREATS AND COUNTERMEASURES IN SMART CITIES

For the possible human or computer errors, automated cities will be able to offer cyber risks actors with a huge attack prevention surface to mark and possibly feat and integrate into wider campaigns as described in Table 5.2.

FIGURE 5.3   Cybersecurity Challenges for Smart Cities

5.6   A NOVEL FRAMEWORK FOR CYBER SECURE SMART CITY

The proposed framework is broadly distributed into two categories i.e., *Smart City Architecture* and the *Cybersecurity Central Control* which are illustrated in Figure 5.4.

A. *Smart City Architecture*
  (1) *Layer 1 – Strategic Vision*. Strategic Vision is the top-level layer which consists of five components, which are leadership awareness, vision for cyber secure Smart City, public-private corporation, regulatory framework for cyber secure Smart Cities, engagement of stake holder's management.
      a) **Leadership awareness:** The leaders should be aware of cyber secure Smart City governance benefits and aim to implement them in different cities.. To cope in the contemporary world realm, there is a dire need that leadership should follow their footsteps and

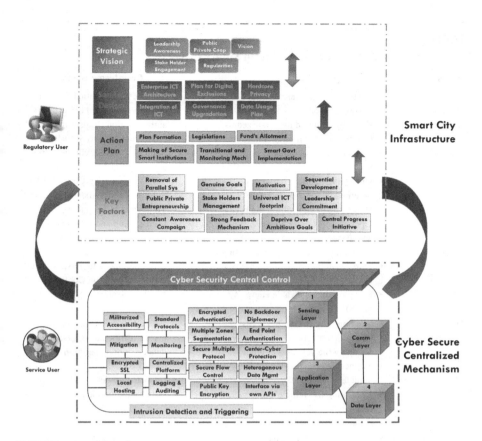

FIGURE 5.4   Cyber Secure-Smart City Framework [41]

adopt the possible fastest tracks to convert traditional cities into Smart Cities.

b) **Strategic Vision:** It requires a clear vision by Federal Government to adopt new smart systems. In developed countries like in the European Union and the US, this implementation is a bit different as cities have independent initiatives and processes are mostly bidirectional. In underdeveloped countries, control and implementation would be central and unidirectional.

c) **Regulatory Framework:** Creation of a regulatory framework for design and development of cyber secure Smart Cities is the next step which would facilitate further progress.

d) **Collaboration:** Development of accountable public-private partnership, without which this initiative will never be able to be materialized.

TABLE 5.2

Cyber Threats and Countermeasure in Smart Cities

Sector	Threat	Countermeasures
Smart Building Sector	• Infection by malware • System failure • Fraud by staff and unauthorized users • Controlling the fire system • Causing physical damage such as flooding • Disrupting building temperature (overheating or overcooling) • Damaging or controlling the lifts • Open window and doors • Modifying smart meters • Disabling water and electricity supplies • Starting/stopping the irrigation water system • Stopping the renewable energy system (RES)	• Two-factor authentication and one-time password for stronger authentication (Imprivata OneSign, Comodo Security Solutions, and STMicroelectronics Secure MCU) • IoT forensics (DigiCert IoT PKI Solutions and Symantec solutions) • Threat and risk modeling • Data backup and recovery solutions to ensure reliability and continuity of services (CommScope solutions, Socome solutions, Johnson Controls and Newtron System)
Transport Sector	• Sending false emergency messages • Disrupting a vehicle's braking system • Stopping the vehicle's engine • Triggering false displays in the vehicle's dashboard • Disrupting the vehicle's emergency response system • Changing GPS signals	• Public key infrastructure (PKI) digital certificates (ECDSA) and data encryption solutions (ECIES and AES) • Misbehavior detection solutions • Pseudorandom identities
Government Sector	• Preventing a cybercrime • Identity theft • Disrupting critical infrastructure • Fiscal fraud • Altered files	• Data leakage prevention (Symantec, Fortinet) • Risk assessment (MEHARI, EBIOS) • Insider threat analysis • Awareness training
Healthcare Sector	• Modifying patient record or information • Exposing sensitive data unintentionally • Disrupting the monitoring system • Disrupting the emergency services • Sending false information • Jamming attacks • Sending an emergency alert • Eavesdropping sensitive information	• Secured Wi-Fi networks to guarantee safe handling of confidential information and personal data (AirTight Networks solutions, Aerohive security solutions) • Risk assessment (Rapid7 solutions, Helath Security Solutions , SafeNet's data security solutions, Intel healthcare security solutions)

(Continued)

TABLE 5.2

Cyber Threats and Countermeasure in Smart Cities

Sector	Threat	Countermeasures
Energy Sector	• Spoofing addresses and user names • Unauthorized access and controls • Zero data attack • Botnets (Zeus, ZeroAccess, Conficker, etc) • Denial of service and distributed denial of service (DDoS)	• Intrusion detection and prevention techniques (Radiflow, Snort) • Risk assessment (MEHARI, EBIOS) • Insider threat analysis • Cybercrime intelligence
Financial Sector	• Loss of privacy • Accounting fraud • Disrupting fraud • Disrupting business processes • Accessing confidential company information • Accessing confidential customer information • Damaging reputation • Defacing websites • Financial and reputation concerns due to fraud and data leakage • Denial of service and DDoS • Phishing • Mobile banking exploitation • SQL injection • Trojan	• Anti-malware solutions (McAfee, Symantec) • Encrypted files and firewalling • Fraud detection and prevention • Risk assessment (MEHARI, EBIOS) • Insurance to mitigate cybercrime Risk. • Cybercrime intelligence. • IBM Enterprise insight Analysis

e) **Engagement:** Finally, stake holders' engagement must be managed otherwise unfavorable forces would interfere and even affect the supportive stakeholders' community by adverse propaganda.

(2) *Layer 2 – Service Architecture*. Integration of ICT and its governance is considered to be a core component in the cyber secure Smart City and this aspect is common in discussed frameworks. An efficient ICT service architecture is mandatory for cyber secure Smart City deployment. Its components are: Integration and Governance of ICT in respective echelons, Enterprise City ICT architecture plan, Data Usage plan, Hardcore Privacy and Security plan, Outreach plan for Digital exclusions and finally the strategy to up gradate governance towards the cyber secure Smart City governance.

(3) *Layer 3 – Action Plan*. Change is difficult with superlative degrees in our scenario so to drive change a comprehensive action plan should be chalked out which should not only implement change but would also have

mechanisms in place to sustain and maintain it. It comprises of different components, namely, Legislation of Smart Governance, Formation of Smart Institutions, Development of Detailed Deployment Plans, Budget Allocations, Application and Employment of Smart Cities and finally Transformation and Monitoring Mechanism of a Secure Smart City.

(4) *Layer 4 – Key Success Factors*. It shows the basic key success factors which should be considered for successful application and employment of a cyber secure Smart City initiative in Pakistan. Those factors are, namely: Leadership Intent, Simple and Clear Goals, Phased Implementation, Cultural Transformation, Central Development Initiative, Citizen Centric Design, Circumvention of Over Ambitious Goals, Strong Feedback Mechanism, Elimination of Parallel Systems, Continuous Awareness Campaign, Ubiquitous ICT Foot Print and finally the Ownership by City Governments.

B. *Cybersecurity Central Control*

Learning from the Indian security mechanism being adopted for the Smart Cities Framework, it is devised to adopt the same end to end data exchange and processing in an encrypted way via the securing of all types of communicational channels adoptive to the standards being defined by the governing body centrally for all the smart cities under its control. In that case the framework is being devised and the functional and operational peculiarities are as under [41]:

(1) *Operational Peculiarities*

   a) Cybersecurity to be given the top most priority for all the stakeholders involved during different operational phases of Smart City development.

   b) Baseline security guidelines to be governed and implemented by the centralized governing body for implementation and configuration of all security related modules.

   c) Risk profile of different components of Smart City to be assessed considering business driven risks analysis to verify the selection of security products in a sequential manner.

   d) Mechanism for the continual security assessment of Smart City setup for identification and mitigation of security risks.

   e) Development and grooming of cybersecurity awareness in the Smart City stakeholders so that they should be capable to maintain the hard core and soft core modules of cyber secure Smart City components with defined or authorized cybersecurity capabilities.

   f) Cybersecurity budget allocation to be the part of the overall Smart City budget which should match the risk profile of smart city components to develop the mechanism to defend their systems .

(2) *Functional Peculiarities*

   a) All message exchange among different applications would be fully encrypted and authenticated and all communication from the exterior world would be done via predefined and exported APIs only.

b) Convergence of multiple platforms into the central platform for the ease of management in which adequate-authentication and role based access control is to be exercised.

c) In the multi-tenant architecture, there should be provision of data flow for normalized data and authorized by using adequate authenticity methods based on valid encryption mechanism.

d) Management of heterogeneous data administrated and managed via various methods by using different communication protocols.

e) Data layer should be capable to provide data communicate services to the different types of sensors and devices for processing, migration and transportation among different supported systems.

f) The entire IT Infrastructure deployed as a cyber secure Smart City should follow standards like ISO-27001, ISO-22301, ISO-37120, BSI-PAS 182, for Wi-Fi access PEAP (Protected Extensible Authentication Protocol, 3GPP (3rd Generation Partnership Project) and related.

g) Generic APIs should be published and application should be based on standard protocols like JSON / XML / Html.

h) At network security level the information and data flow must be authenticated and secure via valid encryption and confidentially to be maintained at all the communication end ports and end points.

i) Plan for the wireless broadband architecture should be Fiber Optical System based and should be interoperable and connective with other land and wireless communication devices.

j) Authentication system to be present at the nodal end points of all echelons of processing and communication system capable of heterogeneous data management. To minimize the latency issues, standard network protocols to be used at different communication layers for data flow. All deployed applications should be indigenously hosted and developed.

k) Updating of all software and firmware, all modules to be proficient in auditing and logging, elimination of backdoors and undocumented hard cored accounts to ensure compliance with vendor, peer to peer solution with full service availability for which a service agreement should be materialized for minimum period of three years since systems operations.

l) Appropriate teams to be in place for monitoring and mitigation of cyber incidents and information of such to be shared with Emergency Response Team and Federal Critical Information Protection Infrastructure Centre for recovery in any eventuality.

5.7 CONCLUSION

Smart Cities are full of advanced technologies, but they come with many security vulnerabilities. If the data is compromised, then it can expose the sensitive information to the people with malicious intent all over the world and can cause havoc for users. The automated data related to external and internal operations, finance and security can be a big concern if breached. This chapter aims to provide a detailed overview of the cybersecurity threats, possible vulnerabilities and the best practice for prevention of them. These Smart Cities are highly dependent on the efficiency, portability and working of these devices because every device is part of the system and their alerts/responses generate the appropriate output. In this chapter the threats that are a real security vulnerability to these systems and the concerns of the different smart city developers have been analyzed. Even now, security is the biggest concern when it comes to Smart Cities and their development. One potential breach can jeopardize the whole concept and is a feature of the Smart Cities which can further lead to the loss of trust and revenue. Even if the Smart City is equipped with best of the tools, it would be useless if it is not secured.

REFERENCES

1. Albino, V., U. Berardi, and R. M. Dangelico. 2015. Smart cities: Definitions, dimensions, performance, and initiatives. *Journal of Urban Technology*, 22(1), pp. 3–21.
2. Qureshi, K. N., and A. H. Abdullah. 2013. A survey on intelligent transportation systems. *Middle-East Journal of Scientific Research*, 15(5), pp. 629–642.
3. Barth, S., and M. D. de Jong. 2017. The privacy paradox–Investigating discrepancies between expressed privacy concerns and actual online behavior–A systematic literature review. *Telematics and Informatics*, 34(7), pp. 1038–1058 (2017).
4. Qureshi, K. N., A. H. Abdullah, and R. W. Anwar. 2014. The evolution in health care with information and communication technologies. In 2nd International Conference of Applied Information and Communications Technology-2014. Oman: Elsevier.
5. Batty, M. et al. 2012. Smart cities of the future. *The European Physical Journal Special Topics*, 214(1), pp. 481–518.
6. Edwards, L. 2016. Privacy, security and data protection in smart cities: A critical EU law perspective. *European Data Protection Law Review*, 2, p. 28.
7. Efthymiopoulos, M.-P. 2016. Cyber-security in smart cities: the case of Dubai. *Journal of Innovation Entrepreneurship*, 5(1), p. 11.
8. Falconer, G., and S. Mitchell. 2012. Smart city framework A systematic process for enabling smartconnected communities. *Cisco Internet Business Solutions Group*, Cisco IBSG.
9. Gretzel, U., M. Sigala, Z. Xiang, and C. Koo. 2015. Smart tourism: Foundations and developments. *Electronic Markets*, 25 (3), pp. 179–188.
10. Ijaz, S., M. A. Shah, A. Khan, and M. Ahmed. 2016. Smart cities: A survey on security concerns. *International Journal of Advanced Computer Science and Applications*, 7(2), pp. 612–625.
11. Kumar, S., U. Dohare, K. Kumar, D. P. Dora, K. N. Qureshi, and R. Kharel. 2018. Cybersecurity measures for geocasting in vehicular cyber physical system environments. *IEEE Internet of Things Journal*, 6(4), pp. 5916–5926.

12. Tousley, S., and S. Rhee. 2018. Smart and secure cities and communities. In 2018 IEEE International Science of Smart City Operations and Platforms Engineering in Partnership with Global City Teams Challenge (SCOPE-GCTC) (pp. 7–11). IEEE.

13. Stergiou, C., K. E. Psannis, B.-G. Kim, and B. Gupta. 2018. Secure integration of IoT and cloud computing. *Future Generation Computer Systems*, 78, pp. 964–975.

14. Van Zoonen, L.. 2016. Privacy concerns in smart cities. *Government Information Quarterly*, 33(3), pp. 472–480.

15. Sen, M., A. Dutt, S. Agarwal, and A. Nath. 2013. Issues of privacy and security in the role of software in smart cities. In 2013 International Conference on Communication Systems and Network Technologies (pp. 518–523). IEEE.

16. Wen, M., J. Lei, and Z. Bi. 2013. Sse: A secure searchable encryption scheme for urban sensing and querying. *International Journal of Distributed Sensor Networks*, 9(12), p. 302147.

17. Clastres, C. 2011. Smart grids: Another step towards competition, energy security and climate change objectives. *Energy Policy*, 39(9), pp. 5399–5408.

18. Ling, A. P. A., and M. Masao. 2011. Selection of model in developing information security criteria on smart grid security system. In 2011 IEEE Ninth International Symposium on Parallel and Distributed Processing with Applications Workshops (pp. 91–98). IEEE.

19. Goel, S.. 2015. Anonymity vs. security: The right balance for the smart grid. *Communications of the Association for Information Systems*, 36(1), p. 2.

20. Su, K., J. Li, and H. Fu. 2011. Smart city and the applications. In 2011 International Conference on Electronics, Communications and Control (ICECC)(pp. 1028–1031). IEEE.

21. Suciu, G., A. Vulpe, S. Halunga, O. Fratu, G. Todoran, and V. Suciu. 2013. Smart cities built on resilient cloud computing and secure internet of things. In 2013 19th International Conference on Control Systems and Computer Science (pp. 513–518). IEEE.

22. Martínez-Ballesté, A., P. A. Pérez-Martínez, and A. Solanas. 2013. The pursuit of citizens' privacy: A privacy-aware smart city is possible. *IEEE Communications Magazine*, 51(6), pp. 136–141.

23. Galdon-Clavell, G.. 2013. (Not so) smart cities?: The drivers, impact and risks of surveillance-enabled smart environments. *Science Public Policy*, 40(6), pp. 717–723.

24. Pan, G., G. Qi, W. Zhang, S. Li, Z. Wu, and L. T. Yang. 2013. Trace analysis and mining for smart cities: Issues, methods, and applications. *IEEE Communications Magazine*, 51(6), pp. 120–126.

25. Qureshi, K. N., F. Bashir, and A. H. Abdullah. 2017. Provision of security in vehicular ad hoc networks through an intelligent secure routing scheme. In 2017 International Conference on Frontiers of Information Technology (FIT) (pp. 200–205). IEEE.

26. Aliero, M. S., I. Ghani, K. N. Qureshi, and M. F. A. Rohani. 2020. An algorithm for detecting SQL injection vulnerability using black-box testing. *Journal of Ambient Intelligence Humanized Computing*, 11(1), pp. 249–266.

27. Kobie, N. 2015. Why smart cities need to get wise to security–and fast. *The Guardian*. Retrieved from http://www.theguardian.com/technology//may/13/smart-cities-intern et-things-security-cesar-cerrudo-ioactive-labs.

28. Abouzakhar, N. 2013. Critical infrastructure cybersecurity: A review of recent threats and violations. In 12th European Conference on Information Warfare and Security (ECCWS). School of Computer Science, College Lane, University of Hertfordshire, Hatfield, UK

29. Qureshi, K. N., S. Din, G. Jeon, and F. Piccialli. 2020. Link quality and energy utilization based preferable next hop selection routing for wireless body area networks. *Computer Communications*, 149, pp. 382–392.

30. Anwar, M. et al. 2018. Green communication for wireless body area networks: Energy aware link efficient routing approach. *Sensors*, 18 (10), p. 3237.

31. Iqbal, S., A. H. Abdullah, K. N. Qureshi, and J. Lloret. 2017. Soft-GORA: Soft constrained globally optimal resource allocation for critical links in IoT backhaul communication. *IEEE Access*, 6, pp. 614–624.

32. Wan, J., D. Li, C. Zou, and K. Zhou. M2M communications for smart city: An event-based architecture. In 2012 IEEE 12th International Conference on Computer and Information Technology (pp. 895–900). IEEE.

33. Qureshi, K. N., A. H. Abdullah, R. W. Anwar, and M. Bukhari. 2015. SSNM-smart sensor network model for vehicular ad hoc networks. In 2015 International Conference on Smart Sensors and Application (ICSSA) (pp. 82–87). IEEE.

34. Gross, R., and A. Acquisti. 2005. Information revelation and privacy in online social networks. In Proceedings of the 2005 ACM workshop on Privacy in the electronic society (pp. 71–80). ACM.

35. Qureshi, K. N., F. Bashir, and S. Iqbal. 2018. Cloud computing model for vehicular ad hoc networks. In 2018 IEEE 7th International Conference on Cloud Networking (CloudNet) (pp. 1–3). IEEE.

36. Ahmad, A., A. Paul, M. Rathore, and H. Chang. 2016. An efficient multidimensional big data fusion approach in machine-to-machine communication. *ACM Transactions on Embedded Computing Systems*, 15(2), p. 39.

37. Ahmad, A., A. Paul, M. M. Rathore, and H. Chang. 2016. Smart cyber society: Integration of capillary devices with high usability based on cyber–physical system. *Future Generation Computer Systems*, 56, pp. 493–503.

38. Aliero, M. S., K. N. Qureshi, M. F. Pasha, I. Ghani, and R. A. Yauri. 2020. Systematic review analysis on SQLIA detection and prevention approaches. *Wireless Personal Communications*, 112, pp. 1–37.

39. Aggarwal, R., and M. L. Das. 2012. RFID security in the context of "Internet of Things". In Proceedings of the First International Conference on Security of Internet of Things (pp. 51–56). ACM.

40. Rawat, D. B., and K. Z. Ghafoor. 2018. *Smart Cities Cybersecurity and Privacy*. Elsevier.

41. Tahirkheli, A.I. 2019. A Novel Framework for Cyber Secure Smart City.*International Journal of Computing and Communication Networks*, 1(2), pp.10–18.

6 Contemplating Security Challenges and Threats for Smart Cities

Kashif Naseer Qureshi and Abeer Iftikhar

CONTENTS

6.1   INTRODUCTION

The privacy and security terms may look same at first glance to protect any asset of user, but both terms are entirely different. A Smart City has to ensure both privacy and security features. Privacy is a term related to an individual's personal data that he wants to keep undisclosed and it truly depends upon the security measures that are taken to protect any harm to assets. Security and privacy are interdependent terms. Security of a Smart City is an attempt to prevent direct or indirect harm to either the Smart City or its inhabitants and thus ensuring the personal privacy feature as well [6, 7].

Smart Cities aim to bring a higher quality of life for individuals through interconnectivity and fefficiency and reliability will improve significantly. The citizens and all other components of Smart City are going to be more intelligent and connected [11]. All efforts towards a Smart City promise to make the cities more efficient, reliable and more sustainable. With all these features, privacy of citizens during data collection and dissemination is always on priority all the time. If the privacy of a Smart City system were not ensured, individuals would be reluctant to participate. In the construction of a secure Smart City, privacy concerns are to be considered in parallel to the design and development of secure Smart Cities. In the long run, the more the Smart City concept fascinates the users, the more it is important to provide a defense against privacy threats [13].

Figure 6.1 is an illustration of Smart City interconnectivity. It shows the components of the Smart City and their interconnectivity with the Internet and the cloud. The components of a Smart City are school, bank, police station, home, shopping mall, drone, hospital, transport, restaurant, etc., where each component is further constituted of smart devices as shown in Figure 6.2.

Presently, the cities that are practicing Smart City technologies include New York, Toronto, Barcelona, Copenhagen and Paris [16]. The importance of privacy concerns in Smart Cities can be best understood with the help of some practical examples. A Smart City relies on information of two types: real time data and aggregated data. There are many examples of gathering real time data with the intention to keep focus on individuals. In 2013, a company named "Renew London" started a

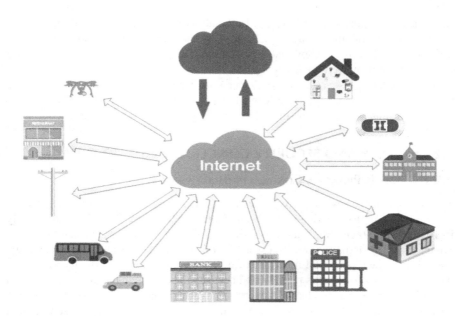

FIGURE 6.1   Smart City Interconnectivity

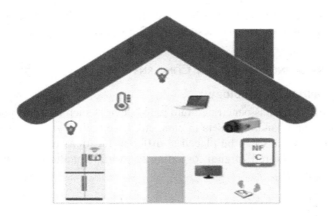

FIGURE 6.2   A Smart Home in a Smart City

program in which sensors were installed in recycling bins. These sensors tracked the Wi-Fi signals from phones passing nearby. The unique media access control (MAC) addresses of phones were used by the sensors to target the user's movement-based advertisements within the range of the sensor network. For instance, if a particular store or restaurant comes frequently in the range of a user's phone, the user would see more ads related to user requirements. In Singapore, the government is establishing a satellite navigation system for transport so that the location, direction and speed will be monitored at any given time. This tracking system will also facilitate automatic charging for parking fees and tickets. In the above given examples, and many more of such kind, companies may be selling personal information for advertising and marketing, or indirectly allow hackers to gain access to information that users did not even know they were giving up [18].

This chapter provides a study on the personal privacy concerns that are applicable to Smart City development. Privacy must be protected from the time the data is captured from sensors to the time the knowledge has been taken and deleted.

6.2 PRIVACY AND SECURITY CONCERNS IN SMART CITY

6.2.1 WHY IS PRIVACY A CONCERN IN SMART CITY?

The question of privacy concerns in the Smart City has come into the picture since the developments in information and communication technology (ICT) have drastically increased. An integrative framework has been proposed in Ref. [21] to understand a Smart City. The authors have discussed eight factors that characterize a Smart City. One of these factors is built infrastructure. In this domain, one of the technological barriers in e-government is privacy and security. The challenges in this dimension are threats from intruders, hackers, worms, Trojans, privacy of personal data and the cost of the solutions to provide security against all these. With the expansion of ICT, information flows have drastically increased and with this expansion in information flows, threats to information privacy have become a point of concern [23]. In Ref. [15], the authors have discussed the three potential threats related to personal privacy that have been posed by smart cities: the IoT, Big Data and the cloud.

6.2.2 CONSEQUENCES OF PRIVACY CONCERNS

6.2.2.1 Bluetooth Technology

Bluetooth technology has penetrated into many devices such as smart phones, navigation systems and hands-free sets in cars, etc. Bluetooth devices emit signals and readers of these signals can be placed at different locations and the movement of devices can be monitored. Digital forgetting is an IoT domain of research in these privacy concerns [26].

6.2.2.2 Health Sector

The privacy of patients' health data is very important because a patient may face serious problems if his/her health information is disclosed and misused [28]. In this study, the authors have highlighted the fact that training in handling patient data must be provided to ensure privacy but these training programs fade away when it comes to the importance and effectiveness of the use of security algorithms for access control, anonymity and authentication [29].

6.2.2.3 Big Data Analytics

The widespread participation of all citizens makes the network based Smart City a success, but privacy concerns are a challenge to this achievement [32]. When research is carried out on big data analytics to characterize the trajectories followed by humans, privacy is a concern when data is not anonymous. In such research, data must be anonymized through analysis and confidentiality.

6.2.2.4 Cloud System

In Ref. [33], the privacy attributes of a security service are termed as privacy preservability. In a cloud system, outsourcing makes the consumers lose control of their own data. The authors have shown privacy as a separate attribute than security revealing its importance and understanding as a separate entity. Guaranteeing the confidentiality of user data in cloud is required for privacy preservation [14]. It has been discussed that even if the data is encrypted, critical information about the raw data can be revealed by the access patterns that each corresponding application exhibits. Not only should the encrypted data can be unauthorized but it should also hide the statistical properties of original data. Although cloud storage is a resource that facilitates collection and mining of data as a result of integrating big data with cloud storage, this integration is a threat to privacy due to the involvement of a third party. And what if a security breach occurs, would the cloud service be fully accountable? Thus it is a challenge to share the responsibility of data sharing with the government [35].

6.2.2.5 Internet of Things

Privacy concerns in IoT at different layers like front end, back end and network have been summarized in Ref. [36]. Privacy of an entity needs to be protected at different stages, i.e., in device, in storage, in processing and in communication.

6.2.2.6 Smart Card

Smart cards provide an easy to use way of gaining a service. Smart card consolidation with the advancements towards improved Smart City has been discussed in Ref. [5]. Many cities are now launching contactless smart cards but with this gradual development in smart card technology, privacy concerns are arising.

6.2.2.7 Smart Tourism

Current trends in smart tourism have been discussed in Ref. [4]. One of the drawbacks of smart tourism is the lack of privacy protection. The location-based services provided by smart tourism on one hand are very useful for tourists but on the other hand they make the consumers vulnerable to privacy threats. The digital footprints of a traveler make it possible to perform data mining on the digital traces and exploit the privacy of information.

6.2.2.8 Drones

In the future, Smart Cities' drones are going to play a major role in goods transportation, mobile hotspots and maintenance of security and surveillance of Smart Cities [8]. The use of drones also brings challenges and concerns of privacy. This paper presents results of cyber-attacks using drones. This implies that not only are the drones vulnerable to cyber-attacks, but they can also be used in harmful and malicious ways to launch cyber attacks. In DEFCON 21 [9], DJI phantom mounted with a wi-fi pineapple was used by a researcher to sniff wireless signals using a virtual private network. The cost of drones is falling and therefore UAVs are being launched in any territory for constant monitoring of that area. They can also cause danger to aircrafts as seen in the near collision incident of a Boeing 737 in a British airport [10].

6.2.2.9 Mobile Applications

The privacy concerns linked to the actual online behavior of users have been analyzed in Ref. [37]. In the systematic literature review in this paper, the authors have used the privacy paradox to explore different theories. The majority of papers studied by the authors focused on online media and social networks in the context of the privacy paradox, but when compared with the results it came up that the privacy paradox is even more complex in the context of mobile applications. An individual can restrict his/her profile on a social networking website to protect his/her data from intrusions and other security threats but there are no such measures of protection available while downloading and installing mobile applications.

6.2.2.10 E-Govennance

In Ref. [38], the authors have discussed privacy concerns in e-governance. The design of a smart building has control systems that include water heater and coolers, light and motion sensors, escalators, etc. These control systems interconnect with other systems hence increasing the security and privacy concerns. The e-government sector is facing challenges of privacy, trust and availability.

6.2.2.11 Online Social Networks

The study carried out by authors in Ref. [39], reveals how Smart Cities are affected by the risks associated with online social networks (OSN). The privacy of an individual on an OSN consists of the individual's privacy of identity, anonymity, personal space and communication. Privacy concerns will certainly arise with the use of individuals' data.

6.2.2.12 Biometrics

Biometrics technology must be integrated in social media so as to authenticate individuals. Biometrics technology is used for identity verification and hence protects privacy of the entity.

6.2.3 Concept and Cardinals of Smart City in the World

The world population is growing tremendously and in particular is going through urban growth. Roughly half of the world's population lived in an urban area in 2010. By 2050, according to the World Health Organization, nearly seven out of ten people will live in an urban environment. By 2025, there will be 37 mega-cities with a population expected to be over and above 10 million inhabitants as per a statement of the UN's Environmental Program. There will be a dire need for Smart Cities having the central, more robust management and administration of infrastructural resources and interactions among the city components and technological elements.

Cities across the globe have transformed from simple urban centers to complex urban ecological systems. The city governments are faced with a multitude of challenges. The leaders at the helm of city affairs need to provide opportunities for city dwellers to earn wealth, health, security, sustainability, improve living conditions and above all carry out the public office functions in an improved manner. The field of a Smart City is still in nascent stages and a diverse technological framework is under development. There is no clarity or central benchmarking system for the implementation of Smart City systems. The underlying Information and Communication Technologies (ICT) systems are complex and vulnerable to security breaches. This inherent void merits a full-fledged research for transforming the current Smart City frameworks into secure Smart City frameworks. These new technologies are producing smarter alliances among urban actors and are improving the way cities are effectively functioning, but the cybersecurity has been an afterthought, which makes these systems vulnerable.

Smart City can be defined as a "Collection of smart computing technology applied to critical infrastructure components and services, which includes the City administration, education, healthcare, public safety, real estate, transportation, and the related utilities, more intelligent, interconnected and efficient" [40]. This scientific application, once supervised and coupled with the existing government policies and smart urban manpower adaptive to such a delicate technological adoption, is the spirit of the Smart City implementation. A Smart City is a concept of a technical modernized city where people enjoy the best life qualities where services are efficient, effective and sustainable while they meet the needs and requirements of the civilization. The Smart City components are interconnected for monitoring, control and automation purposes (Figure 6.3). They are intended to improve the quality of life, accessing information anywhere and anytime. Smart means performing in a forward looking way. The forward looking development approach to a Smart City considers issues such as, awareness, flexibility, transformability, synergy, individuality, self-decisiveness and strategic behaviour.

Another inclusive definition is presented by Caragliu et al. in 2011: "City is considered to be declared a Smart city when investments in human, social capital and traditional (transport) and modern (ICT) communication infrastructure fuel sustainable economic growth and a high quality of life, with a visionary management of available natural resources, through participatory governance" [41]. Since the last decade, the cities are in the process of transformation from a legacy system into the automated and Smart Cities in areas like serving individuals or citizens, buildings and traffic systems. This concept has been improving, which enables us to monitor, control, recognize, analyze, comprehend and plan the city for the future to improve the efficacy, impartiality, economic equity and quality of life for its city inhabitants in real-time systems [42]. Smart City concepts are illustrated in Figure 6.4.

6.2.4   Why Is Security a Concern in Smart City?

From the beginning of this century, there has been an evolution in modern ICT and advancement in a large number of devices connected to the Internet. A huge amount

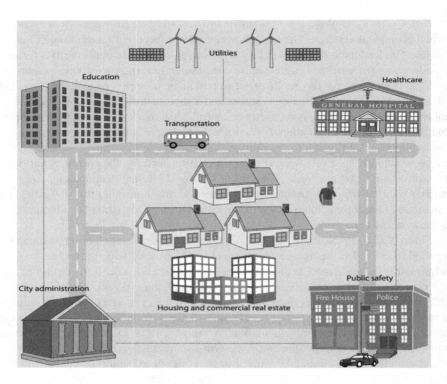

FIGURE 6.3   Smart City Blueprint [40]

of data in volume with different formats and from several sources gets generated. The concept of ICT has enabled the government and industrial leaders to embark upon an innovative and unique path for technological utilization for the transmission from legacy based cities into modernized Smart Cities. The exponential development and improvement rate in ICT technology has proved that these technologies are ubiquitous across the cities. This technological modernization has improvised the world leaders to opt for implementing the Smart City initiatives and hence all the international metropolitan cities have been urged to convert into Smart Cities at the earliest opportunity [43].

The new concept of Smart Governance to transform the old legacy city into a smarter city is the order of the day. Smart Cities have gained importance as a means of making ICT enabled services and applications available to the citizens, and authorities that are part of a city's system [44]. The sole aim is increasing citizens' quality of life and improving the efficiency, Quality of Services (QoS) and Quality of Effort (QoE) provided by governing entities and businesses. By 2050, a great number of people who live in big cities will be almost as large as the world's entire population today, and meanwhile, the bulk of the cities will be transformed into Smart Cities. The prime concern for all the city administrations is the security of these ICT systems and the huge data being gathered and produced by these systems [45]. A fair portion of literature is rather naïve in its supposition that the Smart City systems are

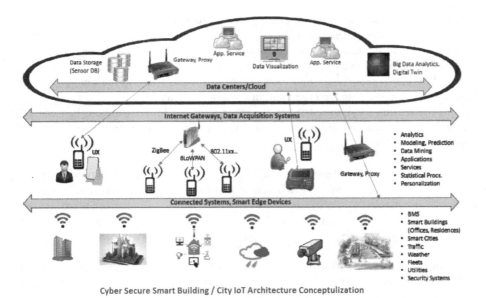

Cyber Secure Smart Building / City IoT Architecture Conceptulization

FIGURE 6.4   Cyber Security Smart City Conceptualization

secure systems. Security is a significant requirement for Smart City implementation. Mostly in academia, more emphasis is being placed on the implementation and development of infrastructures of the Smart Cities and security frameworks [46, 47].

Security is a global idea tied to safety (life, property and rights) as an assurance that a person may go about their life without injury. Cybersecurity is a subset of security that focuses on the computing systems, data exchange channels and the information they process. Information security interlaces with cybersecurity with the focus of information processed. Security is an emerging area in the era of ICT. It is a continuous challenge between two parties, the good one (the protectors) and the bad one (the attackers) [48]. The tools and techniques available for each side are conclusive and the root cause of the decision between the leading and winning sides. Both parties are continuously developing new methods to overcome the defending or attacking methods that have been implemented by the other party. This results in developing new methods for protection and at the same time new ways for compromising the protection methods and vice versa. However, it is well recognized that no defensive method exists that can be used to defeat all security threats to the system; therefore, it is vital to think of developing new methods against new threats [49].

In general, there are three major reasons for establishing and modernizing security mechanisms and in particular within the Smart City networks. Firstly, "Perfect security does not exist" [50]; by this researchers get the leads to develop additional security measures to guard against emerging attacks while supporting the existing security mechanism. Secondly, "New technology always brings new threats" [51], which necessitate the development and designing of new countermeasures against emerging threats. Thirdly, to date it is not possible to create a single security measure which could ensure security against all types of existing or perceived threats [52]. Hence, security is a vital and active concept whose establishment and development requires tangible financial funding for security system designing, development, integration, thought process, technology and tools procurement and training the man power for ensuring and upholding the organization's system security [53].

In the realm of cybersecurity in the essence of the Smart Cities, it is a critical issue due to the increasing potential of cyber attacks and incidents against critical sectors in the Smart City. Different types of threats are as follows [54] (Figure 6.5).

1. Data: personally identifiable information (PII) at risk like the natural disasters, malicious activities of internal and external entities like the DDoS, Sybil attacks.
2. Systems: malicious and unintentional compromise that may cause service interruption.

Cybersecurity intends to achieve the following objectives like protecting a Smart City in a proper way where the cumbersome systems and nodes have to face numerous security problems which are required to be tackled according to a specific design/plan. Intruders are everywhere and may take any number of forms. The key is knowing they are out there and applying the countermeasures necessary to prevent them where possible, detect them when prevention is unsuccessful and respond to threat indicators effectively. Major – specifically cyber – security issues:

a. Availability;
b. Emergency Plan;
c. Engagement of Security Algorithm;
d. Key Management.

6.2.5 SECURITY THREATS AND CHALLENGES [55]

From a security perspective, Smart City networks and the related IoT applications offer numerous innovative advancements; still many devices are susceptible to being connected and captured by the Hackers, Crackers, Script-kiddies, etc., over much bigger attacking space. Either being motivated due to financial gaining objectives, or revenge, they now have ample objectives and opportunities to snatch whatever they desire, to disrupt the institutional hubs and business elements, etc. In the recent past, more than 100,000 Internet-connected smart "things," including edge phones, media players, smart televisions and at least one refrigerator, were part of a network of computers used to send 750,000 spam emails a day. Likewise, it was discovered that the Samsung smart TV line was capturing all audio clips of the deployed rooms or localities via voice recording all the time based upon the voice recognition technology by utilizing the utility used via verbal commands. It is not even just TVs any more – as it turns out, "Hello Barbie" is a doll that can have a two-way conversation with children. It features speech recognition and progressive learning features that

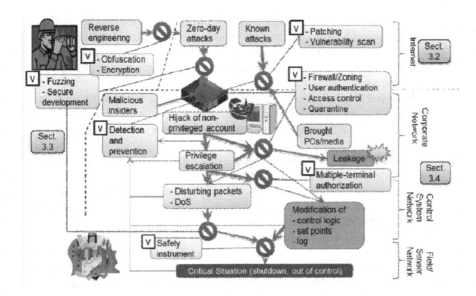

FIGURE 6.5   Cyber Attacks

provide the child with an engaging and unique Barbie experience. It plays interactive games, tells jokes and inspires storytelling. On close observation, it is found that some devices show one or numerous system vulnerabilities which can further be exploited for infiltration and the whole network of the connected domestic devices, e.g. during configuration, device ID and MAC address of the data processing element, is sent in plain form whereas this clear and unciphered transaction among devices and applications via the manufacturer's servers, deprives the unprotected hotspot from properly securing the transaction with weak login credentials. Such unprotected mechanisms are kept active even after the configuration and make the devices deployed with by default installation packages like basic telnet client workstations for sharing the login information [56].

Smart City networks are exclusively vulnerable to advanced persistent threats (APTs), i.e., complex attacks involving a combination of techniques. For example, an APT campaign can combine to involve zero-day exploits and malware with multiple access points. Attacks on smart devices sometime implicate damage over the point of non-recovery. For example, an attack on street lights can be used to mask a criminal operation, leaving the area unserviceable. The city then needs to replace or reinstall the hardware.

Some common internal and external attacks that Smart Cities face are as follows:

1) **Data and identity theft**—this involves pilfering the personally identifiable information (PII) from insecure and open smart city infrastructures, e.g., an attacker can extract sensitive credentials from EV charging stations and use them for fake transactions.

2) **Device hijacking**—the attacker assumes control of a device. In a Smart City, an attacker can hijack smart meters to siphon energy from a municipality.

3) **Man-in-the-middle (MiM)**—an attacker interrupts or redirects communications between two systems, like attacking a smart wastewater system valve to disrupt operations.

4) **Distributed Denial of Service (DDoS)**—floods the target with superfluous requests, disrupting services. As a result, users cannot gain access. An attacker can breach the net of interconnected devices and overwhelm a city system.

5) **Credential theft**—an attacker can get credentials to critical systems, and use them to conduct a ransom ware attack.

6) **Miscellaneous attacks**—like phishing, malicious code, website intrusions and Denial of Service (DoS). Administrations and those in charge of designing, building, operating, maintaining and using the Smart City and its services must therefore include security from the conceptual stage.

Cybersecurity specialist Krishnan was of the opinion that: "For security leaders, this throws up an interesting challenge, as it requires state-of-the-art deployment of the latest technology, dynamic practices and well-trained staff." Likewise, in the opinion of director of India and SAARC at FireEye: "Practitioners should re-imagine their approach, creating an adaptive architecture protecting against advanced attacks and CISOs must focus on early detection, prevention, analysis and appropriate response."

Major challenges for security arise from higher connectivity, opening up new risks and vulnerabilities. The topmost challenge is to ensure the fundamental cybersecurity of thousands of interconnected smart devices or smart systems operating over the hundreds of applications over the world wide web, over the heterogeneous networks vulnerable to multiple types of attacks. A major security constraint is that security is brought under consideration too late in project development. At the network gateway level, the Smart City networks are risk-prone due to ineffective authentication methods which are unable to deprive the information and data theft, espionage and sabotage.

6.2.6 Cybersecurity Challenges in Smart Cities [54]

Various cybersecurity challenges being faced or that are likely to be encountered in normal Smart City functioning are as follows (Table 6.1, Figure 6.6):

1. Non-existence of cryptographic methods and measures.
2. Weak and unreliable ciphering key management.
3. Fictional and absence of secure device on boarding facilities.
4. Weaponized machine learning technologies by the cyber and cipher attackers.
5. Incorrect interpretation of social engineering.
6. Absence of safeguard against the DDoS attacks which are just are some of the key issues contributing to the amplification of cyber-threats in Smart City responsive and querying systems.

TABLE 6.1
Smart City Threats, Vulnerabilities [55]

Vulnerabilities	Threats	Consequences
Lack of awareness of all authorized and unauthorized devices/assets	National-state and state-sponsored actors	Disruption of government services to citizens
Poorly-implemented encryption or lack of encryption management practices	Organized crime and other criminal and terrorist groups	Loss or leakage of citizen personally identifiable information (PII)
Inability to patch or update software/firmware	Hacktivists	Financial loss or expense (e.g., lawsuits, regulatory penalties, theft of funds, cost of response and remediation)
Use of default administrator passwords	Insiders/employees – whether malicious, unintentional, or negligent	Facilitation of terrorist event – whether physical, digital, or combined
Susceptibility to distributed denial of service (DDoS) attacks	External suppliers, service providers, vendors, and partners (e.g., supply chain risk, interdependence and integration risk)	Degradation of trust in government and government services
Lack of security assessment and software code testing	Other individual hackers or hacking groups	Danger to public health or safety
Inadequate security and privacy awareness and training	Natural and man-made disasters	
Weak or immature supply chain risk management practices		

7. Deficiency of financial aiding in digital security which jeopardized the pivotal elements of intelligence, efficiency and sustainability of future Smart City deployments.
8. Sophisticated attacks caused due to hardware in-capabilities, virtualization and advanced cryptographic techniques vastly used in network attacks.
9. Software product bugs and security vulnerabilities which exist due to poor/defective software design, configuration errors, and/or unsecure isolation techniques, legislation issues and complexity.
10. Smart software with legislation issues, i.e., the laws for Smart Cities cannot be developed and applied properly if existing laws are not reviewed in light of new demands (e.g., user privacy, Smart Cities leadership, and law e-health devices supporting healthcare applications).
11. Application constraints such as the computational limitations due to low-speed processors in sensors and smartphones, memory limitations, energy limitations and mobility concerns.

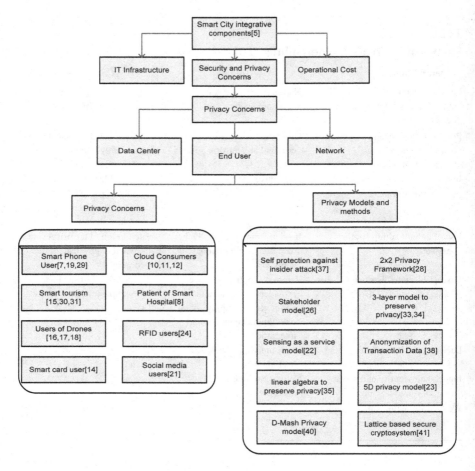

FIGURE 6.6 Cybersecurity Challenges in Smart City

12. Collectively the novel security requirements, discovery of new art crafted attacks and legislation issues further increase the complexity of Smart City technical administration and management.

6.2.7 COUNTERMEASURES AND PROBABLE STRATEGY FOR SECURITY CONCERNS [57]

Smart City security is a multi-stakeholder activity that takes leadership and engagement. It is very important not only to protecting the data and the information but also to securing and protecting the users and the citizens and everything that a citizen interacts upon and depend upon. It is a multi-disciplinary activity with security touching every part of Smart City planning, development, maintenance and operations. Industry desires and demands to work on Smart City systems and smart devices security standards so we can be confident in the devices deployed in Smart Cities. The security planning and strategy applicable in different dimensions could be as follows:

- Development of a clear structure for risk evaluation and management.
- Develop threat models for threat assessment.
- Document and review risk acceptance and exceptions.
- Make risk assessment and management an ongoing process.
- Crafting and deploying a risk based approach to enhance cybersecurity.
- Train the ICT administration to recognise and support the secure Smart City principles and to manage the technical priorities.
- Consider the flexibility for being resilient.
- Set clear objectives and nominate priorities to practice moderate procurement policies to imitate risk and associated priorities and risks.
- Establishment of minimal baseline standards to achieve security.
- Define clear roles and hold the processes accountable for supporting a security baseline.
- Establishing an autonomous system for parallel and uninterrupted security monitoring.
- Designing a minimal security baseline for ICT.
- Set expectations for sharing threat and vulnerability information.
- Building an interoperable and intercity transformable data sharing mechanism.
- Plan and execute cyber drills to experiment the game plans.
- Accentuate the privacy and civil liberty safeguards in sharing the threat credentials.
- Application of relevant national or international standards for information distribution.
- Sharing and coordinating the threat matrix and vulnerability information.
- Develop and propose an automated Disaster Response Team (DRT).
- Craft a clear asset ownership.
- Clearly defined roles and responsibilities.
- Develop a security approach by design based on employment of the privacy impact assessments, vendor management and partnership and engagement with authorities.
- Engagement of the private sector and national resources.
- Facilitate consistent and persistent classification of the threats and incidents.
- Test and quantify the incident response skills and processes.
- Build incident response capabilities.
- Development of public awareness campaigns.
- Cultivate employee development and workforce training programs.
- Enhancement of public awareness, education and staff training.
- Take advantage of private sector resources.
- Partner with universities and academia.
- Sponsor events to connect the public and private sector.

- Promote cooperation in law enforcement agencies while guarding private and civil liberties.
- Promote a culture of technological innovation.
- Empower public, private and academic cooperation and facilitation.
- Ensure engagement of security professionals from the initiation of an idea.
- Defining a novel and robust approach to security architecture.
- Ensuring consultation and consideration of relevant security standards and that minimum standards are defined.
- Inspiring vendors and suppliers to meet the security standards.
- Making security criteria part of quality criteria.
- Ensure testing the security at logical points with clear acceptance criteria.
- Considering an accreditation strategy.
- Planning and designing the disaster management incidents to serialize the events with high risk occurrence and low impact low risk occurrence and high impact.
- Managing the incident management processes.
- Managing the business continuity and emergency management processes.
- Managing residual risk.

To summarize, a good competent Smart City security system requires to prepare a protective shield against internal and external cyber attacks by designing, planning, deploying and developing different technical steps like using the virtual private network, encryption and hashing of the data, incorporation of the network intrusion detection systems, physical and logical protection of software and hardware based protection, application and redistribution of access control lists over all the systems and network devices, event sending and alarm triggering surveillance system, information security policy development and employment, maintaining activity logs and the backup of the data, regular auditing of the system and the data, and proper rehearsing and adoption of the shutdown procedures and data purging technique nomination and development [58].

6.2.8 COUNTERMEASURES FOR PRIVACY CONCERNS

6.2.8.1 Sensing as a Service Model

Sensing has been introduced as a service model in Ref. [17]. The Smart City and Internet of Things have different origins but the sensors make them move into each other. To preserve the privacy of sensor data, sensor owners can define restrictions such as who can access what data. Also, sensitive information collected by sensors such as location data needs to be altered implicitly to anonymize the data.

6.2.8.2 5D Model for Privacy

In Ref. [19], authors have identified some privacy breaches in the context of Smart Cities. The concept of Smart City citizen privacy is presented in the form of a model. A 5D model for privacy of Smart City proposed in the research. The five dimensions are identity, query, location, footprint and owner.

6.2.8.3 User Awareness

In Ref. [1], privacy protection mechanisms have been discussed. Prerequisites to distribution of data are the user awareness and consent.

6.2.8.4 Privacy Protection in RFID

Privacy protection in the RFID systems requires both physical and cryptographic mechanisms [24]. With the help of physical mechanisms like kill code, faraday cage and blocker tag, tags can be blocked and disabled when not in use. Cryptographic mechanisms have been proposed that are helpful in reducing privacy risks. The proposed cryptographic mechanisms are hash lock, randomized id, efficient identification and encryption.

6.2.8.5 Data Aggregation

Data aggregation is another means to protect the individual's privacy [59]. Application specific data analysis can be performed in a cloud.

6.2.8.6 Stakeholder Model

The security and privacy framework proposed by Zareen Khan et al. proposes a stakeholder model of a Smart City in which privacy aspects are dealt with according to the stakeholder's viewpoint [24]. User consent acquisition, freedom of choice and control and anonymity technology are sources of preserving privacy [60]. The major stakeholders that are responsible for user privacy protection are individual consumers and non-consumers, device manufacturers, IOT cloud services and platform providers, third party application developers and government and regulatory bodies.

6.2.8.7 2 × 2 Framework

A 2 × 2 framework, proposed in Ref. [20], hypothesizes which technologies and data applications are likely to raise the concerns of privacy. The four types of sensitivities people have about their data are represented as a 2x2 framework. These four dimensions are personal data for service purpose, personal data for surveillance purpose, impersonal data for surveillance purpose and impersonal data for service purpose. The authors have explained how an innocent technology can be transformed into a sensitive one.

6.2.8.8 Mobile Cloud Framework

Data over-collection in smart phones has a become a big cause of privacy leakage [12]. Data over-collection means that apps in smartphones collect more user data than their capacity. The authors have presented cases of data over-collection in smartphones and a framework of mobile-cloud is presented that is a proposed scheme for data over-collection eradication.

6.2.8.9 Changing Pseudonyms in Intelligent Transport System

In an intelligent transport system there is an information of start and end points [2] and this may be required by an attacker to keep the vehicle track record for some malicious intention. A proposed solution to this issue is provided in Ref. [3] where pseudonyms have to be changed frequently for the solution of location privacy.

6.2.8.10 Homomorphic Encryption

Homomorphic encryption is a very good solution in the e-health sector that provides privacy protection to patient's health data maintained at cloud [61].

6.2.8.11 Three-Layer Model

The authors of [30] have proposed the where, who, what model for location-based services. A three-layer model proposed in Ref. [31], protects user privacy and introduces user-friendly systems.

6.2.8.12 Linear Algebra

The authors of Ref. [27] have proposed a solution based on linear algebra. They have proposed two-party protocols and compute inner products, determinants, eigenvalues and eigenvectors. These protocols produce the output results while the privacy of the inputs is preserved.

6.2.8.13 Continuous Streaming Data

The traditional security technologies are not sufficient in the management of dynamic natured data; they can only deal with static data. It is a challenge to ensure privacy in continuously streaming data due to the large amount of data generation [62].

6.2.8.14 Protection of DBMS from Insider Attacks

Database management systems can be secured from outside threats by the use of firewalls, password mechanism, penetration testing, etc., but the insider's intent is difficult to monitor [22]. The authors in this paper have provided a solution of self-protection against the insider's attacks through the implementation of policies. The authors enforce the access control, encryption and database auditing in their proposed model. The reason for enforcing these policies is to protect the database management system from malicious insider attacks.

6.2.8.15 Anonymization of Transaction Data

The transaction logs stored in a medium have many levels. An IT manager gets an insight of data that moves between levels. The authors in Ref. [6] have proposed a novel technique based approach in which anonymized transaction data can be analyzed by the mining tools.

6.2.8.16 D-Mash Model

Due to its advantages, data as a service (DaaS) is an emerging area in the field of research [63]. Enterprises do not opt for DaaS because of the two threats linked to it; the threat of hackers and the threat of data privacy compromise. To prevent privacy leakage one of the proposed privacy models is D-Mash. This is also known as data mashup. By virtue of this model the data providers are enabled to integrate their relevant data on demand while preserving data privacy [25].

6.2.8.17 Lattice Based Secure Cryptosystem

This system is proposed for healthcare in Smart Cities in Ref. [34]. The authors have proposed a model for communication between doctors and patients and the cloud. The scheme is designed for constrained nodes of Smart Cities and works efficiently due to low computation and communication costs as compared to other schemes presently in use.

6.2.8.18 Taxonomy Diagram

Figure 6.7 represents the taxonomy diagram that completely provides an insight to the research classification. The independent boxes represent the name of studied field and the references of the studied document are provided along with the name. Two boxes at the bottom constitute multiple boxes. Each area studied has been mentioned along with the references of papers studied.

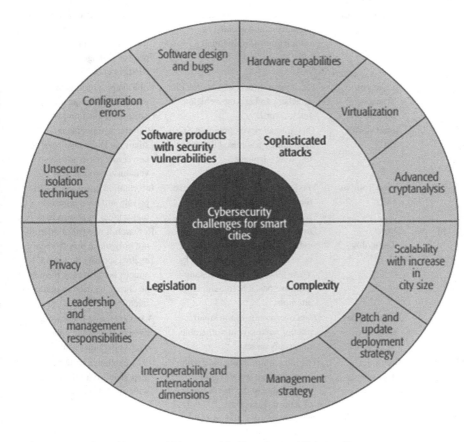

FIGURE 6.7 Classification of User-specific Security and Privacy Concerns

6.3   TABULAR REPRESENTATIONS

The research carried out is summarized in two tables. Table 6.2 provides the list of Smart City technologies and the security compromise and privacy leakage consequences linked to each technology is provided. Table 6.3 enlists the studied models, frameworks and methods that provide countermeasures of consequences discussed in Table 6.2.

TABLE 6.2
Smart City Technologies and Privacy Concerns

Paper Reference	Technology	Privacy Concerns	Recommendations / Comments
[1]	Radiofrequency Identification (RFID)	Data from multiple RFID readers can be correlated to reveal the movement and social interactions of individuals.	Physical mechanisms can disable the RFID when not in use and cryptographic mechanisms can reduce privacy leakage risks when RFID is in use.
[2-4]	Intelligent Transport System (ITS)	The issue in this system is that an attacker can keep the vehicle track record.	Solution proposed is to change pseudonyms frequently for protecting location privacy.
[5]	Smart Card (SC)	This gradual development in SC technology has raised the threat of privacy leakage.	With the advancements in ICT, smart cards are also coming in newer and more advance versions as contactless SC.
[4, 7]	Smart Tourism (ST)	The location-based services make the consumers vulnerable to privacy threats.	Information governance and privacy are the suggested major areas of research.
[8-10]	Drone Technology (DT)	Drones are not only prone to cyber attacks but also they can be used to launch cyber attacks. Their falling costs are making their use possible in malicious attempts.	Research is needed in order to not only make drones secure against security and privacy attacks but also they must not be able to be used in malicious intentions.
[12]	Smart Phones (SP)	Data over-collection in smart phones makes them vulnerable to privacy attacks.	A mobile cloud framework is presented to solve data over-collection problem.
[14, 15]	Cloud Technology (CT)	The integration of big data with cloud storage is a threat to privacy due to the involvement of a third party. Data accountability is the problem in cloud services.	It is a challenge to share the responsibility of data sharing with the government.

TABLE 6.3

Privacy Protection Models and Frameworks

Reference number	Model/Method/ Framework	Main Function / Purpose	Details
[17]	Sensing as a Service	Smart city and Internet of things are from different origin but sensors make them move into each other.	In this model, sensor data privacy is preserved if sensor owner defines restrictions to access.
[19]	5D model for privacy in smart cities	. The proposed model has the quality of preserving privacy in the 5 dimensions; identity, query, footprint, owner, location.	This model is based on the proper handling of coexistent domains and secures transportation of information.
[20]	2x2 framework	The four types of sensitivities that people have about their data are represented as a 2x2 framework	This framework is used to hypothesize if the smart city technologies provide privacy concern among citizens of the smart city.
[22]	Self Protection Against Insider Attacks	Self-protection model of database management systems against insider's attacks is provided.	The self protection model proposed by authors enforces the implementation of policies for access control, encryption, and database auditing.
[24]	Stake-holder model	The authors presented a framework based on the stakeholder model for providing secure and privacy aware services in smart cities.	Smart city is essentially comprised of citizens from different cadres and having different point of views. This model brings forth the necessity of dealing the aspects of data security and privacy from the point of view of different stakeholders.
[25]	A framework for privacy preserving D-Mash	To fulfill the request of a consumer, mashing the data from different sources is carried out. This involves the risk of revealing sensitive information of users.	The proposed DaaS mashup framework is an effective solution to data privacy concerns.
[27]	Linear algebra to preserve privacy	Privacy preserving of distributed data.	The proposed protocols are computationally efficient. Privacy invasion is protected.
[30, 31]	a three-layer model of user privacy concerns	Guidelines have been developed for the construction of privacy-friendly systems.	Two approaches are distinguished: privacy by policy and privacy by architecture.

(Continued)

TABLE 6.3 (CONTINUED)
Privacy Protection Models and Frameworks ´

Reference number	Model/Method/ Framework	Main Function / Purpose	Details
[6]	Anonymized transaction techniques	Raw data can be a cause of identity theft and information leakage. The anonymization of raw data is necessary.	Adaptive Differential Privacy (ADiffP) algorithm has been proposed for sharing sanitized data instead of raw data.
[34]	Lattice Based Secure Cryptosystem for smart healthcare	This privacy preserving technique is designed for constrained nodes of smart cities.	This scheme works more efficiently as compared to other schemes presently in use. Although the scheme is introduced for smart healthcare I smart cities, it can be practically implemented in other infrastructures of smart cities.

6.4 OPEN ISSUES

- Security and privacy awareness activities and programs are needed to educate citizens of the Smart City. Security and privacy awareness is the basic thing required. It is all about understanding the risks and threats around the cyber world. It is to be educated that the hackers are deliberately trying to steal, misuse and damage the information of the users and that everyone is aware of the associated risks and that they work accordingly to protect them from these risks [64].
- Security and privacy vulnerabilities of the involved technologies must first be analyzed before they are installed and used in a Smart City.
- With the advancements in technology, new, improved and more reliable versions of software and hardware products/solutions are being developed that solve many problems of the previous versions including privacy issues and security concerns. Keeping this in view, the installed/deployed technology must be upgraded to the latest and safest one [65].

6.5 CONCLUSIONS AND RECOMMENDATIONS

In this chapter, the security and privacy concerns linked to Smart City technologies have been discussed. The security threats and privacy concerns vary for different stakeholders. The privacy protection models, security and threat perceptions, methods and frameworks have been explored and enlisted. These countermeasures are beneficial in the security and privacy protection strategy of a Smart City construction/development. In future, this research will be helpful in the development of a hybrid approach that will use salient features of each or some of the discussed methods/models and the implementation of security risk management tools and security awareness techniques to ensure cybersecurity metrics at each and every layer. This hybrid design will provide privacy protection, cryptanalysis with improvised legislation in the form of a single unified solution. In short, the maximized integrated and interoperable and trusted technology can be achieved for public adoption if we can fight against the cyber-crime and security threats in the Smart City.

REFERENCES

1. Cheng, Y., M. Naslund, G. Selander, and E. Fogelstrom. 2012. Privacy in machine-to-machine communications a state-of-the-art survey. In 2012 IEEE International Conference on Communication Systems (ICCS) (pp. 75–79). IEEE.
2. Hoh, B., M. Gruteser, H. Xiong, and A. Alrabady. 2010. Achieving guaranteed anonymity in gps traces via uncertainty-aware path cloaking. *IEEE Transactions on Mobile Computing*, 9(8), pp. 1089–1107.
3. Lu, R., X. Lin, T. H. Luan, X. Liang, and X. Shen. 2012. Pseudonym changing at social spots: An effective strategy for location privacy in vanets. *IEEE Transactions on Vehicular Technology*, 61(1), p. 86.
4. Gretzel, U., M. Sigala, Z. Xiang, and C. Koo. 2015. Smart tourism: Foundations and developments. *Electronic Markets*, 25 (3), pp. 179–188,.
5. Belanche-Gracia, D., L. V. Casaló-Ariño, and A. Pérez-Rueda. 2015. Determinants of multi-service smartcard success for smart cities development: A study based on citizens' privacy and security perceptions. *Government Information Quarterly*, 32 (2), pp. 154–163.
6. Zaman, A., C. Obimbo, and R. A. Dara. 2018. Information disclosure, security, and data quality. In *International Conference on Industrial, Engineering and Other Applications of Applied Intelligent Systems* (pp. 768–779). Springer.
7. Iqbal, S., A. H. Abdullah, and K. N. Qureshi. 2019. An adaptive interference—aware and traffic—aware channel assignment strategy for backhaul networks. *Concurrency Computation: Practice Experience*, 32(11), p. e5650.
8. Vattapparamban, E., İ. Güvenç, A. İ. Yurekli, K. Akkaya, and S. Uluağaç. 2016. Drones for smart cities: Issues in cybersecurity, privacy, and public safety. In 2016 International Wireless Communications and Mobile computing Conference (IWCMC) (pp. 216–221). IEEE.
9. Shepard, D. P., J. A. Bhatti, T. E. Humphreys, and A. A. Fansler. 2012. Evaluation of smart grid and civilian UAV vulnerability to GPS spoofing attacks. In *Radionavigation Laboratory Conference Proceedings*. The University of Texas.
10. Liberatore, S.. 2015. How do you catch a drone? with an even bigger drone and a giant net. *Daily Mail*.
11. Elmaghraby, A. S., and M. M. Losavio. 2014. Cyber security challenges in smart cities: Safety, security and privacy. *Journal of Advanced Research*, 5 (4), pp. 491–497.
12. Li, Y., W. Dai, Z. Ming, and M. Qiu. 2016. Privacy protection for preventing data over-collection in smart city. *IEEE Transactions on Computers*, 65(5), pp. 1339–1350.
13. Kumar, S., U. Dohare, K. Kumar, D. P. Dora, K. N. Qureshi, and R. Kharel. 2018. Cybersecurity measures for geocasting in vehicular cyber physical system environments. *IEEE Internet of Things Journal*, 6(4), pp. 5916–5926.
14. Tari, Z.. 2014. Security and privacy in cloud computing. *IEEE Cloud Computing*, 1(1), pp. 54–57.

15. Edwards, L.. 2016. Privacy, security and data protection in smart cities: A critical EU law perspective. *European Data Protection Law Review*, 2, p. 28.
16. Ijaz, S., M. A. Shah, A. Khan, and M. Ahmed. 2016. Smart cities: A survey on security concerns. *International Journal of Advanced Computer Science and Applications*,7(2), pp. 612–625.
17. Perera, C., A. Zaslavsky, P. Christen, and D. Georgakopoulos. 2014. Sensing as a service model for smart cities supported by internet of things. *Transactions on Emerging Telecommunications Technologies*, 25(1), pp. 81–93.
18. Geib, C. 2017. The rise of the smart city. Available: https://futurism.com/privacy-smart-cities.
19. Martínez-Ballesté, A., P. A. Pérez-Martínez, and A. Solanas. 2013. The pursuit of citizens' privacy: a privacy-aware smart city is possible. *IEEE Communications Magazine*, 51(6), pp. 136–141.
20. Van Zoonen, L. 2016. Privacy concerns in smart cities. *Government Information Quarterly*, 33(3), pp. 472–480.
21. Chourabi, H. et al. 2012. Understanding smart cities: An integrative framework. In *2012 45th Hawaii International Conference on System Science (HICSS)* (pp. 2289–2297). IEEE.
22. Zaman, F., B. Raza, A. K. Malik, and A. Anjum. 2017. Self-protection against insider threats in DBMS through policies implementation. *International Journal of Advanced Computer Science and Applications*, 8(3), pp. 239–249.
23. Smith, M. L.. 2009. Viktor Mayer-Schönberger, delete: The virtue of forgetting in the digital age. *Identity in the Information Society*, 2(3), pp. 369–373.
24. Khan, Z., Z. Pervez, and A. Ghafoor. 2014. Towards cloud based smart cities data security and privacy management. In *2014 IEEE/ACM 7th International Conference on Utility and Cloud Computing (UCC)* (pp. 806–811). IEEE.
25. Arafati, M., G. G. Dagher, B. C. Fung, and P. C. Hung. 2014. D-mash: A framework for privacy-preserving data-as-a-service mashups. In *2014 IEEE 7th International Conference on Cloud Computing (CLOUD)* (pp. 498–505). IEEE.
26. Gubbi, J., R. Buyya, S. Marusic, and M. Palaniswami. 2013. Internet of things (IoT): A vision, architectural elements, and future directions. *Future Generation Computer Systems*, 29(7), pp. 1645–1660.
27. David, B., R. Dowsley, J. van de Graaf, D. Marques, A. C. Nascimento, and A. C. Pinto. 2016. Unconditionally secure, universally composable privacy preserving linear algebra. *IEEE Transactions on Information Forensics and Security*, 11(1), pp. 59–73.
28. Farzandipour, M., F. Sadoughi, M. Ahmadi, and I. Karimi. Security requirements and solutions in electronic health records: Lessons learned from a comparative study. *Journal of Medical Systems*, 34(4), pp. 629–642.
29. Hasan, A. and K. Qureshi. Internet of things device authentication scheme using hardware serialization. In *2018 International Conference on Applied and Engineering Mathematics (ICAEM)* (pp. 109–114). IEEE.
30. Pérez-Martínez, P. A., and A. Solanas. 2011. W3-privacy: The three dimensions of user privacy in LBS. In *12th ACM International Symposium on Mobile Ad Hoc Networking and Computing*. ACM.
31. Spiekermann, S. and L. F. Cranor. 2009. Engineering privacy. IEEE Transactions on Software Engineering, 35(1), pp. 67–82.
32. Batty, M. et al. 2012. Smart cities of the future. *The European Physical Journal Special Topics*, 214(1), pp. 481–518.
33. Xiao, Z. and Y. Xiao. 2013. Security and privacy in cloud computing. *IEEE Communications Surveys & Tutorials*, 15(2), pp. 843–859.

34. Chaudhary, R., A. Jindal, G. S. Aujla, N. Kumar, A. K. Das, and N. Saxena. 2018. LSCSH: Lattice-based secure cryptosystem for smart healthcare in smart cities environment. *IEEE Communications Magazine*, 56(4), pp. 24–32.

35. Thoke, O. 2016. Cloud and mobile device security: Challenges for 2016. Available: https://www.lifewire.com/cloud-mobile-device-security-challenges-3473908.

36. Kumar, J. S. ,and D. R. Patel. 2014. A survey on internet of things: Security and privacy issues. *International Journal of Computer Applications*, 90(11), pp. 20–26.

37. Barth, S., and M. D. de Jong. 2017. The privacy paradox–Investigating discrepancies between expressed privacy concerns and actual online behavior–A systematic literature review. *Telematics and Informatics*, 34(7), pp. 1038–1058.

38. Khatoun, R. and S. Zeadally. 2017. Cybersecurity and privacy solutions in smart cities. *IEEE Communications Magazine*, 55(3), pp. 51–59.

39. Moustaka, V., Z. Theodosiou, A. Vakali, and A. Kounoudes. 2018. Smart cities at risk!: Privacy and security borderlines from social networking in cities. *Athena*, 357, p. 25870072.

40. Washburn, D., U. Sindhu, S. Balaouras, R. A. Dines, N. Hayes, and L. E. J. G. Nelson. 2009. Helping CIOs understand "smart city" initiatives. *Growth*, 17(2), pp. 1–17.

41. Caragliu, A., C. Del Bo, and P. Nijkamp. 2011. Smart cities in Europe. *Journal of Urban Technology*, 18(2), pp. 65–82.

42. Batty, M. et al. 2012. Smart cities of the future. *European Physical Journal*, 214, pp. 481–518.

43. Ferro, E., B. Caroleo, M. Leo, M. Osella, and E. Pautasso. 2013. The role of ICT in smart cities governance. In Proceedings of 13th International Conference for E-Democracy and Open Government(pp. 133–145). Donau-Universität Krems.

44. Albino, V., U. Berardi, and R. M. Dangelico. 2015. Smart cities: Definitions, dimensions, performance, and initiatives. *Journal of Urban Technology*, 22(1), pp. 3–21.

45. Efthymiopoulos, M.-P.. 2016. Cyber-security in smart cities: The case of Dubai. *Journal of Innovation and Entrepreneurship*, 5(1), p. 11.

46. Stergiou, C., K. E. Psannis, B.-G. Kim, and B. GuptaGupta. 2018. Secure integration of IoT and cloud computing. *Future Generation and Computer Systems*, 78, pp. 964–975.

47. Qureshi, K. N., A. H. Abdullah, and R. W. Anwar. 20124The evolution in health care with information and communication technologiesIn 2nd International Conference of Applied Information and Communications Technology-2014, Oman. Elsevier.

48. Han, G., J. Jiang, L. Shu, J. Niu, H.-C. Chao. 2014. Management and applications of trust in wireless sensor networks: A survey. *Journal of Computer and System Sciences*, 80(3), pp. 602–617.

49. Chakrabarty, S., and D. W. Engels. 2016. A secure IoT architecture for Smart Cities. In 2016 13th IEEE annual Consumer Communications & Networking Conference (CCNC) (pp. 812–813). IEEE.

50. https://www.dw.com/en/perfect-it-security-does-not-exist/a-18514534. 2015.

51. Al-Hamami, A. H. 2012. The state of the art and future prospective of the network security. In *Simulation in Computer Network Design and Modeling: Use and Analysis* (pp. 358–376). IGI Global.

52. Jang-Jaccard, J., and S. Nepal. 2014. A survey of emerging threats in cybersecurity. *Journal of Computer and System Sciences*, 80(5), pp. 973–993.

53. Seigneur, J.-M. 2005. Trust, security and privacy in global computing. (Ph.D. thesis).

54. Dickens, C., P. Boynton, and S. Rhee. 2019. Principles for designed-in security and privacy for smart cities. In Proceedings of the Fourth Workshop on International Science of Smart City Operations and Platforms Engineering (pp. 25–29).

55. Tousley, S., and S. Rhee. 2018. Smart and secure cities and communities. In 2018 IEEE International Science of Smart City Operations and Platforms Engineering in Partnership with Global City Teams Challenge (SCOPE-GCTC), (pp. 7–11). IEEE.

56. Qureshi, K. N., F. Bashir, and A. H. Abdullah. 2017. Provision of security in vehicular ad hoc networks through an intelligent secure routing scheme. In 2017 International Conference on Frontiers of Information Technology (FIT) (pp. 200–205). IEEE.

57. Rhee, S. 2020. *2019 Global City Teams Challenge: Smart and Secure Cities and Communities Challenge Expo.* National Institute of Standards and Technology.

58. Yang, L., N. Elisa, and N. Eliot. 2019. Privacy and security aspects of E-government in smart cities. In *Smart Cities Cybersecurity and Privacy* (pp. 89–102). Elsevier.

59. Bischof, S., A. Karapantelakis, C.-S. Nechifor, A. P. Sheth, A. Mileo, and P. Barnaghi. 2014. Semantic modelling of smart city data. Wright State University.

60. Perera, C., R. Ranjan, L. Wang, S. U. Khan, and A. Y. Zomaya. 2015. Big data privacy in the internet of things era. *IT Professional*, 17(3), pp. 32–39.

61. Cheon, J. H., and J. Kim. 2015. A hybrid scheme of public-key encryption and somewhat homomorphic encryption. *IEEE Transactions on Information Forensics and Security*, 10(5), pp. 1052–1063.

62. Moreno, J., M. A. Serrano, and E. Fernández-Medina. 2016. Main issues in big data security. *Future Internet*, 8(3), p. 44.

63. Jacobsen, O., and M. Van Vugt. 2017. A literature review of data as a service: Defining schools of thought, Department of Engineering, Natural Sciences and Economics, Faculty of Marketing, Halmstad University, Halmstad, Sweden.

64. Qureshi, K. N., M. M. Idrees, J. Lloret, and I. Bosch. 2020. Self-assessment based clustering data dissemination for sparse and dense traffic conditions for internet of vehicles. *IEEE Access*, 8, pp. 10363–10372.

65. Iqbal, S., A. H. Abdullah, K. N. Qureshi, and J. Lloret. 2017. Soft-GORA: Soft constrained globally optimal resource allocation for critical links in IoT backhaul communication. *IEEE Access*, 6, pp. 614–624.

7 Self-Monitoring Obfuscated IoT Network

*Ajay Biswas, Dipnarayan Das
and Souvik Bhattacharyya*

CONTENTS

7.1   INTRODUCTION

In today's world of computer science, "Artificial Intelligence (AI) research" deals with the study of intelligent agents, a device that perceives its environment and takes actions that maximize its chances of successfully achieving its goals. Smart Cities, as the name suggests are cities that are not only governed by the people but are also governed by smart devices. We had seen supercars in the 1970s, although the commercial implication of the self-driving car was not available until 2014 [1]. Building a self-driven car requires years of research and has to pass various industry standards to be available and labelled safe for average consumers. Similarly, building a Smart City requires years of research and planning also requires acceptance of people. A Smart City must convince people about its security, applications and its intelligence compared to humans [2–4].

The purpose of this chapter is to provide an intelligent, secured, obfuscated network, which can maintain itself to give optimum stability in present Smart City cyber communication. The proposed system is different from existing technologies because it provides an unconventional approach of communication. In this system, every new device which connects to the network is bounded to follow some protocols to maintain the signature of the network. This is achieved by the process of knowledge-infecting the devices [5]. In order to main the security of inter-module communication, the communication takes place within the system by using images having control signals embedded within it. These signals help in identifying threat, allowing the main server to take necessary action and adjust automatically to protect itself from the future threats.

This chapter has been organized into the following sections: Section 2 discusses some of the related works carried out by the previous researchers. Section 3 deals with proposed method. Section 4 discusses he approach of implementation of the proposed method with the results of the various analyses conducted. Finally, section 5 draws the conclusion.

7.2   RELATED WORKS

This section reviewed various existing techniques used for Smart City communications based on different cyber protocols. Masanobu Katagi et al. [6] provided an efficient implementation of lightweight cryptography for IoTs for end-to-end communication which requires less resources. Another work in the area of lightweight cryptography was proposed by Tapalina Bhattasali in 2013 [7]. In this work she highlighted the advantages of lightweight cryptography known as LICRYPT and also showed its trade-off among security, cost and performance.

In 2016 Tanya Singh et al. [8] provided a methodology to secure IoTs in 5G using audio steganography implemented using Least Significant Bit Insertion (LSBI) method. The audio signals used in this scheme were in the form of music files. This method is extremely useful for sharing passwords and keys over a 5G network.

In 2018, Mohamed Elhoseny et al. [9] proposed a secure method of transmitting medical data for IoT-based healthcare systems. This method works by using Haar-DWT and hybrid Advanced Encryption Standard (AES) and RSA algorithm for implementing the steganography approach. This method is used for sending confidential medical data with high imperceptibility and capacity with minimum distortion. Sung Ryoung Kim et al. [10] in 2018 proposed an "Anti-reversible dynamic tamper detection" technique which uses a distributed image steganography concept. This method also uses a digital watermarking technique to detect tampering with Android Application Packages (APK) and provides a great resistance in reverse engineering approaches.

7.3   PROPOSED METHOD

In this paper a new approach to Smart City cyber communication using "Self-Monitoring Obfuscated IoT Network" (SMOIN) has been proposed. This strategy works in two layers; the first layer uses conventional techniques of communication and the second one uses a steganography channel for secret communication. Steganography strategy is implemented by hiding secret information into shared files, common between the modules like audio input from multiple microphones or images captured from a CCTV camera. Apart from these two layers, each server has its own processing unit and each module can be connected to one or more LANs and must have a dedicated stego-circuit embedded within it. A stego-circuit [11] is a combinational circuit that adds stego-information into the signals that pass through it.

It is natural that every network-connected device like computers, smartphones, tablets, different smart home gadgets and many more must have an IP address and a unique MAC address that will identify it on that particular network. Similarly, when an authorised device gets connected to our network it will bear a unique signature. On the other hand, if any unauthorized device connects to the network through a particular node then that node (it may be an IoT device or a router) will stop all communication until the device is authorized and otherwise it will reject that device. The cyber-network makes a real-time map with all the devices connected to it making requests. The real-time map contains details of connected nodes such as their IP addresses, subnet masks and load balancing factors. It also makes a colour map to detect the amount of payload for each device. The basic principle of the proposed method is based on the following key concepts [12, 13].

In any arithmetic calculations, if the numbers in a group with equal value are averaged, their average will remain the same regardless of their quantity. Conceptually, if the communicators are increased in any network then the signature should remain unaffected. In case of malfunction of a device, the network will stop all the incoming connection from it and alert the administrator using that real-time map. The communication layer is composed of multiple layers of routers, repeaters and IoT devices along with, centrally located, the main server. In order to establish a connection with the main server a specific path needs to be followed for only one instance or we have to identify the actual IP address of the main server, which may be quite impossible because the server information needs to be propagated throughout the obfuscated network. Therefore, for all attacks, the server will not be accessed directly.

Figure 7.1 depicts the case where any IoT device is under attack and the connected routers are not receiving any important information like the IP address of the server. Figure 7.2 discusses the case when the router is under attack and if the router is also connected to the server then the server will reject every incoming connection request from that router and responses using "hard restart interrupt". Figure 7.3 describes the case when the attacker targets an IoT device and tries to connect to the router. But

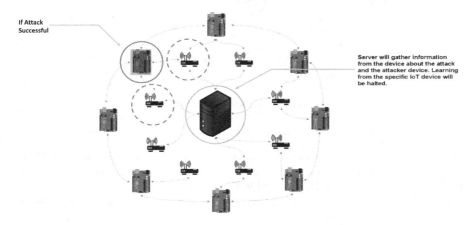

FIGURE 7.1   Router isolation protocol when device under attack

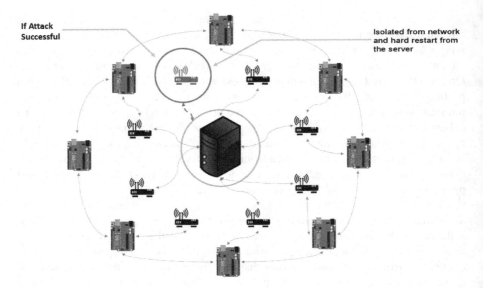

FIGURE 7.2   Server pinging for authentication

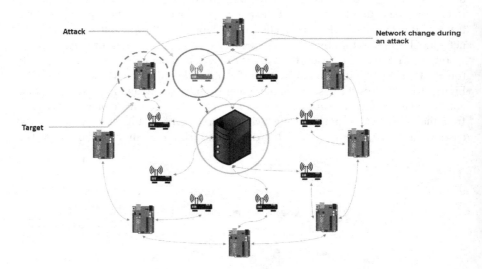

FIGURE 7.3   Attack unsuccessful due to propagation of connection

as soon as the attacker connects the router he/she will find out the targeted device has left the router. Still, if any unauthorized device gets connected then all incoming traffic from that device will stop totally. Finally, in Figure 7.4 the colour map representation of the proposed architecture has been shown. The module circled in red signifies "connection limit has reached" whereas the yellow colour warns the system about the high amount of connections to a particular module.

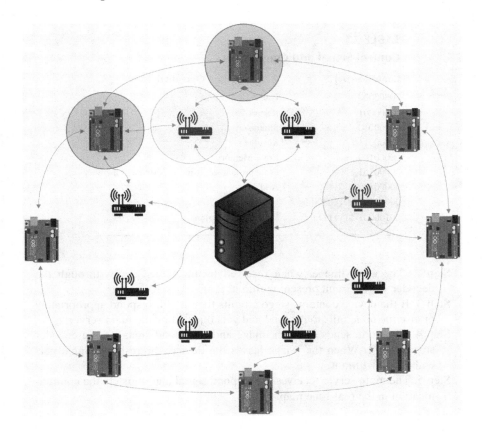

FIGURE 7.4   Colour map for payload amount at real-time

7.3.1   THE INTER-MODULE STEGANOGRAPHY PROTOCOL

Steganography is the art and science that hides the information in an appropriate cover carrier like image, text, audio and video media. The proposed steganography modules connected in the common network can exchange stego information in the form of a stream of bits embedded in an image at the regular intervals which allow remote control of a specific IoT module using another IoT module existing in the network. Table 7.1 provides the concept of various control signals that can be used in an inter-module network. Consider also the case, when an attacker is trying to physically modify a device he may accidentally trigger the malfunction operation. Complexity can be further increased by differently assigning the control signals for each module.

The algorithm below demonstrates the steps that occur when the control signals get embedded into the images.

7.3.1.1   Control Signals Embedding Technique

Step 1. The main server sends a stego-image to a node (IoT module), containing some control signal and expects a similar stego-image back from it.

TABLE 7.1

Control Signal and Operations

Control Signal	Operation
00000000	Pause
00000001	Restart
00000010	Shutdown
00000011	Resume
00000100	Erase Memory
00000101	Store present status in the permanent memory
00000110	Add delay
00000111-00100000	Ignore
00100001-11111111	Report Malfunction

Step 2. The stego-image, when received by the node, passes through the decoder stego-circuit present within it, if any.

Step 3. If the device contains stego circuits then it will respond appropriately or else the node fails to respond and gets rejected by the main server.

Step 4. The node sends back an image and a respond signal to the encoder stego-circuit. When the image leaves the device, the respond signal gets embedded within it.

Step 5. The main server receives the respond signal and registers the communication in the real-time map.

7.3.2 Behaviour Learning

AI is rapidly changing our lifestyle and continues to grow at an incredible rate, which makes an AI-equipped machine different from robots in its ability to learn and exercise judgment. A Smart City is not considered smart if it only hires dumb robots which cannot go beyond its capabilities. Similarly, the proposed system has the capability of taking decisions and learning from its mistakes. In this system, when a device works perfectly, the data received from it during a finite interval will have some similarities. While processing these data in the main server, if any irregularity is observed whether it is a delay in communication, malfunctioning, accessing unassigned networks, etc., then the main server will command that module and other neighbouring modules to take appropriate actions. The processing is done using ensemble type machine learning algorithms which continuously collect data and generate a pattern for checking irrelevancy, if any. In this system, no external data gets executed and can only be executed at the edges of the networks. During communication, every data chunk is sent along with some headers and no transmission is allowed without it. Whenever the header data is added to the transmitted file, the data becomes non-executable as it is treated as unknown metadata. This header part of the network architecture actually contains the signature. If any data has to be

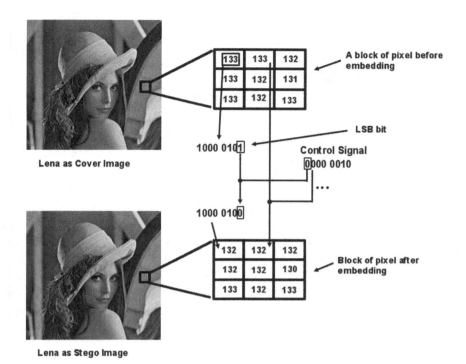

Lena as Cover Image

Lena as Stego Image

FIGURE 7.5 Embedding of the Control Signals into an image using LSB steganography

executed in this network then some additional protocols should be present so as to achieve an environment virtually isolated from the real world.

7.4 RESULTS AND ANALYSIS

The proposed system was tested using a personal computer as the main server, some wi-fi routers, and some IoT devices like Arduino, Node MCU, Raspberry Pi, [14] etc. The stego-circuits were implemented using Raspberry Pi. The cost of the complete setup is low as it can be implemented on cheap, low powered IoT devices. The extra cost is contributed by multiple routers and the stego circuits (can be implemented by software too) only. To check the integrity of the signature, 20 images were embedded with a text message (control signal), where each control signal is preceded by a signature. Therefore, two entities, the steganography algorithm, and the control signal is common among the 20 images. If someone else tries to tamper with the communication, a different pattern of data gets embedded as the attacker is unaware of the steganography protocol (Figure 7.5). The following equation describes the embedding process.

$$Z_i = y * x_i, i \in [1, 20]$$

where Z_i are the stego images, y is the control signal and x_i are the cover images. The * operator denotes the steganography operation.

TABLE 7.2
Classification of Cover and Stego

			Stratified cross-validation					
Summary								
Correctly Classified Instances	3	15	%					
Incorrectly Classified Instances	17	85	%					
Kappa statistic	-0.1333							
Mean absolute error	0.3979							
Root mean squared error	0.4797							
Relative absolute error	102.97%							
Root relative squared error	107.44%	%						
Total Number of Instances	20							
Detailed Accuracy By Class								
TP Rate	FP Rate	Precision	Recall	F-Measure	MCC	ROC Area	PRC Area	Class
0.4	0.333	0.286	0.4	0.333	0.061	0.493	0.267	a
0.2	0.267	0.2	0.2	0.2	-0.067	0.427	0.268	b
0	0.2	0	0	0	-0.243	0.42	0.232	c
0	0.333	0	0	0	-0.333	0.167	0.181	d
Weighted Avg.	0.15	0.283	0.121	0.15	0.133	-0.146	0.377	0.237
Confusion Matrix								
a b c d	<-- classified as							
2 0 1 2 | a = a								
0 1 2 2 | b = b								
2 2 0 1 | c = c								
3 2 0 0 | d = d								

TABLE 7.3

Classification of Cover and Stego Images through Logit Boost

Stratified cross-validation		

Summary

Correctly Classified Instances	3	15 %
Incorrectly Classified Instances	17	85 %
Kappa statistic	-0.1333	
Mean absolute error	0.4333	
Root mean squared error	0.529	
Relative absolute error	112.16%	
Root relative squared error	118.48%	
Total Number of Instances	20	

Detailed Accuracy By Class

TP Rate	FP Rate	Precision	Recall	F-Measure	MCC	ROC Area	PRC Area	Class
0.4	0.4	0.25	0.4	0.308	0	0.393	0.25	a
0	0.133	0	0	0	-0.192	0.167	0.217	b
0.2	0.333	0.167	0.2	0.182	-0.126	0.3	0.208	c
0	0.267	0	0	0	-0.289	0.227	0.212	d
Weighted Avg. 0.15	0.15	0.283	0.104	0.15	0.122	-0.152	0.272	0.222

Confusion Matrix

```
a b c d   <-- classified as
2 0 1 2 | a = a
2 0 2 1 | b = b
1 2 1 1 | c = c
3 0 2 0 | d = d
```

TABLE 7.4

Classification of Cover and Stego Images through Naïve Bayes

Stratified cross-validation

Summary

Correctly Classified Instances	1	5 %
Incorrectly Classified Instances	19	95 %
Kappa statistic	-0.2667	
Mean absolute error	0.475	
Root mean squared error	0.6892	
Relative absolute error	122.94%	
Root relative squared error	154.35%	
Total Number of Instances	20	

Detailed Accuracy By Class

TP Rate	FP Rate	Precision	Recall	F-Measure	MCC	ROC Area	PRC Area	Class
0.2	0.867	0.071	0.2	0.105	-0.63	0.14	0.214	a
0	0.067	0	0	0	-0.132	0.3	0.25	b
0	0.133	0	0	0	-0.192	0.493	0.267	c
0	0.2	0	0	0	-0.243	0.413	0.24	d
Weighted Avg.	0.05	0.317	0.018	0.05	0.026	-0.299	0.337	0.243

Confusion Matrix

```
a b c d   <-- classified as
1 0 1 3 | a = a
4 0 1 0 | b = b
4 1 0 0 | c = c
5 0 0 0 | d = d
```

TABLE 7.5

Classification of Cover and Stego Images through Random Forest

Stratified cross-validation

Summary

Correctly Classified Instances	1	5 %
Incorrectly Classified Instances	19	95 %
Kappa statistic	-0.2667	
Mean absolute error	0.4108	
Root mean squared error	0.4886	
Relative absolute error	106.32%	%
Root relative squared error	109.43%	%
Total Number of Instances	20	

Detailed Accuracy By Class

TP Rate	FP Rate	Precision	Recall	F-Measure	MCC	ROC Area	PRC Area	Class
0	0.467	0	0	0	-0.424	0.227	0.195	a
0	0.133	0	0	0	-0.192	0.2	0.195	b
0.2	0.4	0.143	0.2	0.167	-0.182	0.393	0.236	c
0	0.267	0	0	0	-0.289	0.107	0.173	d
Weighted Avg. 0.05	0.05	0.317	0.036	0.05	0.042	-0.272	0.232	0.2

Confusion Matrix

```
a b c d   <-- classified as
0 1 2 2 | a = a
3 0 2 0 | b = b
2 0 1 2 | c = c
2 1 2 0 | d = d
```

TABLE 7.6
Classification of Cover and Stego Images through SMO

Stratified cross-validation ===

Summary

Correctly Classified Instances	3	15 %
Incorrectly Classified Instances	17	85 %
Kappa statistic	-0.1333	
Mean absolute error	0.4333	
Root mean squared error	0.529	
Relative absolute error	112.16%	
Root relative squared error	118.48%	
Total Number of Instances	20	

Detailed Accuracy By Class

	TP Rate	FP Rate	Precision	Recall	F-Measure	MCC	ROC Area	PRC Area	Class
	0.4	0.4	0.25	0.4	0.308	0	0.393	0.25	a
	0	0.133	0	0	0	-0.192	0.167	0.217	b
	0.2	0.333	0.167	0.2	0.182	-0.126	0.3	0.208	c
	0	0.267	0	0	0	-0.289	0.227	0.212	d
Weighted Avg.	0.15	0.15	0.283	0.104	0.15	0.122	-0.152	0.272	

Confusion Matrix

```
a b c d   <-- classified as
2 0 1 2 | a = a
2 0 2 1 | b = b
1 2 1 1 | c = c
3 0 2 0 | d = d
```

A good signature should be powerful enough to keep its existence even after the carrier medium faces abuses like manipulation, noise addition, etc. The data received from the signature will help us to identify any abnormal behaviour arising from a module. All the images were fed to a feature extractor called SPAM686 [15] which extracts 686 features of each image. These features can be used to detect steganography and will help in classifying normal and abnormal system behaviour. Although we know that all images contain the same embedded data and have been implemented with the same steganography algorithm, the majority of the image data consists of its own unmodified data, typically, its pixel intensity values. To prove that the signature has kept its existence in the images, four clusters of five images each were made and were fed to the five well-known classifiers namely Naïve Bayes, Random Forest, Sequential Minimal Optimization (SMO), Decision Table, Logit boost [16–19]. If the classifiers fail to classify the clusters correctly, i.e., differentiate cover images with stego images, that means the signature has successfully obfuscated itself.

The results for each classifier are given in Table 7.2 to Table 7.6. On analysing the results, a maximum of 15% correctly classified instances through SMO, Decision Table, and Logit boost and a minimum 5% of correct classified instances through Naïve Bayes and Random Forest.

On analysing these results, it can be observed that the applied signature has successfully obfuscated its identity throughout the 20 images as most of the stego images appear clean to the machine learning classifiers.

7.5 CONCLUSION

From the analysis point of view, we can conclude that the proposed network architecture is secure and resilient. This system is based on horizontally scalable technology which ensures performance boost with each iteration in technology. Compared with the existing works it can be concluded that the proposed architecture is superior in terms of self-maintenance and learning. From the results, we can see that only 15% of the images containing the signature could be successfully classified which shows the obfuscation of the signature into the network. The obfuscated architecture along with the application of steganography provides a high level of security which is resistant to tampering and has the capability of reporting it too. The integration of this architecture in the Smart Cities will not only increase their security but will also make them smarter and self-maintainable.

REFERENCES

1. Howard, D., and D. Dai. 2014. Public perceptions of self-driving cars: The case of Berkeley, California. In Transportation Research Board 93rd Annual Meeting (Vol. 14, pp. 1–16). Transportation Research Board.
2. Jawhar, I., N. Mohamed, and J. Al-Jaroodi. 2018. Networking architectures and protocols for smart city systems. *Journal of Internet Services and Applications* 9(1), p. 26.
3. Baig, Z. A., P. Szewczyk, C. Valli, P. Rabadia, P. Hannay, M. Chernyshev, M. Johnstone, et al. 2017. Future challenges for smart cities: Cyber-security and digital forensics. *Digital Investigation* 22, pp. 3–13.

4. Theoleyre, F., T. Watteyne, G. Bianchi, G. Tuna, V. C. Gungor, and A.C. Pang. 2015. Networking and communications for smart cities (editorial). *Computer Communications*, 58, pp. 1–3.

5. Das, D., and S. Gupta. 2020. IntelliNet: An intelligence delivery network. In *Advances in control, signal processing and energy systems* (pp. 55–66). Singapore: Springer.

6. Katagi, M., and S. Moriai. 2008. Lightweight cryptography for the internet of things. *Sony Corporation* 2008, pp. 7–10.

7. Bhattasali, T. 2013. Licrypt: Lightweight cryptography technique for securing smart objects in internet of things environment. *CSI Communications*, pp. 26–36.

8. Singh, T., S. Verma, and V. Parashar. 2016. Securing internet of things in 5G using audio steganography. In International Conference on Smart Trends for Information Technology and Computer Communications (pp. 365–372). Singapore: Springer.

9. Elhoseny, M., G. Ramírez-González, O. M. Abu-Elnasr, S. A. Shawkat, N. Arunkumar, and A. Farouk. 2018. Secure medical data transmission model for IoT-based healthcare systems. *IEEEAccess* 6, pp. 20596–20608.

10. Kim, S. R., J. N. Kim, S. T. Kim, S. Shin, and J. H. Yi. 2018. Anti-reversible dynamic tamper detection scheme using distributed image steganography for IoT applications. *The Journal of Supercomputing* 74(9), pp. 4261–4280.

11. Walia, E., P. Jain, and N. Navdeep. 2010. An analysis of LSB & DCT based steganography. *Global Journal of Computer Science and Technology* 4(10), pp. 4–8.

12. Dumitrescu, S, X. Wu, and Z. Wang. 2002. Detection of LSB steganography via sample pair analysis. In International workshop on information hiding (pp. 355–372). Berlin: Springer.

13. Bhattacharyya, S. 2011. A survey of steganography and steganalysis technique in image, text, audio and video as cover carrier. *Journal of Global Research in Computer Science*, 2(4), 1–16.

14. Ferdoush, S., and X. Li. 2014. Wireless sensor network system design using Raspberry Pi and Arduino for environmental monitoring applications. *Procedia Computer Science*, 34, pp. 103–110.

15. Pevny, T., P. Bas, and J. Fridrich. 2010. Steganalysis by subtractive pixel adjacency matrix. *IEEE Transactions on Information Forensics and Security*, 5(2), pp. 215–224.

16. Rish, I. 2001. An empirical study of the naive Bayes classifier. In IJCAI 2001 workshop on empirical methods in artificial intelligence (Vol. 3, pp. 41–46). https://www.cc.gatech.edu/.

17. Safavian, S. R., and D. Landgrebe. 1991. A survey of decision tree classifier methodology. IEEE Transactions on Systems, Man, and Cybernetics, 21(3), pp. 660–674.

18. Keerthi, S. S., S. K. Shevade, C. Bhattacharyya, and K. R. K. Murthy. 2001. Improvements to Platt's SMO algorithm for SVM classifier design. *Neural Computation*, 13(3), pp. 637–649.

19. Kotsiantis, S. B. 2005. Logit boost of simple bayesian classifier. *Informatica*, 29(1), 53–59.

8 Introduction to Side Channel Attacks and Investigation of Power Analysis and Fault Injection Attack Techniques

Shaminder Kaur, Balwinder Singh and Harsimranjit Kaur

CONTENTS

8.1   INTRODUCTION

Security has become a big concern in today's modern world of IOT and cloud computing. This era of IOT has given advent to the field of hardware security. Security is required at every level ranging from hardware level to software level as shown in Figure 8.1. Embedded circuits comprise of both software and hardware parts. Software security deals with securing software against attacks such as virus, etc. Hardware security, on the other hand, focuses on attacks and protection of hardware. This chapter deals with security at hardware level, hence known as hardware security. Hardware security is a field which deals with securing a device at hardware level (circuit level, system level, transistor level, etc.).

Side channel attacks are a sub-class of hardware security. These are also known as physical attacks. It has been observed that the security of cryptographic devices is threatened by side channel attacks, which further leak secret information. Side channels attacks have become a major industrial concern for the last 15 years and have resulted in intensive research efforts to develop suitable countermeasures that can at least make attacks more difficult and time consuming to perform [1].

Figure 8.1 shows the hierarchy of security that is required and important at every level. Gathering information from computers (information such as power consumption, voltage fluctuation) rather than algorithms is known as side channel attacks. Side channels attacks are called side channels because these attacks do not take part actively but they leak information through physical interfaces such as power consumption, EM radiations, and timings attacks.These physical interactions (power, EM waves, etc.) can be instigated and monitored by adversaries, like Eve, and may result in information that is not intended for the attacker. This type of information is called sidechannel information, and the attacks exploiting sidechannel information are called sidechannel attacks. The main principle of (SCA) side channel attacks is retrieve secret information through side channel leakage information. Side channel attacks work because there is a correlation between the physical measurements taken during computations (e.g., power consumption, computing time, EMF radiation, etc.) and the internal state of the processing device, which is itself related to the secret key. It is the correlation between the side channel information and the operation related to the secret key that the side channel attack tries to find.

There are various tools and methods used to extract the secret key/information [2, 3]. By doing simple analysis and advanced analysis the adversary can easily detect

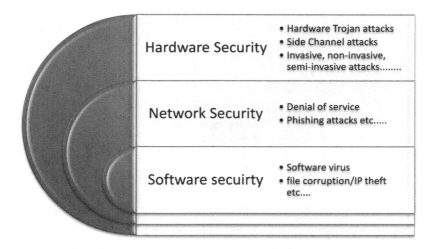

FIGURE 8.1 Hierarchy of Hardware Security.

secret information [4]. Brute force analysis is one of the methods. Brute force analysis is done in order to obtain the secret key. Brute force analysis requires an adversary to perform lots of experiments to have access to secret key.

- *This chapter covers power analysis tools and fault injection techniques in detail.*

8.1.1 BRIEF HISTORY OF SIDE CHANNEL ATTACKS

It was in late 90s when Kocher et al. proposed Side Channel Attacks [5]. In 1996, Kocher introduced the first passive attack based on the execution's timing measurements. It showed a new method to extract secret data from smart cards while processing. Figure 8.2 shows an example of a passive attack where an attacker gathers information about an embedded device through side channel leakage. Boneh, DeMillo and Lipton then published the first active attack know as "bellcore attack". Both attack types are opposite in nature. Active attacks tamper the parameters of IC such as variation in clock, power supply, etc., that leads to the erroneous behavior of the device, whereas passive attacks are based on observation of information leaked during the normal operation of the device such as power consumption, EM waves, temperature, computation time of different instructions, observing the sound of the fan used in the microprocessor, etc.,while the cryptographic operation is still taking place.

8.2 STATE OF THE ART IN HARDWARE SECURITY

8.2.1 MELTDOWN ATTACK

This is a kind of attack that enables an adversary to read the memory of other processors which are not intended for him. This attack is independent of the operating system and does not rely on software vulnerabilities. Its root cause is hardware.

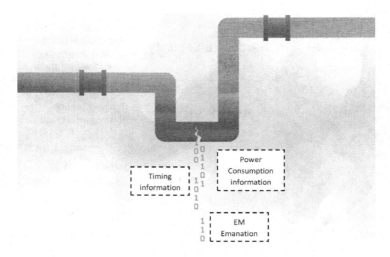

FIGURE 8.2 Information Captured by Attacker through Side Channel Leakage [6].

8.2.2 SPECTRE ATTACK

Spectre breaks the isolation between different applications. It allows an attacker to trick error-free programs, which follow best practices, into leaking their secrets. In fact, the safety checks of said best practices actually increase the attack surface and may make applications more susceptible to Spectre [7].

> "Spectre is harder to exploit than Meltdown, but it is also harder to mitigate. These attacks come under the category of timing attacks."

Both these attacks exploit processors and steal data. These malicious programs get hold of secret data which is not intended for them. Moreover these attacks do not leave any traces in traditional files. More information about these attacks can be found on the link given in the references.

8.2.3 ACOUSTIC CRYPTANALYSIS

Sound which is produced during computation is exploited in this kind of attack. By listening to the sound of the computer the attacker gets an idea of the secret key.

8.2.4 PAGE CACHE ATTACK

The page cache is a pure software cache that contains all disk backed pages, including program binaries, shared libraries and other files, thus works across cores and CPUs [8].

8.3 SIDE CHANNEL ATTACK MODEL

Side channel attacks breaks the security of systems by exploiting signals that are unknowingly emitted during the execution of cryptographic operation such as power

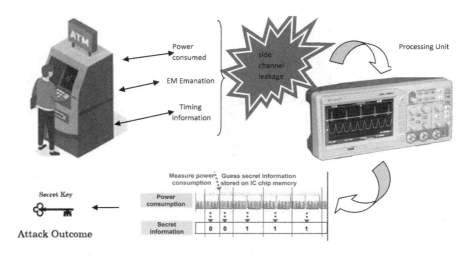

FIGURE 8.3   A Simple Side Channel Attack Model.

consumption, memory and timing information, EM emanation etc as shown in the Figure 8.3. These so-called physical attacks do not necessarily aim at mathematical weaknesses of algorithms or implementations but rather take advantage of physically observable or manipulable parameters. After gathering side channel information they are further processed. By performing several iterations on this data the attacker collects lot of information and is successful in extracting the secret key. Figure 8.3 represents the process of extracting the data. Attacker observes the power consumption of device and captures waveforms. Bits 0s and 1s are easily distinguishable from the power waveforms leading to key extraction.

8.3.1   CLASSIFICATION OF SIDE CHANNEL ATTACKS

Side channel attacks are called "side channel" because they do not intrude actively but take part passively without tampering with the device. The person will not even know about the attack. Figure 8.4 shows the categorization of side channel attacks. Side channel attacks can be categorized as: Active and Passive attacks.

"Active attacks are more harmful as compared to passive attacks."

The literature categorizes side channel attacks as Active vs Passive attacks.

8.3.1.1 Active vs Passive Attacks: They aim at inducing faults in a circuit to get slightly different or erroneous behavior. There are several means to inject faults into a circuit, either by modifying chips' parameters or by modifying its external environment: variation in clock frequency, under powering, over powering, glitches, laser shots, etc [9]. Passive attacks are based on observation of information leaked during normal operation of device such as power consumption, EM waves, temperature,

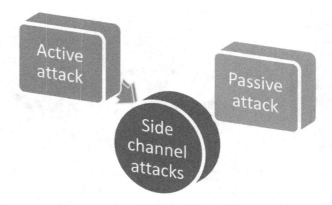

FIGURE 8.4   Categorization of Side Channel Attacks.

sound, etc. These attacks can retrieve secret data using statistical analysis, which are discussed later.

- **Power attacks**: As shown in Figure 8.3, attacker tries to capture the information from the target device. Resistor is connected across the target device. Since

$$V = IR$$

$$P = VI$$

$$P_{load} \alpha V_{series}$$

From the above equation, we can easily find out power traces and can find out the secret key. Attacker doesnot need to discover the exact power consumption, he just needs to determine when target is consuming more power and when less.

8.3.1.2   Invasive vs Non-invasive:

Invasive attacks are the ones which require direct access to the chip. They are penetrative attacks, which leave tamper evidence of attack or even destroy the device. They may harm the chip physically leaving the device damaged permanently. Noninvasive attacks are less destructive as compared to invasive attacks and they do not harm the chip physically. They are also known as non-penetrative attacks. In this, attacker interacts with the device via its interface (voltage, current, I/O, etc.). They just observe and manipulate the device without physical harm to it [9]. These types of attacks leave no evidence of attack. The device remains undamaged. Skorobogatov and Anderson add a new distinction with what they call *semi-invasive attacks*. It is a kind of attack which is less destructive than invasive one. In this, it requires depackaging of the chip but they do not tamper with passivation layer – they do not require electrical contact to metal surface.

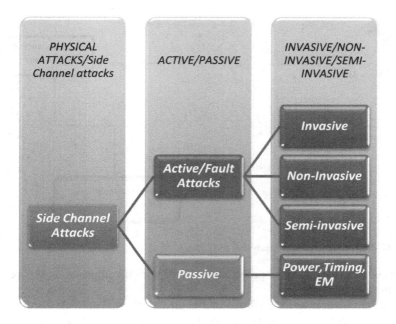

FIGURE 8.5 Classification of Side Channel Attacks.

Between invasive and non-invasive, non-invasive attacks are interesting because the equipment and hardware specific knowledge necessary to perform them is minimal. Strong expertise is not required to perform such types of attacks. This is why these types of attacks are gaining a lot of attention in the scientific community. Figure 8.5 shows classification of side channel attacks.

8.4 POWER ANALYSIS TECHNIQUES

There are various power analysis techniques as discussed below [9]:

1. *SPA (Simple Power Analysis)*
2. *DPA (Differential Power Analysis)*
3. *CPA(Correlation Power Analysis)*
4. *MIA(Mutual Information Analysis)*
5. *Horizontal & Vertical power analysis*
6. *CIA (Combined Implementation Attacks)*

8.4.1 SIMPLE POWER ANALYSIS AND DIFFERENTIAL POWER ANALYSIS

These techniques were proposed in 1999 [9,10]. Simple power analysis is done by adversary to reveal secret information just by observing the power waveforms. Data is leaked through side channels such as timing, power, EM waves, etc., as shown in Figure 8.6. It simply involves interpreting power traces or graphs during normal

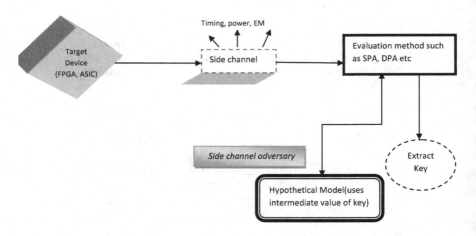

FIGURE 8.6 Side Channel Analysis DPA Attack.

execution [11]. Small set of power traces with relevant information are obtained directly from trace patterns.

Attacker captures the waveforms and compares them with leaked information. By using hamming weight distance model the secret key is revealed. This is a basic technique used to do analysis. After this much more advanced techniques arrived.

Figure 8.6 shows how an attacker can steal the secret key by doing simple analysis such as SPA. Figure 8.7 shows a RSA asymmetric cryptographic standard used for key exchange. It uses modular exponentiation as its basis. RSA is implemented using a method where a square function is used if the key byte is odd, and square and multiply is used if the key byte is even. An attacker by observing the waveform can guess these operations of square and multiply and can get information about the

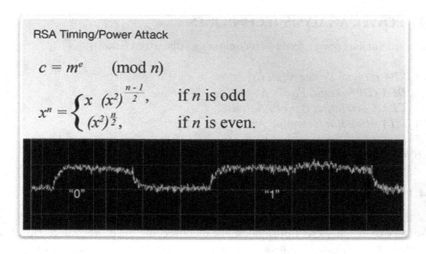

FIGURE 8.7 Example of Side Channel Attack on Crypto Function [12].

secret key. Others techniques such as DPA or more advanced techniques can also be used for easy recovery

Advantage: Small traces are required.
Disadvantage: Lots of manual effort is required along with detailed supervision.

8.4.2 DIFFERENTIAL POWER ANALYSIS

It was introduced by Paul Kocher [13, 14]. This is an advanced method as compared to SPA in which the attacker uses statistical properties of traces in order to recover secret data. It is based on the evaluation of many traces with varying input data for the targeted algorithm. Then a brute force attack with additional information is performed on a part of the algorithm. Hence, it is also called a divide and conquer strategy.

8.4.2.1 Basic Approach of DPA: It is a statistical technique which takes several power consumption traces of a cryptographic device as one of its inputs and determines the validity of a guess made on the cipher key. This attack relies on the assumption that a correlation exists between the device operation and the power consumed by the device while performing that operation. DPA is a powerful attack because it is non-invasive, it does not require expensive equipment and it is independent of the algorithm implementation.

8.4.2.2 Steps to perform DPA: It can be divided into two steps:

1. Measurement phase;
2. Evaluation Phase.

8.4.2.3 Countermeasure against DPA: Power consumption of the device should be made independent of data since they are correlated.

- Noise generators.
- Insertion of random delays which will further makes power measurement task for attacker more time consuming and difficult.
- Another approach is to randomize the intermediate results.
- Masking: It can be applied at algorithm level or gate level.

8.4.3 CORRELATION POWER ANALYSIS

An improved DPA technique. In CPA [15, 28, 29] based power attacks, an adversary encrypts multiple plaintexts and measures the power consumption during the encryption (Figure 8.8). He then constructs a power model based on hamming weight (HW) or hamming distance (HD) of intermediate state(s) by using the plaintexts and a guess for the target key byte. The measured power traces are correlated with the power model and the highest correlation reveals the secret key byte.

For linear power model, Pearson's correlation coefficient is a good choice [2].

- Other models: difference of means, mutual information.

Concept of CPA:

Correlation coefficient (measured power, hypothetical power)

FIGURE 8.8 Concept of CPA.

8.4.3.1 Steps to Perform CPA Attack

1. The intermediate value is chosen.
2. Based on chosen values power traces are measured
3. Choose a power model.
4. Calculate the hypothetical intermediate value and corresponding hypothetical power consumption.
5. Apply the statistic analysis between measured power consumption and hypothetical power consumption. The value having highest correlation will be considered as secret key.

8.4.4 MUTUAL INFORMATION ANALYSIS

It is one of the most established techniques. Techniques discussed before are quite complicated and they need to consider many factors while doing power analysis such as[16]:

- Device power consumption characteristics;
- Attackers power model;
- The distinguisher by which measurements and model predictions are compared;
- The quality of the estimations.

In contrast to CPA, MIA can capture non-linear dependencies between predicted power consumption and measured values and hence improve the success rate of side channel attacks in certain situations [17].

8.4.5 HORIZONTAL AND VERTICAL POWER ATTACK

A different kind of evaluation method called *horizontal* and *vertical* power analysis is also there which is based on detecting and utilizing correlations within a single trace, e.g., to identify the processing of similar values in a cryptographic algorithm [18]. These methods apply to both symmetric and asymmetric cryptographic primitives.

According to literature review, all kinds of countermeasures become ineffective if attacks are performed with *modus operandi* called *Horizontal*. Classic attacks require several traces; however, these kinds of attacks require single observation trace. Colin Walter at CHES 2001 originally introduced these attacks [19]. Vertical attack differs from horizontal attack in the way that information is obtained from different algorithm executions.

8.4.6 Combined Implementation Attack

Different kinds of attacks such as side channel attacks and fault injection attacks are considered as separate attacks [20]. Adversary may successfully combine them to overcome countermeasures against them. This category is known as combined implementation attack [21].

8.4.6.1 Basic Principle of Combining Active and Passive Attacks

By injecting a fault, the computation of the device gets disturbed; further it becomes possible to realize a passive attack on the perturbed execution. The fault is detected at the end of the command. The secret value has already been recovered using classic power analysis. Fault countermeasures are only active after the end of the computation.

8.5 NON-INVASIVE ACTIVE ATTACKS

Fault injection techniques are kinds of *non-invasive active attacks*. These kinds of attacks require more of a skill set as compared to passive attacks. Figure 8.9 categorizes fault injection attacks viz, power tampering, clock tampering, laser glitching, EM emanation.

8.5.1 Fault Injection Attacks

Here we will discuss non-invasive methods of fault injection attack. As compared to invasive and semi-invasive attacks, this attack method does not require much expertise to conduct and therefore is an area of much importance to researchers. In contrast to the passive side-channel attacks, fault attacks actively attack a device and its operation by modifying physical/environmental parameters. Thus, it is possible to enforce faulty behavior or wrong conditions in the attacked device. As a consequence, induced faults typically result in erroneous calculations. This enables an attacker to gain details about the implementation or to even extract secret information.

Figure 8.10 shows a demonstration of the fault injection method. Unlike passive attacks, fault injection is a kind of active attack method which requires expertise to conduct. The main idea behind this attack is to produce faulty behavior and that behavior may lead to some erroneous changes in the embedded device. Fault is produced either by tampering with clock signal, power supply lineor optical injection as shown in the figure. This tampering of external signal may produce some glitch and

TABLE 8.1
Countermeasures Against Various Power Attacks

Countermeasure	Power attack	Drawback
Differential dynamic logic(DDL) [22,23]	equalize the power consumption irrespective of the input vectors	differential logic at least doubles the area or power, does not scale with activity factor and its custom design makes it difficult to scale with respect to digital process technology
power delivery network (PDN) as well as on-chip integrated voltage regulator (IVR) modules to modulate the current signatures generated by the device while it is performing encryptions	IVRs mainly focused on inductor- or capacitor-based switching regulators to enable power attack protection	These require passives which are difficult/ expensive to integrate with the digital circuit.
LDO (low dropout regulator)	Induce current transformations and therefore to provide side-channel attack protection.	-----------
Noise Insertion	This involves introducing noise in the power measurements forcing attacker to make more power measurements.	Requires changes in implementation of cryto-graphic hardware
Temporal De-synchronization	Randomly varying the clock frequency of device.	Requires changes in implementation of cryto-graphic hardware
Masking	Generate random numbers to hide data.	-----------
Supply current shielding	Power supply is isolated from the cryptographic hardware of a smart card.	-----------

if the attacker is smart enough to produce glitches at the desired location then he may be successful in obtaining the secret key.

8.5.2 Effects of Fault Injection Attacks

This code represents security systems for entering a house. A person can only enter into the house if he knows the secret key. Attacker tampers with the security mechanism by varying either its clock signal or its power device. It will further produce glitches (Figure 8.11). If the attacker is smart enough and has the expertise then he may produce a glitch at the point as shown in the code which may skip the instruction:

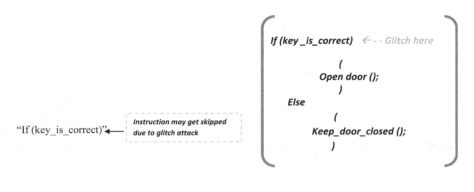

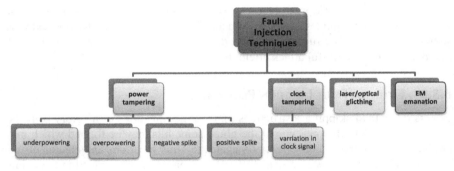

FIGURE 8.9 Types of Non-invasive Active Attacks.

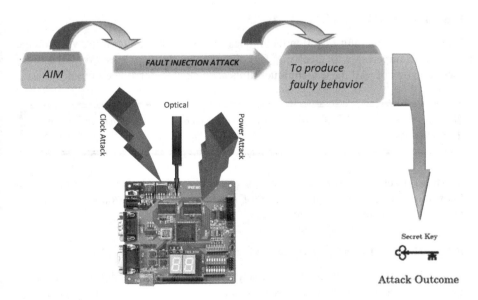

FIGURE 8.10 Illustration of Fault Injection Attack.

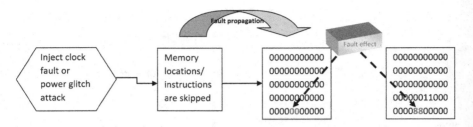

FIGURE 8.11   Faults Effects Propagates and Causes Some Faulty Behavior in Device such as Skipping Instruction or Bit Flip Which May Further Lead to Erroneous Output.

This will lead to a skipped instruction and attacker can easily enter the house without even knowing the secret key. Attacker keeps on doing variations in external signals until it is successful in getting the data. It is the precise injection of the fault that matters in a successful attack attempt.

8.5.3   Effect of Fault Injection Propagation

Effects other than skipping instructions may be modifications of memory or register location. Due to the presence of the glitch some bits may be flipped which may produce faulty outputs. This effect propagates to other locations and creates disturbances while execution is going on. The outputs generated after injecting faults into the embedded device are known as faulty ciphertexts.

8.6   FAULT INJECTION ATTACKS

There are various fault injection techniques discussed in the literature, viz: voltage glitching, tampering with clock pin, EM disturbances, laser attacks. We will discuss them one by one. All these techniques aims at producing corrupted output.

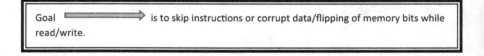

These attacks are more harmful as compared to passive attacks since they require knowledge of the device and some prior information about the operation or algorithm running on cryptographic devices.

8.6.1   Power Tampering/Voltage Glitching

This is the most basic type of fault injection attack. It tampers with the power supply of the device. There are various methods of tampering with the power line of the device, viz: under-powering, over-powering, negative spike, positive spike (Figure 8.12).

FIGURE 8.12   Types of Power Glitch Attacks/Voltage Glitching.

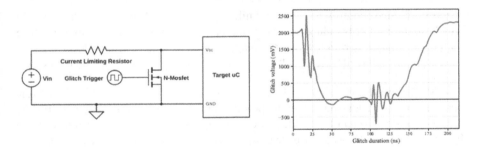

FIGURE 8.13   A Typical Transistor Based V-FI set up and Generated Glitch [24].

8.6.1.1 Under-powering Attack: In this type of attack, the device is basically under-power/under-fed for some time to produce erroneous errors. For some amount of time the power line supplied is lower than the nominal voltage. By doing this,the device may produce faulty output. The success of the attack lies in the precision and exact location where the attacker intends to produce faults. Fault propagation with this kind of attack is uniform and can results in activation of rare events or registers in the device. As shown in Figure 8.13, the power supply range is below the normal range for some time. Lot of circuits are used by attackers for generating such kinds of attacks and one is presented in Figure 8.13.

Figure 8.13 shows a circuit which was used for generating power supply below the nominal range of the device. This circuit is designed using NMOS technology and the corresponding waveform is shown along with it.

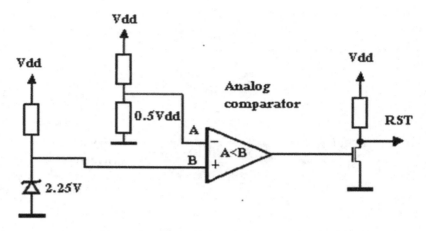

FIGURE 8.14   Microcontroller Brown Out Detection Circuit [26].

Countermeasure: Use of brown out circuit as shown in Figure 8.14.

A "brownout" is a short dip in the power supply. Many microcontrollers have brown-out detection on-chip, often, like in the Atmel AVR, with programmable threshold levels. When a brownout occurs the microcontroller will be reset [25]. Almost all microcontrollers have a built-in brown-out detection (BOD) circuit, which monitors supply voltage levels during operation. BOD circuit is nothing more than the comparator, which compares supply voltage to a fixed trigger level.

If the microcontroller doesnot have an on-chip brown-out detector, then an external circuit can be used.

8.6.1.2 Over-Power Attack: In this type of attack the device is basically over-powered /over-fed for some time to produce erroneous errors as shown in Figure 8.15. For some amount of time the power line supplied is above the nominal voltage. Figure 8.15 shows the case of over-power attack where the power supply at 600 ns shoots above the nominal voltage level. Attacker uses this tampered power supply instead of using the normal supply line to produce faults in the device. If the adversary is smart enough to precisely control the location of the glitch then he may be successful in the attack attempt.

8.6.1.3 Negative/Positive Spikes: A refinement of the aforementioned techniques are negative and positive spikes whereby precisely choosing the location of glitch, it is possible to make it so that some instructions are skipped (Figure 8.16). Over-feeding and under feeding methods just require a basic skill set and their attack location is also not fixed. Negative/ positive spike methods require customized circuits to make the glitch effect more harmful and successful from the attacker's point of view.

8.6.1.4 Tampering with Clock Pin: This is another category of fault injection attack where the clock signal of the device is tampered with. Tampering phenomena of clock signal is clearly observed from Figures 8.17 and 8.18. These attacks can be further divided as over clocking attacks and under clocking attacks. In these types of attacks either the clock signal length is shortened or widened for one or two clock

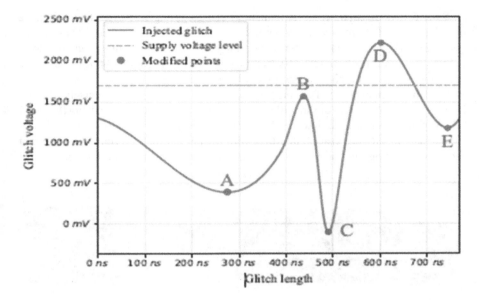

FIGURE 8.15 Over-Power Attack.

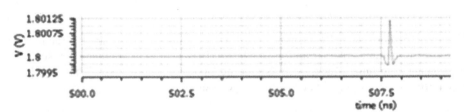

FIGURE 8.16 Generation of Positive Spike.

cycles as shown in the figures below. For this modification with clock signal to take place, attacker needs direct access to it, which is the case with smart cards. Hence today's smart cards have an in built clock signal so that attackers cannot alter it.

- *"It is not possible to attack a chip that generates its own clock signal."*

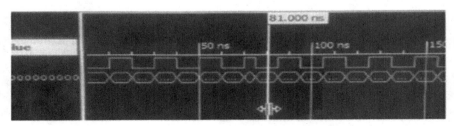

FIGURE 8.17 Under Clock Glitch Attack at 81.000 ns [27].

8.6.1.5 EM disturbances: This method causes strong EM disturbances near a device causing it to produce faulty output. Due to this EM disturbance, eddy currents induced in the circuit cause alterations in signal level. These alterations are temporary. By controlling these EM variations enough information about the device's behavior can be gathered resulting in leaking of secret key.

8.6.1.6 Laser attacks: This method makes use of strong and precisely focused light beam which affects the specific area of chip. "It is one of the most costly methods of generation of fault attacks." This method requires some advanced skill sets to precisely locate the position of attack with the help of focused light. The effect of radiation of strong light on silicon areas may result in blanking of erasable EEPROM

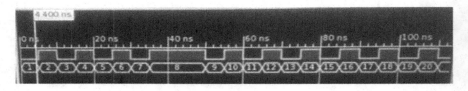

FIGURE 8.18   OverClock Glitch Attack at Glitch Position 2 (35–50 ns) [27].

or flash memory. The effect can be harmful depending on the duration of the illumination of the light. Apart from this, ion beam (FIB) is used as another expensive tool for generating fault attacks such as modification of structures, etc. These methods require reverse engineering causing de-encapsulation of chip.

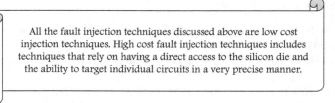

All the fault injection techniques discussed above are low cost injection techniques. High cost fault injection techniques includes techniques that rely on having a direct access to the silicon die and the ability to target individual circuits in a very precise manner.

- One of the methods is changing device operating temperature. Extreme temperatures are known to facilitate fault injection and side channel attacks on several targets like MCU, etc. Every device has some operating temperature. If we hinder the operating ambient temperature of device then fault will be induced leading to produce corrupted output which again facilitates and caters the needs of attacker. It has been found in literature survey that even small variation in ambient temperature of device affects the attack performance.

8.7 HANDS-ON-EXPERIMENTS: FAULT INJECTION ATTACKS

8.7.1 OBJECTIVES

This experiment is designed for students to produce various types of fault injection attacks viz: positive, negative, positive/negative.

8.7.2 METHOD

This experiment focuses on the fault injection attack, where students will deliberately inject faults into the module inorder to analyze and see effects of these attacks on embedded devices. Various circuits are presented which students can simulate on any platform such as HSPICE, PSPICE, CADENCE, MENTOR GRAPHICS that generate various fault attacks.

CIRCUIT 1: TO PRODUCE UNDER-POWER ATTACK [24]

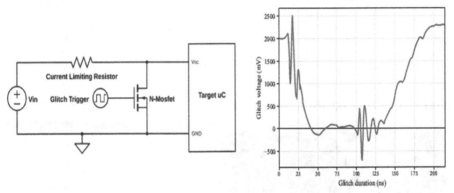

CIRCUIT 2: TO PRODUCE POSITIVE SPIKE ATTACK[27]

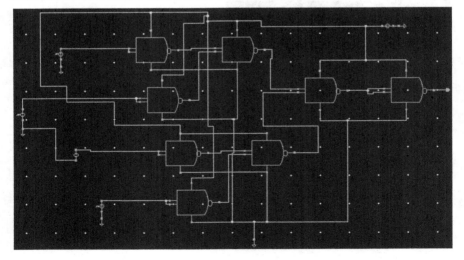

CIRCUIT 2: *EXPECTED OUTCOME*

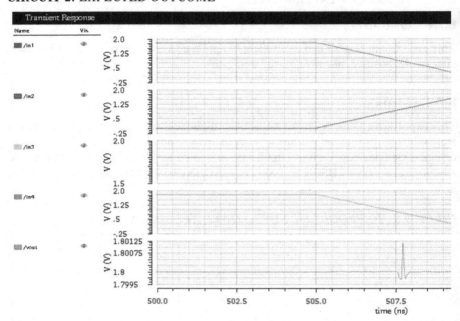

CIRCUIT 3: *TO PRODUCE NEGATIVE SPIKE ATTACK[27]*

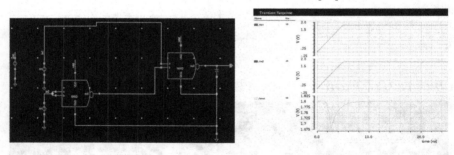

CIRCUIT 4: *TO PRODUCE POSITIVE/NEGATIVE SPIKE ATTACK[27]*

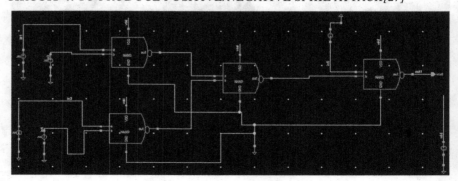

CIRCUIT 4: EXPECTED OUTCOME

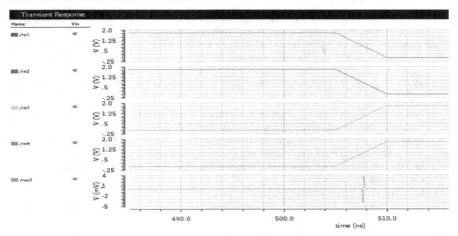

8.7.3 LEANING OUTCOME

By performing the specific steps of the experiments, the students will understand how FAULTS are induced using several methods discussed above. They will understand the analysis steps and the mechanisms for fault injection. They will also explore the level of information that can be extracted through side-channel analysis.

8.8 EXERCISES

8.8.1 SHORT ANSWERS TYPE QUESTIONS

1. What tools/kits are available online for generating fault injection attacks?
2. Differentiate low cost and high cost methods of generation of fault attacks?
3. Why are side channel attacks known as side channel attacks?
4. How are side channel attacks different from others types of attacks such as software attacks, network layer attacks?
5. How are power and timing attacks performed? Explain them with help of some model.
6. Categorize various kinds of fault injection attacks methods.
7. Describe various tools available to perform power attacks along with their countermeasures.
8. Under what conditions do clock attacks become unsuccessful?
9. It is possible to protect embedded devices against all kinds of side channel attacks. Comment on this statement.
10. What tools/kits are available to perform timing, power and EM attacks?

REFERENCES

1. Barenghi, A. et al. 2012. Fault injection attacks on cryptographic devices: Theory, practice and countermeasures. *Proc. IEEE*, 100(11), pp. 3056–3076.
2. Yanci, A. G. et al. 2008. Detecting voltage glitch attacks on secure devices. In *ECSIS symposium on bio-inspired learning and intelligent systems for security (BLISS-2008)* (pp.75–80). IEEE.
3. Endo, S. et al. 2011. On chip glitch clock generator for testing fault injection attacks. *Journal of Cryptographic Engineering*, 1(4), pp. 265–270.
4. Karaklajić, D. et al. 2013. Hardware designer guide to fault attacks. *Journal of Very Large Scale Integration Systems*, 12, (12), pp. 2295–2306.
5. Biham, E. et al. 1997. Differential fault analysis of secret key cryptosystems. In *Proceedings CRYPTO* (Vol. 1294, pp. 513–525). Springer.
6. https://web.eecs.umich.edu/~genkin/papers/physical-key-extraction-cacm.pdf.
7. https://meltdownattack.com/.
8. https://arxiv.org/pdf/1901.01161.pdf.
9. https://www.igi-global.com/book/implementing-computational-intelligence-techniqu es-security/236581#table-of-contents.
10. Courrege, J. C. et al. 2010. Simple power analysis on exponentiation revisited. In *Lecture notes* (Vol. 6035, pp. 65–79). Springer.
11. Giraud, C. et al. 2006. An RSA implementation resistant to fault attacks and to simple power analysis. *IEEE Transactions on Computers*12(4), pp. 241–245.
12. https://www.synopsys.com/designware-ip/technical-bulletin/protecting-against-sid e-channel.html.
13. Kocher, P. C. et al. 1998. Introduction to differential power analysis. *Journal of Cryptographic Engineering*, 1(1), pp. 5–27.
14. Goubin, L. et al. 1999. DES and differential power analysis: The duplication method. In *Lecture notes CHES* (Vol. 1717, pp. 158–172). Springer.
15. https://sci-hub.tw/https://link.springer.com/article/10.1007/s41635-017-0023-0.
16. Gierlichs, B. et al. 2008. Mutual information analysis. In *Lecture notes CHES* (Vol. 5154, pp. 426–442). Springer.
17. Batina, L., B. Gierlichs, E. Prouff, M. Rivain, F.-X. Standaert, N. Veyrat-Charvillon. 2011. Mutual information analysis: A comprehensive study. *Journal of Cryptology*, 24(2), pp. 269–291.
18. Bauer, A., E. Jaulmes, E. Prouff, and J. Wild. 2013. Horizontal and vertical side-channel attacks against secure RSA implementations. *Proceedings of the 13th International Conference on Topics in Cryptology* (pp. 1–17). Springer.
19. Bauer, A. et al. 2013. Horizontal and vertical side-channel attacks against secure RSA implementations: Extended version (to appear on the Cryptology ePrint Archive, LNCS, volume 7779).
20. Amiel, F. et al. 2007. Passive and active combined attacks: Combining fault attacks and side channel analysis. In *FDTC* (pp. 92–102). IEEE.
21. Kulikowski, K. J. et al. 2006. DPA on faulty cryptographic hardware and countermeasures. In *FDTC* (pp. 211–222). Springer.
22. Cilio, W. et al. 2013. Mitigating power- and timing-based side-channel attacks using dual-spacer dual-rail delay-insensitive asynchronous logic. In *Microelectronics Journal*44, pp. 258–269.
23. Ravi, S. P. et al. 2015. Delay insensitive ternary CMOS logic for secure hardware. *Journal of Low Power Electronics and Applications*, 5, pp. 183–215.
24. Bozzato, C., R. Focardi, & F. Palmarini. 2019. Shaping the glitch: Optimizing voltage fault injection attacks. In *IACR transactions on cryptographic hardware and embedded systems* (pp. 199–224).

25. https://electronics.stackexchange.com/questions/37561/what-is-a-brownout-condition.
26. https://scienceprog.com/microcontroller-brown-out-detection/.
27. Kaur, S. et al. 2020. Injecting power attacks with voltage glitching and generation of clock attacks for testing fault injection attacks. In International conference on (ETCCS-2020). Springer.
28. Rankl, W., and W. Effing. 1997. *Smart card handbook*. Wiley.
29. Brier, E. et al. 2004. Correlation power analysis with a leakage model. In *Lecture notes, CHES* (Vol. 3156, pp. 16–29). Springer.

9 Collaborative Digital Forensic Investigations Model for Law Enforcement
Oman as a Case Study

Younis Al-Husaini, Haider Al-Khateeb, Matthew Warren, Lei Pan and Gregory Epiphaniou

CONTENTS

9.1 INTRODUCTION

Digital information and the methods used for electronic communication have become more important to people, many of whom would think of them as the most needed personal asset for their daily living. This can be evident in the shift towards online shopping, virtual learning environments and eBanking services. However, it has also triggered digital crimes to evolve rapidly. Online criminal offences increased and, indeed, they led to the emergence of "Digital Forensics" as a new concept and an inevitable speciality within the hierarchy of law enforcement investigation teams (Valjarevic & Venter, 2012). Digital forensics is needed to prosecute cyber criminals because it gives law enforcement the means to support trials conducted and governed by a court of law. This process is facilitated through Digital Forensic Investigations (DFI) to obtain, preserve and submit an acceptable form of evidence (Ballou, 2010; Kruse II & Heiser, 2001). DFI involves a set of procedures and techniques that must be conducted properly by an experienced Digital Investigator to establish facts following a sound methodology. Investigation findings and conclusions are summarised as part of an Expert Witness Report and presented to a court of law in support of a particular prosecution (Selamat et al., 2008). Various DFI methodologies have been developed to brace specific technologies and scenarios; they should be followed thoroughly to maintain evidence integrity and enforce the required level of consistency when identifying relevant artefacts (Ballou, 2010; Kruse II & Heiser, 2001; Noblett et al., 2000). However, these steps differ according to the crime scene environment and the type of crime. A generic approach usually starts with a collection stage that involves a comprehensive and lengthy seek-and-find of various data sources. Once identified, data acquiring techniques are utilised to capture a data source in its entirety; think of tangible devices such as mobile phones and Solid-State Drives (SSD), or capture a snapshot of a running system at that particular moment for devices that cannot be easily disconnected such as large servers. From a data acquisition perspective, a live snapshot has the advantage of preserving artefacts from the volatile memory of the system. This is followed by an analysis stage where the collected data is examined to answer a selected number of investigation questions. Finally, the last stage involves reporting and presenting findings to a trial (Ballou, 2010; Palmer, 2001; Reith et al., 2002; Selamat et al., 2008; Valjarevic & Venter, 2012). Since there are various data sources to consider, and various legislation requirements to meet in different countries, there is no standard DFI model to be utilised globally (Al Husaini et al., 2018, 2019; Valjarevic & Venter, 2012).

The complex, dynamic and highly interconnected Cyber-Physical-Natural (CPN) world has redefined our ecosystem introducing many difficulties and challenges for Digital Forensics and Incident Response (Al Husaini et al., 2018). This has affected the work of law enforcement authorities globally, and in the Sultanate of Oman in particular due to the required level of resources and training, but also new processes needed to address and cope with new technologies used in the cyber world. This chapter aims to report and discuss the development and implementation of a bespoke DFI model for ROP as a case study to conclude recommendations in this area for other regional (or similar) law enforcement executive authorities. This research will address the shortcomings in an existing model and propose an alternative approach.

In the remainder of this chapter, section 2 covers a literature review of related work such as examples of existing DFI models and relevant standards. In section 3 we introduce and discuss the implementation of the CDFIR model; and finally, section 4 shares conclusions and recommendations.

9.2 LITERATURE REVIEW

9.2.1 DEFINITIONS OF DIGITAL FORENSICS

Several researchers have defined digital forensics. Table 9.1 presents a list of the most common definitions.

Based on the definitions listed in Table 9.1, we can further summarize the concept of DF (see Table 9.2) as the use of scientific methods in acquiring digital evidence from its source while maintaining its integrity to avoid questioning or doubt in its integrity and credibility. To analyze and reconstruct events and document the scientific facts extracted from the evidence to confirm or deny the allegations.

9.2.2 DIGITAL FORENSICS FOR LAW ENFORCEMENT

The concept of digital forensics is relatively new compared to other branches of forensic science that can be dated back to the early 1920s (Baryamureeba & Tushabe, 2004). Since the emergence of electronic crimes, the notion appeared and evolved parallel to various emerging crimes performed by cyber offenders around the globe. The impact of this problem has intensified by the accelerated development of information technology. Therefore, "digital forensics emerged in response to the growth of crimes committed by the use of computer systems either as an object of the crime, a tool used to perpetrate a crime or a repository of evidence related to a crime" (National Institute of Justice, 2001). In 1984, the Federal Bureau of Investigation (FBI) laboratory started to develop programs dedicated to the examination of computer evidence. Consequently, professional initiatives such as the Computer Analysis and Response Team (CART), the Scientific Working Group on Digital Evidence (SWGDE), the Technical Working Group on Digital Evidence (TWGDE) and the National Institute of Justice (NIJ) emerged, and this has contributed to further develop and define Digital Forensics as a discipline and proposed the need for a standardized approach to performing examinations on the variety of digital devices we used at the time (Kruse II & Heiser, 2001).

The prime purpose of Digital Forensics is to facilitate the reconstruction of events and actions which are found to be criminal or helping to anticipate any malicious actions shown to be troublesome to planned operations. Therefore, the credibility of digital evidence is at the core of the digital forensic process because it is how a forensic conclusion is either accepted or rejected (Selamat et al., 2008).

TABLE 9.1

Digital Forensics Definition in the Literature

Reference	Definition
Palmer (2001)	"The use of scientifically derived and proven methods toward the preservation, collection, validation, identification, analysis, interpretation, documentation and presentation of digital evidence derived from digital sources to facilitate or further the reconstruction of events found to be criminal, or helping to anticipate unauthorised actions shown to be disruptive to planned operations".
(Wolfe-Wilson & Wolfe, 2003)	"The methodologies used to capture and authenticate data at its source, analyse that captured data for evidence relevant to the case at hand, produce an understandable report that can be introduced into evidence in a court of law, and testify as to the authenticity of evidence presented".
(Danielsson & Tjostheim, 2004)	"Digital evidence is present in disputes and crimes where (i) computers and the information they store have been targeted, (ii) computers have been used as tools, and (iii) computers have been used as repositories for information used or generated in the commission of crimes or disputed events".
(Kentet al., 2006)	"Generally, it is considered the application of science to the identification, collection, examination, and analysis of data while preserving the integrity of the information and maintaining a strict chain of custody for the data. It comprises four basic phases: collection, examination, analysis, and report".
(Grobler & Louwrens, 2007)	"The efficient use of analytical and investigative techniques for the preservation, identification, extraction, documentation, analysis, and interpretation of computer media which is digitally stored or encoded for evidentiary and/or root-cause analysis and presentation of digital evidence derived from digital sources for the purpose of facilitating or furthering the reconstruction of events found to be criminal, or helping to anticipate unauthorised actions shown to be disruptive to planned operations".

Despite many assertions by researchers of the importance of an international standard for digital forensics (Du et al., 2017; Kohn et al., 2013; Reith et al., 2002), there is no international digital forensics standard to unify the process. However, we have a series of attempts to consolidate procedures in given legislation such as the Association of Chief Police Officers (ACPO) *Good Practice Guide for Digital Evidence* (Williams, 2012) in the United Kingdom, and the "Electronic Crime Scene Investigation: A Guide for First Responders" in the United States (Ballou, 2010). Both guidelines attempt to highlight key principles and define best practices when dealing with digital evidence. Furthermore, several International Organization for Standardization (ISO) standards have been developed. For example, the ISO/IEC 27037 provides guidelines for the identification, collection, acquisition and preservation of digital evidence while the ISO/IEC 27043 provides guidelines based on idealised models for common incident investigation principles and processes.

Nonetheless, various digital forensic frameworks and models can be found in academic literature (Agarwal et al., 2011; Al-Husaini, 2015; Baryamureeba & Tushabe, 2004; Carrier & Spafford, 2003; Gary, 2001; ISO 27037, 2012; ISO/27043, 2015;

TABLE 9.2
Simplification of some of the critical concepts of DF

Term	Definition	Reference
Acquisition	"The process of creating a copy of data within a defined set".	(ISO 27037, 2012)
Activity	"A set of cohesive tasks of a process".	(ISO 12207:2008)
Analysis	"The process of evaluating potential digital evidence to assess its relevance to the investigation".	(ISO/IEC 27042)
Collection	"Process of gathering the physical items that contain potential digital evidence".	(ISO 27037, 2012)
Digital evidence	"Information or data, stored or transmitted in binary form, that may be relied on as evidence".	(ISO 27037, 2012)
Identification	"Process involving the search for, recognition, and documentation of potential digital evidence".	(ISO 27037, 2012)
Interpretation	"Synthesis of an explanation, within agreed limits, for the factual information about evidence resulting from the set of examinations and analysis making up the investigation".	(ISO/IEC 27042)
Preservation	"Process to maintain and safeguard the integrity and/or original condition of the potential digital evidence and digital evidence".	(ISO 27037, 2012)
Readiness	"Process of being prepared for a digital investigation before an incident has occurred".	(ISO/27043, 2015)
Validation	"Confirmation, through the provision of objective evidence, that the requirements for a specific intended use or application have been fulfilled".	(ISO 27004:2009)
Verification	"Confirmation, through the provision of objective evidence, that specified requirements have been fulfilled".	(ISO/IEC 27041)
Volatile data	"Caused by data that is especially prone to change and can be easily modified".	(ISO 27037, 2012)
Hash value	"String of bits which is the output of a hash function".	(ISO/IEC 10118-1)
Imaging	"Process of creating a bitwise copy of digital storage media".	(ISO 27037, 2012)
Timestamp	"Time variant parameter which denotes a point in time with respect to a common time reference".	(ISO 11770-1:1996)

Perumal, 2009; Pollitt, 1995; Pollitt, 2007; Rogers et al., 2006; Satti & Jafari, 2015; Yusoff et al., 2011). They differ in their scope and level of detail, hence their ability to address miscellaneous technologies and crime scene scenarios.

9.2.3 THE EVOLUTION OF EXISTING DIGITAL FORENSIC INVESTIGATION (DFI) MODELS

Developing a model for DFI requires a thorough elaboration on the rules and responsibilities of the forensics team. This should be incorporated as part of the organizational structure of a given party (e.g., Police) and thus each model adjusts its own set of procedures to accomplish the investigation processes while establishing a balance between resources and the core requirement of the investigation principles (e.g., ACPO Guidelines) (Williams, 2012). Additionally, new models are presented in response to new electronic crime scenes such as the Internet of Things (IoT) as umbrella terms for various sub environments including but not limited to connected cars, the cloud and smart homes. By reviewing the literature, many models for DFI have been devised. Each of these models differs in the number of steps or phases used in the investigation process.

In 1984, Pollitt (Pollitt, 1995; Pollitt, 2007; Yusoff et al., 2011) proposed a methodology called the Computer Forensic Investigative Process. The essence beyond proposing this methodology was to deal with the digital evidence in an investigation to produce scientifically reliable and legally acceptable results. Pollitt's methodology consists of four main phases. The first phase is called the acquisition phase in which evidence can be gathered or acquired in a way that can be accepted and approved by a named authority. Then, the acquired artefact is identified and converted into a format that can be imported into a software tool for further analysis. Then, phase three evaluates and determines whether the identified artefact is relevant and whether it can be supportive of the case being investigated. Finally, the admission phase presents the acquired and extracted evidence to a court of law.

In 2001, further research (Palmer, 2001; Yusoff et al., 2011) presented during the first Digital Forensics Research Workshop (DFRWS) introduced a general-purpose digital forensics investigation methodology. This model involved six phases (shown in Table 9.3). Unlike Pollitt's model from 1984, the new model starts with an identification phase to detect profiles and anomalies, monitor systems and analyze audits to initiate the investigation process. Next, the preservation phase involves setting up a proper case management procedure and ensures the quality of the output at the end. One of the key objectives of this phase is to ensure that the collected data is not corrupted. Thereafter, the collection phase enforces pre-approved methods for data recovery. After the collection phase, there are two crucial phases, namely the examination phase and the analysis phase. They cover chores such as preservation, traceability, validation, filtering, data mining, recovery of hidden/encrypted data, timeline, etc. Similar to the previous model, the investigation is concluded with a presentation phase which involves documentation.

In 2003, Carrier & Spafford proposed the Integrated Digital Investigation Process (IDIP) as shown in Figure 9.1 (Carrier & Spafford, 2003; Yusoff et al., 2011). The author introduced the concept of a virtual environment that is a digital crime scene. In the methodology of Carrier & Spafford, the first phase requires preparation for the physical and operational infrastructure so that it could support any future investigation. This phase involves the preparation of the equipment needed in the investigation, and the individual who is "responsible" must have the capability to use the equipment effectively. Moreover, this phase is divided into two sub-phases, which are named as operational readiness and infrastructure readiness. Next, the deployment phase comes to offer a procedure for detection and confirmation of an incident. In common with the previous phase of this model, this phase can be partitioned

TABLE 9.3
The DFRWS Framework

Identification	Preservation	Collection	Examination	Analysis	Presentation	Decision
Event/Crime Detection	Case Management	Preservation	Preservation	Preservation	Documentation	
Resolve Signature	Imaging Technologies	Approved Methods	Traceability	Traceability	Expert Testimony	
Profile Detection	Chain of Custody	Approved Software	Validation Techniques	Statistical	Clarification	
Anomalous Detection	Time Synch.	Approved Hardware	Filtering Techniques	Protocols	Mission Impact Statement	
Complaints		Legal Authority	Pattern Matching	Data Mining	Recommended Countermeasure	
System Monitoring		Lossless Compression	Hidden Data Discovery	Timeline	Statistical Interpretation	
Audit Analysis		Sampling	Hidden Data Extraction	Link		
Etc.		Data Reduction		Spatial		
		Recovery Techniques				

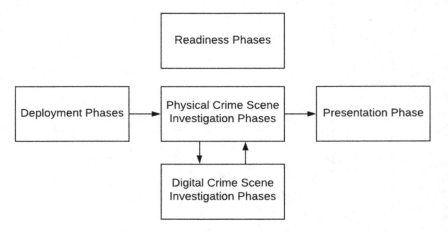

FIGURE 9.1 Graphical Representation of IDIP Model.

to cover detection, notification, confirmation and authorization respectively. After preparing the infrastructure and detecting the incident, in a physical crime scene the collection and analysis of physical evidence are performed followed by preservation, review, documentation, exploration, collection, restoration and demonstration. The last phase of this model is called the review phase to identify areas of improvement that may result in new procedures or new training requirements.

In 2004, the Enhanced Digital Investigation Process Model (EDIP) was proposed by Baryamereeba & Tushabe as shown in Figure 9.2 (Baryamureeba & Tushabe, 2004; Yusoff et al., 2011). From its name, the model is based on IDIP. However, the EDIP model introduced one significant phase known as the Trackback, which allows the investigator to hit back to the actual devices used in committing the crime. Like IDIP, the investigation process starts with the readiness phase that is responsible for preparing the infrastructure. Then, it comes to the deployment phase which performs

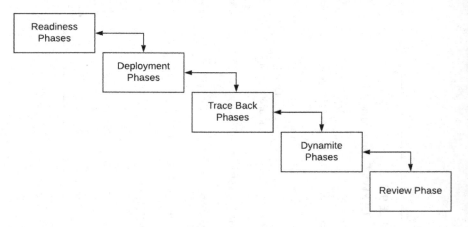

FIGURE 9.2 Process of the EIDIP Model.

the same function as the deployment phase in IDIP. It consists of five sub-phases, namely as detection, notification, physical crime scene investigation, digital crime scene investigation, confirmation and submission. Unlike DIP, this phase includes both physical and digital crime scene investigations and demonstration of findings to legal entities. The extra phase in this model is called the "trackback", which covers all the electronic devices and their location for tracking and reverse engineering purposes. Another difference is the inclusion of a "Dynamite" phase to identify the prospective convicts. It consists of four other phases, namely the physical crime scene investigation, digital crime scene investigation, reconstruction and finally communication.

In 2006, the Computer Forensics Field Triage Process Model (CFFTPM) was developed by Rogers and his colleagues as shown in Figure 9.3 (Rogers et al., 2006;

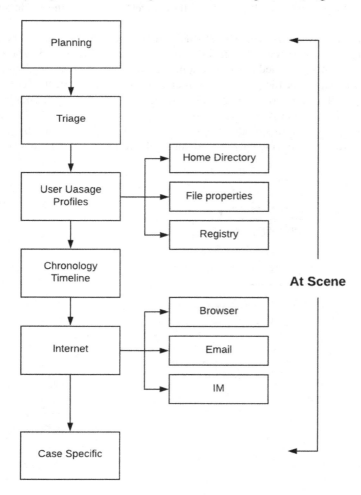

FIGURE 9.3 Process of (CFFTPM) Model.

Yusoff et al., 2011). An on-site approach is proposed which, in a fairly short time frame, aims to provide the identification, analysis and explanation of electronic evidence. There is no need to take the devices or media back to the lab and there is no need to acquire a complete forensic image. Instead, the CFFTPM ranks the identified shreds of evidence to investigate the most informative first. This model incorporates a user usage profile phase which focuses on evidence attribution. The model guides the investigator to adjust the focus of the examination to the case essentials; for example, the essentials in child pornography would be different from those of financial crime essentials.

In 2009, Perumal proposed the Digital Forensic Model based on Malaysian Investigation Process (DFMMIP) as shown in Figure 9.4 (Perumal, 2009; Yusoff et al., 2011). The DFMMIP model consists of seven phases. The model has a reconnaissance phase to address challenges with the investigation of running devices (live forensics).

In 2011, the Systemic DFI Model (SRDFIM) was proposed by Agarwal et al. (Agarwal et al., 2011; Satti & Jafari, 2015) as shown in Figure 9.5. There are 11 phases in this model named as preparation, securing the scene, survey and recognition, documentation of the scene, communication shielding, evidence (both volatile and non-volatile) collection, preservation, examination, analysis, presentation, result and review. This model is comprehensive and aims to act as a benchmark for DFI. The documentation in this model was presented as a continuous loop back activity. Revisions are permitted and encouraged during the full life cycle of the investigation

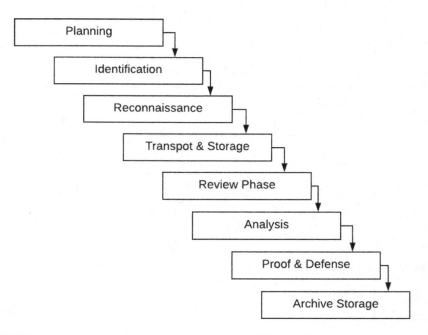

FIGURE 9.4 Malaysian Investigation Process based on the Digital Forensic Model.

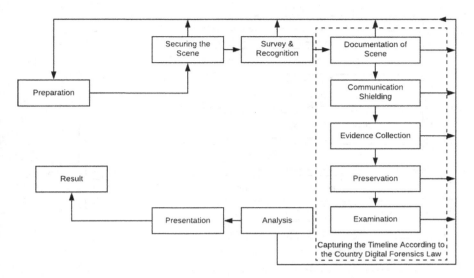

FIGURE 9.5   A Systemic Digital Forensic Investigation Model.

to maintain a Chain-of-Custody (CoC) while realising the properties of reliability and testability during the analysis of digital crime.

However, the investigatory process becomes complex due to the incorporation of additional phases, which in certain cases is the rate-limiting step in combating cybercrime.

More recent proposals recognise the need for application-specific models. For example, the Domain Specific Cyber Forensic Investigation Process Model (DSCFIPM) (Satti & Jafari, 2015) tailors DFI procedures to the particular domain of Higher Education (HE) institutes (see Figure 9.6). There are 10 phases in total in this model. The first phase forms a standard of procedures for the institutional cyber forensic investigation teams. The second phase is related to strategic planning and scope definition. The crime scene is addressed as part of phase three, evidence collection in phase four, evidence preservation in phase five, and evidence extraction in phase six. The last four phases cover evidence analysis, presentation of findings, archiving of case records and post case review, respectively. Other recent attempts such as Van Baar et al., 2014 aimed at reducing the case backlogs by moving from the traditional process towards a service-oriented approach by introducing Digital-Forensics-as-a-Service (DFaaS) where collaborative activities between the team become the key characteristic of the DFI model.

9.2.4   ISO Standards

As an international body for setting standards, ISO has addressed this area of application with several standards to comply with. For instance, the ISO/IEC 17025 "General requirements for the competence of testing and calibration laboratories" was introduced as the recommended checklist for digital forensics laboratory testing.

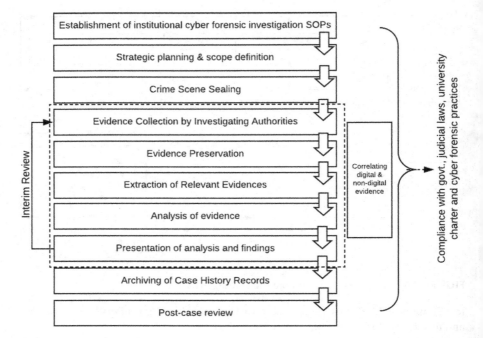

FIGURE 9.6   Domain-specific Cyber Forensics Investigation Process Model.

Compliance and certification can be crucial under certain jurisdictions such as the United Kingdom where non-compliance must be declared on each issued report. Non-compliance with the regulator's standards introduces risk and affects the credibility of the findings concluded by the DFI process. ISO/IEC 17025 helps to develop the laboratory's management system for administrative, quality and technical operations. However, various other security standards can be relevant to forensics labs for a sound establishment, the list could include ISO/IEC 9000 and ISO/IEC 27001 to support quality management, and to implement the required level of security controls and best practices for existing Information Security Management Systems (ISMS).

Other standards addressing digital forensics include ISO/IEC 27050, which is meant to focus on eDiscovery; the discovery of Electronically Stored Information (ESI), with ISO/IEC 27050-3:2017 offering guidance on ESI identification, preservation, collection, processing, review, analysis and production. Likewise, ISO/IEC 27043 (ISO/27043, 2015) offers guidelines for the broader incident investigation process, which includes activities from pre-incident preparation through investigation closure; therefore, we think of it as the most relevant to the design of our model. Moreover, it provides general advice related to practical aspects. The guidelines of this standard describe processes to various types of investigations such as unauthorized access and data corruption. ISO documents tend to contain references to other related standards. For instance, ISO/IEC 27037 covers crucial practices for fulfilling or handling digital evidence, ISO/IEC 27042 covers the process after the collection of digital evidence, and ISO/IEC 27041 covers assurance aspects that the relevant forensically sound methods and tools have been utilised properly.

9.3 TOWARDS A NEW COLLABORATIVE DFI MODEL

9.3.1 WHY ROP NEEDS A NEW MODEL

As discussed earlier, there are several ISO standards and initiatives to develop generic cross border investigation models. However, these are extended at the operational level to comply with local procedures, policies and principles in a given country (Kebande & Venter, 2016). Local models are further influenced by the responsibilities of each stakeholder involved in the forensic investigation. Not all models are developed for non-profit state-funded agencies such as law enforcement laboratories and public prosecution labs; there are several private digital forensic laboratories such as the Digital Forensics Laboratory – South Australia (DFLAB, 2018), which provides digital forensic services for law firms, small and medium-sized enterprises (SMEs) and individuals.

ROP is the main representative and the frontline for law enforcement in the Sultanate of Oman. Their work is geographically spread to various cities and rural areas. Examples of the types of police directorates and specializations include, but are not limited to, customs, drug control, coast guard, traffic and public security, all of which require DFI services. Therefore, the National Digital Forensics Laboratory was established as part of ROP to provide the required support. However, several investigation cases have since been highlighted as challenging or incomplete. The reason was attributed to the gap and inconsistencies between first responders and the investigators at the digital forensic laboratory. This gap was further studied by conducting a focus group attended by all the forensics investigators based at the laboratory. This qualitative approach was found suitable due to the small sample size ($n=8$). Emerging themes and conclusions suggest that the existing model implemented at the laboratory was generic and therefore left the details to be interpreted differently by the team including the incident responders in the field. Additionally, there was no case management system to facilitate communication and collaborative tasks which were found to be a much needed element to work more efficiently and reduce the number of pending or incomplete cases.

The risk associated with the lack of details mentioned earlier can be demonstrated by incomplete notes written for some cases, which shows the different interpretation of how to maintain a Chain-of-Custody (CoC) (Al-Khateeb et al., 2019). The time it took to identify a problem associated with the CoC was also discussed. Further to the lack of a method to facilitate collaborations, these issues were then partially attributed to the lack of a clear and unified responsibility and accountability matrix.

9.3.2 PHASES WITHIN THE CDFIR MODEL

The proposed CDFIR acknowledges lessons learned from existing models following a review of the literature. It is compatible with local laws in the Sultanate of

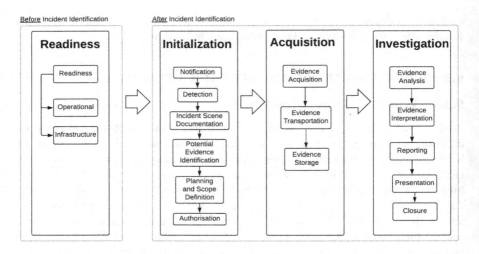

FIGURE 9.7   The Key Phases covered by the CDFIR Model.

Oman and designed to accommodate internal processes while flexibly incorporates the requirements of international standards to support compliance and cross-border investigations. Overall, the model has been designed to include four main phases with each of these containing a set of sub-phases as shown in Figure 9.7.

9.3.3   Readiness

The proposed methodology starts with a readiness phase, which should be available before handling any case. Digital Forensic Readiness (DFR) stands out to preparing digital forensic strategies (for instance, what evidence is needed?) well before an incident happens. DFR enables efficient and cost-effective investigations, and effective corporate cyber hygiene best practices (Rowlingson, 2004). We distinguish between two parts for this phase. Firstly, operational readiness, which covers the preparation / training of individuals who are responsible for completing the investigation process. They should be well qualified to test and evaluate the tool kit used, they should also have adequate awareness around what they must do in each duty. Secondly, infrastructure readiness, which involves the preparation of the technical environment (hardware / software) to be utilized in any investigation. Specifically, it involves the preparation of the equipment that is needed in the investigation process such as hardware components; servers, network devices, firewalls and software components; operating systems, virtual environments and other forensics software.

9.3.4   Initialization

Initialization often occurs once the incident is detected and it includes six main phases.
   Notification phase. In the new proposed methodology, the notification phase is considered to be at the base phase in the investigation procedures due to its

significance. All incidents will need to start from a notification, whether that notification comes from the victim directly or it issues from the public prosecution or any law enforcement agencies. In this context, the digital forensic investigation team in Royal Oman Police must receive a notification regarding the incident from the victim directly that alerts or informs the cybercrime department in ROP if the crime has any associated digital evidence; they must receive a notification before starting in the investigation procedures of the case. The notification will only be received by well-trained employees as stated in the operational readiness stage above; the recipient will ask for certain details that might be of huge value to the case at a later stage. Once the notification is received by the digital forensic team, the recipient will then register the details about the incident and offer these details to the team administrator to make a confirmation and then send the first responder to start a new phase which is a detection phase.

Detection phase. In this step, an incident is detected, or an anomaly is identified and classified within a valid case type. Incident responders prepare a set of procedures to follow as issued by the ISO/IEC 27037 which standardise procedures suitable for the detection of digital anomalies as reported by the notification phase.

Incident Scene Documentation. It involves documenting any activity performed by the incident responder. The documentation ensures that no details are missed including justification to actions or decisions taken by the team at the crime scene. At this stage, a written document is produced containing associated templates such as CoC forms, sketches, photographs, videos and bag and tag of the potential evidence acquired.

Potential Evidence Identification. The responder identifies potential evidence to be collected. This is mostly a tangible artefact such as memory drives, laptops, mobiles and routers. Therefore, this stage is concerned with collecting the source of evidence rather than identifying the digital evidence itself. This phase requires search-and-seek, and recognition skills to tag all potential sources for digital evidence.

Planning and scope definition. The documentation provided by the first responder so far is utilised to take critical decisions on a bespoke plan to follow. Specific procedures and equipment are identified to perform the investigating, and the appropriate human resources are also identified to build the required team. Each member in the team has clear duties demonstrated by a responsibility matrix as shown in Figure 9.8. Furthermore, the perimeter of the crime scene is defined at this stage as part of establishing the investigation scope.

Authorization phase. After establishing a clear plan of how the investigation process will be deployed, the authorization phase provides authorization to conduct the investigation. This permission is usually supported by a judicial authority. In Oman, the public prosecution service is the judicial authority to give such permissions or warrants.

9.3.5 ACQUISITION

This phase begins in which evidence can be gathered or acquired in a way that can be accepted and approved by a court of law. It includes three steps:

Process class	Activity	Victim	First responder	Admin	Public Prosecution	Judge	Investigator
Readiness	Operational & Infrastructure		R	A	I		R
Initialization	Notification	R	A	I	I		C
	Detection		R	I	I		A
	planning & scope definition	I	R	I	C		C
	Authorization		I	R	A	I	I
Acquisitive	Incident Scene Documentation		R/A	I	I	I	C
	Potential Evidence Identification	I	R/A	I			A
	Evidence Acquisition		R/A	I			A
	Evidence Transportation		R/A	I			A
	Evidence Storage		R	I			A
Investigation	Evidence Analysis			I			R/A
	Evidence Interpretation			I	I	I	R/A
	Reporting		I	A	I	I	R/A
	Presentation	I	I	I	I	A	R/A
	Investigation Closure	I		R	R	A	R
R	Responsible – Who is responsible for the execution of the task?						
A	Accountable – Who is accountable for the tasks and signs off the work?						
C	Consulted – Who are the subject matter experts who to be consulted?						
I	Informed – Who are the people who need to be updated of the progress?						

FIGURE 9.8 Rule and Responsibility RACI Matrix.

Evidence Acquisition. Gathering and collecting relevant digital artefacts from the crime scene while preserving the integrity of any collected data. The first responder is tasked to capture the original evidence where possible and / or create a bit-to-bit copy. Evidence acquisition involves removing the devices that contain the potential digital evidence from the original location (crime scene) to a controlled environment. Different approaches and tools will be utilised dictated by factors such as the state of the device. For example, if the device is power on, then a live acquisition procedure will be followed to preserved data resident in the volatile memory. After creating an identical copy of the original evidence, a hash function (or more) such as MD5 and SHA-2 will be used to produce multiple hashes. This will then be used to validate the integrity of the captured data. It is a legal requirement to reject any altered evidence following the acquisition phase. This responsibility resides with the investigation team; they must provide evidence with means to verify its integrity as an exact copy of the originally captured data.

Evidence Transportation. The evidence should be transported to a location where it can be stored and analysed either physically through traditional procedures or over a network (or Internet) remotely using a secured transportation link secured with protocols such as IPSec and Transport Layer Security (TLS), in addition to encryption at the application layer of the TCP / IP stack model. The CoC should also be involved in this phase by writing the name of the person transporting the evidence, and the name of the person receiving the evidence, with dates, times and signatures.

Evidence Storage. The last phase of the acquisitive stage, is a digital evidence storage process in which the collected and transported evidence can be stored securely to be ready for further investigation. This phase is required if the analysis of the potential evidence cannot start immediately and if there is a legal requirement to keep digital evidence secured for a certain of time. To preserve the integrity in this phase, extreme care must be taken to avoid natural factors from damaging the media that carry the potential digital evidence due to shock, high temperature, humidity, pollution, and loss of power, malfunction and other factors. Any loss of the potential evidence will surely affect the investigation procedure. There is a legal requirement to keep digital evidence secured for a certain amount of time even after a decision on the case is legally concluded in a court of law. Therefore, the evidence store should have antistatic material to radiate any magnetic interruption and Faraday bags for any signal based devices such as mobiles to cut off the connection with the outside world to avoid any changes to the original evidence.

9.3.6 INVESTIGATION

This stage aims at studying the digital evidence to present it within a suitable context that is easy for non-tech people to understand. The investigation process is divided into five sections:

Evidence Analysis. The analysis will be performed on a copy of the original, this should first be verified with a valid verification function (hash function). Then, analysis techniques and tools are used to study the evidence and answer the questions asked as part of the initialization phase in the CDFIR model.

Evidence Interpretation. The findings from the analysis phase are interpreted and mapped to clarify, reject or accept a claim. Evidence interpretation is the most critical part in the investigation process as it could help a judge to conclude.

Reporting. The investigators write a report detailing all the processes and tools used during the analysis phase. They also report the methodology deployed to reach specific findings. The report must be written with simple language understandable by non-technical professionals without omitting or sacrificing important details; the challenge here is to maintain a balance between providing the required level of detail while addressing a multi-disciplinary audience.

Presentation. The results of the analysis will be presented in front of the public prosecution service. An expert witness will share the conclusions and should, therefore, have good communication skills. The presentation may include PowerPoint slides, whiteboard illustrations or simulations to demonstrate the evidence.

Investigation Closure. The final phase in which all the collected and analysed details will be archived for future references. The following Table 9.5 summarizes the proposed methodology phases.

9.3.7 RULES AND RESPONSIBILITIES RACI MATRIX

In response to the feedback received from the focus groups in our case study, the CDFIR model incorporates a RACI Matrix as shown in Figure 9.8. It describes the participation of the different stakeholders including the investigation team. The various roles to complete the tasks and deliverables should be clear to the team. It is

TABLE 9.4

Comparing the phases included in various models to that of CDFIR. This table shows that our model covers the level of details required by the ISO/IEC 27043 standard and introduces further breakdown.

CDFIR phases	Classic	DFWRS	IDIP	EDIP	CFFTPM	DFMMIP	SRDFIM	DSCFIPM	ISO 27043
references	(Pollitt, 1995)	(Palmer, 2001)	(Carrier & Spafford, 2003)	(Baryamureeba & Tushabe, 2004)	(Rogers et al., 2006)	(Perumal, 2009)	(Agarwal et al., 2011)	(Satti & Jafari, 2015)	(ISO/27043, 2015)
Readiness			✓	✓			✓		✓
Notification			✓						
Detection			✓						
Planning & Scope Definition					✓	✓	✓	✓	✓
Authorization			✓						
Incident Scene Documentation							✓		✓
Evidence Identification	✓	✓	✓	✓		✓	✓	✓	✓
Evidence Acquisition	✓	✓	✓	✓		✓	✓	✓	✓
Evidence Transportation						✓			✓
Evidence Storage		✓	✓	✓		✓	✓		✓
Evidence Analysis	✓	✓	✓			✓		✓	✓
Evidence Interpretation									
Reporting							✓		✓
Presentation	✓	✓	✓	✓			✓	✓	✓
Investigation Closure									✓

rather important that one person only can ultimately be accountable for each activity at a time to avoid ownership implications.

9.3.8 FACILITATING COLLABORATION

The first element introduced to enable collaborative activities is a Mobile Application securely connected to a web server to help the DFI team achieve faster incident response as shown in Figure 9.9.

It allows cases to be registered remotely from the crime scene; this is especially useful because the National Laboratory is centralized while a team of First Responders is spread across the country covering several regions. The application includes a registration form to log new cases and help to upload related files including pictures, videos and compressed files. The application works offline since the Internet might not always be available at the crime scene, the included forms are saved and secured on the device but can also be sent to the central Police server for the benefit of the remotely connected team members. Figure 9.10 shows an example of a mobile screen used by the First Responder.

The second element is a web portal presented as a management system for DFI, part of which is shown in Figure 9.11. It helps to manage (accepting, rejecting, amending) cases registered by the mobile application. The portal helps to control the workflow between the CDFIR phases. For instance, the *planning and scope definition* phase will be locked until the *incident scene documentation* phase is fulfilled. Furthermore, the web portal provides means to search for cases based on specific keywords and computes statistics that can be useful to measure the performance of the team or to have a better understanding about the types of investigations and criminal activities taking place.

9.4 CONCLUSION AND RECOMMENDATIONS

As the digital landscape grows rapidly beyond traditional devices, the need to have a collaborative environment is inevitable. A collaborative DFI model should enable communications while complying with all expected criteria set by local and in many cases international standards (Alhaboby et al., 2018). We have introduced CDFIR to our case study with ROP; part of our objective was to put the means to start the analysis more quickly after identifying, extracting and preserving the digital evidence. It is critical to realise that the number of IoT devices is estimated to increase from 8.4 Billion in 2017 to over 20 Billion by 2020, and the CDFIR is, therefore, a step towards readiness in this regard. However, further work is needed, if we consider recent development in the area of Cyber-Physical Systems (CPS), and study connected cars as an example (Al-Khateeb et al., 2018), we realise the level of automation involved and the complexity of attribution for such cases. To elaborate, consider the expansion required to the First Responders' team from a project management point of view to deal with a cyber attack affecting several connected cars in the street of a rural area resulting in a severe accident with damage including both to life and property.

TABLE 9.5

Summary of proposed methodology phases

Phases	Sub-phases	Description
Readiness	Infrastructure	Preparation of the equipment that is needed in the investigation process.
	operation	Training individuals that are responsible for completing the investigation process to be well qualified.
Initialization	Notification	The victim alerts or informs the administrator (the head of the investigation department) about the incident.
	Detection	The victim detects the incident
	planning & scope definition	A plan with the specification of the relevant procedures that are needed for particular incidents.
	Authorization	The investigators must receive authorization from the head of the department to conduct the investigation.
Acquisitive	Incident Scene Documentation	A written document of actions, sketches, photographs, videos of the incident team, and labelling the potential evidence.
	Potential Evidence Identification	The investigators identify the potential evidence to be collected.
	Evidence Acquisition	Gathering or collecting the evidence and preserving the integrity of the collected evidence.
	Evidence Transportation	The evidence can be transported to a location where it can be stored and analyzed.
	Evidence Storage	Securely to be ready for further investigation.
Investigation	Evidence Analysis	Techniques and tools are used to identify the evidence and show how the incident occurred.
	Evidence Interpretation	The findings from the analysis are interpreted clearly in a more understandable way.
	Reporting	A documentation of all processes that are carried out during the investigation process.
	Presentation	The completed report will be presented in the form of expert reports to all stakeholders in the investigation.
	Investigation Closure	All the evidence gathered during the investigation process will be returned to the victim and the case will.

A more traditional example of challenges is malware; recent literature reviews suggest that we are still struggling to detect and mitigate metamorphic malware due to reasons related to code obfuscation, lack of dynamic capabilities to analyze the code and application difficulties (Irshad et al., 2018). Therefore, application and deployment challenges must be planned as part of the readiness stage of the CDFIR model (and other models).

Nonetheless, utilising secure tunnels over the Internet to facilitate collaboration and share or submit case related details should not completely replace transferring the original evidence (and documentation), e.g., by car. This recommendation is to make sure that the legal requirement is satisfied, and therefore the admissibility of

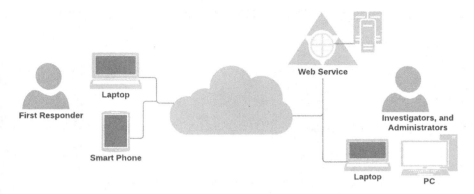

FIGURE 9.9 The Collaborative Elements in CDFIR are Secured over the Internet to Enable Case Registration from Various Regional Areas in the Country.

FIGURE 9.10 Mobile Screen used by the First Responder.

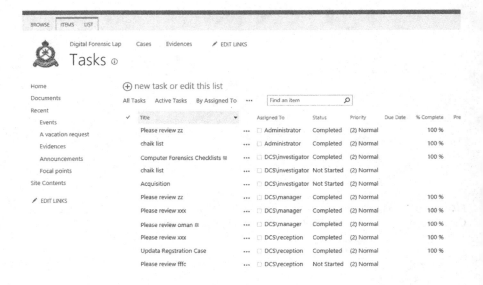

FIGURE 9.11 CDFIR Case Management System.

the evidence is not affected. Therefore, while the investigation starts faster, the incident responder will still have a plan to transport the original evidence obtained from the crime scene to the laboratory. Further work is needed to develop clear guidelines on scenarios where a digital transfer of the case can be accepted on its own. Future work will focus on automating certain parts of the model to streamline the investigative process.

ACKNOWLEDGEMENTS

This chapter was partly based on the first author's Master thesis submitted in 2015 to the University of Bedfordshire in the UK. This work has contributed to the development of the procedures used by the National Digital Forensic Laboratory in the Sultanate of Oman, which was opened in February 2016. In 2017, the laboratory obtained international Accreditation from ANAB (ANSI-ASQ National Accreditation Board) (Anab, 2018).

REFERENCES

Agarwal, A., M. Gupta, S. Gupta, & S. C. Gupta. 2011. Systematic digital forensic investigation model. *International Journal of Computer Science and Security,* 5(1), pp. 118–131.

Al-Husaini, Y. 2015. *Enhancing Digital Forensic Investigations Model within the Royal Omani Police.* (MSc Dissertation). Bedfordshire: University of Bedfordshire.

Al-Husaini, Y., A.-K. Haider, M. Warren, L. Pan. 2018. A model to facilitate collaborative digital forensic investigations for law enforcement: The royal Oman police as a case study. Paper presented at the Cyber Forensic and Security Conference, Tonga.

Al-Husaini, Y., M. Warren, L. Pan. 2018. Cloud forensics relationship between the law enforcement and cloud service providers. Paper presented at the 17th Australian Cyber Warfare Conference (CWAR), Melbourne.

Al Husaini, Y., M. Warren, L. Pan, & M. A. Gharibi. 2019. Cloud forensics investigations relationship: A model and instrument. Paper presented at the 30th Australasian Conference on Information Systems, Perth.

Al-Khateeb, H., G. Epiphaniou, & H. Daly. 2019. Blockchain for modern digital forensics: The chain-of-custody as a distributed ledger. In *Blockchain and Clinical Trial: Securing Patient Data*, H. Jahankhani, S. Kendzierskyj, A. Jamal, G. Epiphaniou, & H. Al-Khateeb (Eds.) (pp. 149–168). Cham: Springer.

Al-Khateeb, H., G. Epiphaniou, A. Reviczky, P. Karadimas, & H. Heidari. 2018. Proactive threat detection for connected cars using recursive Bayesian estimation. *IEEE Sensors Journal*, 18(12), pp. 4822–4831. doi:10.1109/JSEN.2017.2782751.

Alhaboby, Z. A., D. Alhaboby, H. M. Al-Khateeb, G. Epiphaniou, D. K. B. Ismail, H. Jahankhani, & P. Pillai. 2018. Understanding the cyber-victimisation of people with long term conditions and the need for collaborative forensics-enabled disease management programmes. In *Cyber Criminology*, H. Jahankhani (Ed.) (pp. 227–250). Cham: Springer.

ANAB. 2018. ANSI-ASQ National Accreditation Board (ANAB). Retrieved from https://www.anab.org.

Ballou, S. 2010. *Electronic Crime Scene Investigation: A Guide for First Responders*. Diane Publishing.

Baryamureeba, V., & F. Tushabe. 2004. The enhanced digital investigation process model. Paper presented at the Proceedings of the Fourth Digital Forensic Research Workshop.

Carrier, B., & E. H. Spafford. 2003. Getting physical with the digital investigation process. *International Journal of digital evidence*, 2(2), pp. 1–20.

Danielsson, J., & I. Tjostheim. 2004. The need for a structured approach to digital forensic readiness. Paper presented at the IADIS International Conference e-commerce.

DFLAB. 2018. Digital Forensics Laboratory - South Australia - Services. Retrieved from https://www.dflab.com.au/services/.

Du, X., N. A. Le-Khac, & M. Scanlon. 2017. Evaluation of digital forensic process models with respect to digital forensics as a service. https://arxiv.org/abs/1708.01730.

Gary, P. 2001. A road map for digital forensic research. Paper presented at the Digital Forensics Research Workshop.

Grobler, C. P., & C. Louwrens. 2007. Digital forensic readiness as a component of information security best practice. Paper presented at the IFIP International Information Security Conference.

Irshad, M., H. M. Al-Khateeb, A. Mansour, M. Ashawa, & M. Hamisu. 2018. Effective methods to detect metamorphic malware: a systematic review. *International Journal of Electronic Security and Digital Forensics*, 10(2), pp. 138–154. doi:10.1504/ijesdf.2018.090948

ISO 27037. 2012. IEC *Information Technology-Security Techniques-Guidelines for Identification, Collection, Acquisition and Preservation of Digital Evidence*. ISO.

ISO/27043. 2015. *Information Technology - Security Techniques - Incident Investigation Principles and Processes*. ISO/IEC.

Kebande, V. R., & H. Venter. 2016. Requirements for achieving digital forensic readiness in the cloud environment using an NMB solution. Paper presented at the 11th International Conference on Cyber Warfare and Security: ICCWS.

Kent, K., S. Chevalier, T. Grance, & H. Dang. 2006. Guide to integrating forensic techniques into incident response. *NIST Special Publication*, 10(14), pp. 800–886.

Kohn, M. D., M. M. Eloff, & J. H. Eloff. 2013. Integrated digital forensic process model. *Computers & Security*, 38, pp. 103–115.

Kruse II, W. G., & J. G. Heiser. 2001. *Computer Forensics: Incident Response Essentials*. Pearson Education.

National Institute of Justice (US). July 2001. Electronic Crime Scene Investigation: A Guide for First Responders. [online] Second Edition, Available from: https://www.ncjrs.gov/pdffiles1/nij/219941.pdf . [Accessed: 20 September 2020]

Noblett, M. G., M. M. Pollitt, & L. A. Presley. 2000. Recovering and examining computer forensic evidence. *Forensic Science Communications*, 2(4), pp. 1–3..

Palmer, G. 2001. A road map for digital forensic research. Paper presented at the First Digital Forensic Research Workshop, Utica, New York.

Perumal, S. 2009. Digital forensic model based on Malaysian investigation process. *International Journal of Computer Science and Network Security*, 9(8), pp. 38–44.

Pollitt, M. 1995. Computer forensics: An approach to evidence in cyberspace. Paper presented at the Proceedings of the National Information Systems Security Conference.

Pollitt, M. M. 2007. An ad hoc review of digital forensic models. Paper presented at the Second International Workshop on Systematic Approaches to Digital Forensic Engineering, 2007 (SADFE 2007).

Reith, M., C. Carr, & G. Gunsch. 2002. An examination of digital forensic models. *International Journal of digital evidence*, 1(3), pp. 1–12.

Rogers, M. K., J. Goldman, R. Mislan, T. Wedge, & S. Debrota. 2006. Computer forensics field triage process model. Paper presented at the Proceedings of the conference on Digital Forensics, Security and Law.

Rowlingson, R. 2004. A ten step process for forensic readiness. *International Journal of digital evidence*, 2(3), pp. 1–28.

Satti, R. S., & F. Jafari. 2015. Domain specific cyber forensic investigation process model. *Journal of Advances in Computer Networks*, 3(1), pp. 75–81.

Selamat, S. R., R. Yusof, & S. Sahib. 2008. Mapping process of digital forensic investigation framework. *International Journal of Computer Science and Network Security*, 8(10), pp. 163–169.

Valjarevic, A., & H. S. Venter. 2012. *Harmonised digital forensic investigation process model*. Paper presented at the Information Security for South Africa (ISSA), 2012.

Van Baar, R., H. Van Beek, & E. van Eijk. 2014. Digital forensics as a service: A game changer. *Digital Investigation*, 11, pp. S54–S62.

Williams, J. 2012. *ACPO Good Practice Guide for Digital Evidence*. Metropolitan Police Service, Association of chief police officers, GB.

Wolfe-Wilson, J., & H. B. Wolfe. 2003. Management strategies for implementing forensic security measures. *Information Security Technical Report*, 8(2), pp. 55–64.

Yusoff, Y., R. Ismail, & Z. Hassan. 2011. Common phases of computer forensics investigation models. *International Journal of Computer Science & Information Technology*, 3(3), pp. 17–31.

10 Understanding Security Requirements and Challenges in the Industrial Internet of Things
A Review

*Aos Mulahuwaish, Kayhan Zrar Ghafoor
and Halgurd S. Maghdid*

CONTENTS

10.1 INTRODUCTION

The "Internet of Things" has become an increasingly growing topic of conversation both in the workplace and outside of it. The concept, which is often called IoT, means connecting all devices to the Internet. IoT has become prevalent to a variety of industries, but possibly none more than logistics. Ideas such as "connected trucks" equipped with IoT devices to monitor temperature, location, and speed real-time, producing data that can be used to drive predictive analytics, are being vigorously researched and tested.

IoT security [1,30] has become the subject of scrutiny after a number of high-profile incidents where a common IoT device was used to infiltrate and attack the larger network. Implementing security measures is critical to ensuring the safety of networks with IoT devices connected to them. Also, as security and privacy are important factors that will influence the adoption of the IoT paradigm, it is essential to know what are the security and privacy challenges – and benefits – of the distributed approach, and what are the most promising approaches in this field. If the challenges are too complex and the benefits too small, it might make sense to focus mainly on the centralized approach for IoT deployments.

In this chapter, we have discussed the state-of-the-art efforts to secure IoT networks and applications from the attacks and vulnerabilities. The IoT security challenges mainly fall under privacy in IoT, and light-weight cryptographic framework for IoT.

The rest of the chapter is organized as follows. Section 2 discusses privacy issues in IoT. In Section 3, state-of-the-art lightweight cryptographic framework for IoT is discussed. We conclude our paper in Section 3.

10.2   PRIVACY IN IOT

Privacy in IoT is a prime security issue that needs full attention from researchers in academia and industry. There is a dire need to propose protocols and management frameworks to handle privacy in IoT. IoT has become an integral part in various applications like remote patient monitoring, energy consumption control, traffic control and smart parking systems. In all of these applications, users require protection of personal information which is related to their movement, habits and interactions with other people. Internet of Things privacy is the special considerations required to protect the information of individuals from exposure in the IoT environment, in which almost any physical or logical entity or object can be given a unique identifier and the ability to communicate autonomously over the Internet or similar network. With regards to privacy in IoT, every framework or solution must address the following challenges.

The first challenge is profiling and tracking. The association of identity with a specific individual is a threat as this could result in tracking and profiling. Hence, the key challenge is to disallow such activity in IoT and take some preventive measures.

The next challenge is that of localization and tracking. Localization is another threat as systems try to determine and record a person's location through time and space. Design protocols for interactions with IoT are one of the most important challenges of security solutions for IoT that daunt such activity. Profiling information associated with a specific individual to infer interests by the correlation between other profiles and data is extremely common in e-commerce applications. A huge challenge lies in balancing the interests of businesses for profiling and data analysis with user's privacy requirements.

The next challenge is secure data transmission. One more security is to make sure that data are transmitted in an exceedingly secure manner through the public medium without revealing information to anyone and thereby preventing the unauthorized collection of information about things and people.

10.2.1   EXISTING SOLUTION AND DISCUSSION

In this section, we discuss existing research and efforts within the direction of ensuring privacy in IoT applications, especially body sensor networks.

Another recent work that is an attempt to analyze existing privacy-preserving solutions can be found in Ref. [2]. The authors identified the gaps in various proposals and put forward suggestions to remove them.

In Ref. [5], the authors introduced a survey in the existing IoT applications. In this work, the authors proposed a translation in a common system model and that they studied and identified differentiating behavioral patterns of sensor data generated. From the analysis, it had been disclosed that just about all applications gather time

information and location. Whatever data that is gathered is of varied types including audio and video. The authors surveyed up to this point privacy countermeasures. Furthermore, potential threats to user privacy in participatory sensing which ends up from uncontrolled disclosure of private information to untrusted people are discussed. Also, the authors mapped their analysis to a proposed common system model for analyzing security in mobile participatory sensing applications.

A detailed discussion on security threats and privacy in IoT architectures can be found in Ref. [15]. The discussion begins with detail of the layered architecture of IoT. Privacy and security threats at each level of the architecture are analyzed in detail. State of the art in presenting threat scenarios at various levels of the IoT architecture is discussed in detail. Based on the scenarios discussed, the security issues of importance are eavesdropping, man-in-the-middle and other similar attacks that jeopardize the data confidentiality and integrity, and grab control of some components. Along with that the authors also study the emerging EU legislation for IoT. It is important to understand the management domains of the IoT architecture. EU legislation requires that an individual should be able to control his or her information at all levels of architecture. Issues of further study require an in-depth study of how this kind of control is technically supported. Energy aspects of privacy and threats require more in-depth study.

The most recent work that addresses the challenges of privacy and security of cloud- based IoT can be found in Ref. [16]. In this work, authors identify that the privacy and security requirements in cloud-based IoT are identity privacy, node compromise attack, location privacy, forward and backward security, layer removing / adding attack and malicious and semi-trusted cloud security. Another recent work that is an attempt to investigate existing privacy-preserving solutions is found in Ref. [4]. The authors identified the gaps in various proposals and propose suggestions to get rid of them.

In Ref. [12], the authors surveyed privacy enhancements in IoT in various application domains. Key future security requirements for smart home systems are discussed. Also, the authors suggested an appropriate security architecture for IoT. The gateway architecture is nominated to be the most appropriate for resource-constrained devices and high system availability. This architecture implements sophisticated management algorithms on a fairly powerful processor and might operate critical smart home functions. But gateway architecture, other architectures are scrutinized for IoT are middleware architecture and cloud architecture. Two technologies are discussed for a gateway architecture for assisting auto management: firstly, auto-configuration support enhancing system security, and secondly, automatic update of system software and firmware to maintain ongoing secure system operation.

In Ref. [11], security challenges in mobile ad hoc networks are discussed in detail. There are various challenges to security design such as open peer to peer network architecture, shared wireless medium, stringent resource constraints, and highly dynamic network topology. Considering these challenges building a multi-fence security solution that achieves both broad protection and desirable network performance is possible. Security issues and state-of-the-art proposals related to the multihop delivery of packets among mobile nodes are discussed. For a comprehensive security solution, it should span both layers and encompass all three security components of prevention, detection and reaction.

In Ref. [17], the authors discussed thoroughly the enabling technologies for IoT privacy provisioning like RFID on threat analysis of RFID system components. RFID technology is taken into account as good for tracking and keeping stock of items. In order to use this on humans, there must be regulations and laws to operate, and strict imposition to confirm acceptance because it is often abused. The authors conclude, in order to use

RFID to enable IoT, issues with technological and social problems must be resolved. In Ref. [7], the authors introduced an effort in managing privacy for IoT by efficient data tagging through information flow control (IFC). The sensed data are tagged with privacy properties that allow trusted control access supported sensitivity. Because of the resource requirement of IoT, tagging is incredibly expensive, and this work discusses the concerns about tagging resource-constrained IoT. There are four properties of privacy-sensitive IoT applications including sensing valuable data, physical interaction, distributed implementation, and vulnerable sensors are illuminated which makes IFC data tag feasible for privacy preservation. Apart from these four, there are two more properties of such applications that are connected operation and skewed tag use that make the implementation of IFC data tags much easier.

In Ref. [8], authors have proposed a Host Identity Protocol (HIP) and Multimedia Internet Keying protocol enabling secure network alliance with the network in an exceedingly secure manner together with managing keys using a key management mechanism. HIP leverages public key cryptography to produce distinct identification of the IoT devices. Furthermore, the authors have extended HIP to have key management support.

Medical sensor networks (MSNs) require efficient and reliable access control that is a crucial requirement to authorizing staff to access private medical data and ensure productive and dependable access control. The authors in Ref. [10] have proposed an access control system enabling control on access in well-defined medical situations. The proposed system is an extension of the modular traditional role-based access control model. The modular design enables a simpler way of making a decision for access control and effective distribution of access control policies.

10.3 LIGHTWEIGHT CRYPTOGRAPHIC FRAMEWORK FOR IOT

There are new challenges in IoT in terms of the power consumption and also the energy. It is desired that the cryptographic primitives designed for IoT should be lightweight. These primitives must consume fewer resources without compromising the specified level of security. Hence, lightweight cryptography becomes so important, and also the research community has started focusing on it. Different properties of lightweight cryptography are discussed in ISO/IEC 29192 and ISO/IEC JTC 1/SC 27.

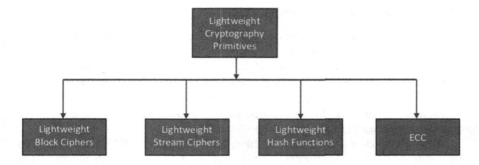

FIGURE 10.1   Lightweight Cryptographic Primitives for IoT.

Also, there's a project of lightweight cryptography (ISO/IEC 29192) under the method of standardization. Lightweight cryptography in ISO/IEC 29192 is described based on the target platform. Chip size and energy consumption are important measures to assess lightweight properties. Furthermore, small code and / or RAM size are preferable for lightweight applications in case of software implementation. Given the constraints of hardware recourses, design a lightweight cryptographic framework for IoT is highly needed. This can be achieved by proposing cryptographic primitives that require to be revisited and designed considering the constraints of IoT devices.

There are mainly four types of lightweight cryptographic primitives that are available for the use. As presented in Figure 10.1 the lightweight cryptography primitives can be classified as Lightweight Block Cipher (LWBC), Lightweight Stream Ciphers (LWSC), Lightweight Hash Functions (LWHF) and Elliptic Curve Cryptography (ECC) [25]. The factors on which the lightweight cryptographic primitives can be analyzed are key size, block size, number of rounds and structures. ECC is another option for lightweight cryptography [26]. Being an asymmetric cipher, it can provide authentication and non-repudiation as well (Figure 10.2).

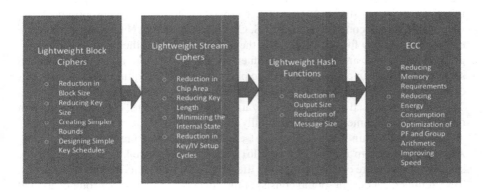

FIGURE 10.2   Research Gaps for LWC Primitives.

10.3.1 EXISTING SOLUTION AND DISCUSSION

In this section, we discuss efforts within the direction of proposing a lightweight cryptographic framework for IoT.

In Ref. [22], authors have proposed architecture for the security that is used to confirm the security objectifies. The proposed solution works in accordance with the smart object lifetime in IoT network. The keying material is managed by TTP infrastructure. The framework has been proposed by the authors is employed to manufacture the smart objects in a secure and protected fashion.

Lightweight key predistribution schemes can be found in Ref. [20]. Such schemes are proposed for IoT. Improvement in resource efficiency of such algorithms is proposed in Ref. [22]. Optimization of the cryptographic operations in the security provisioning of IoT are proposed in Ref. [21] where the authors have shown the equivalence of the Mixing Modular Operations (MMO) problem to finding close vectors in a lattice.

Authors in Ref. [3] have proposed distributed security mechanism for key agreement, recourse friendly, fast and methods to verify the identification parameters in wireless sensor network (WSN). System has proposed by authors are based on "alpha secure polynomials" that have been proposed as a method for the key distribution and establishment. In Ref. [23], authors have introduced some mechanisms to form the computation of polynomials more lightweight for IoT.

In Ref. [19], the authors proposed an efficient scheme of ID-based key establishment. The new scheme is made from a node with an identifier and a trusted third party (TTP) which provides a secret keying material to the node within the network. The identity of the other node and the secret keying material is utilized by other nodes to get a common pairwise key for secure communication. The scheme proposed by the authors is super efficient for the key computation time. In Ref. [24], the authors presented the body sensor networks (BSNs) and that they proposed a key management service for it. The key management service considers low-power devices and inefficient resource of IoT.

Authors in Ref. [14] proposed a lightweight security framework that gives a holistic security approach that contains lightweight authorization and authentication functionality on constrained smart objects. In Ref. [39], the authors proposed a lightweight framework comprising of DTLS, CoAP, and 6LoWPAN protocols to provide end-to-end security for IoT. In Ref. [6], the authors evaluated the lightweight cryptographic framework and proposed a framework that will use to assist the embedded software engineer in choosing the best cipher to match the requirements of an application. In Ref. [18], provided a lightweight framework to supply access control in IoT. The authors proposed a generic authorization framework for IoT devices. Evaluation of the proposed framework is additionally discussed.

Challenges within the security of IoT communication are presented in Ref. [27]. Architectural design for the IP-based IoT security is reviewed. The design for the security architecture can determine the lifecycle of an IoT device and its capabilities. The architectural design should consist of the concept of the type of protocol applied and also the trusted third party. As another requirement, an architecture should scale from small-scale ad hoc security domains to large-scale deployments. Lightweight protocols should be adopted within the architecture. Another point highlighted by the authors is that the security placement at the IoT layers like (link, network, or application layer), as each layer has different communication patterns and security requirements. If security is provisioned at the application layer, then the network is receptive attacks. However, focusing security on the network or link-layer introduces possible inter-application security threats.

The standard-compliant security framework is found in Ref. [9], and also the authors will make it applicable for future IoT paradigm. Another similar work that proposes an end-to-end security framework for IoT is found in Ref. [29].

In Ref. [28], the authors proposed a security scheme for IoT based on established standards and prevailing Internet standards on a low-power hardware platform. The proposed security solution fails in preventing against routing attacks and is simply too heavy for low-power devices. Another effort within the evaluation of resource consumption during the provisioning of security services is found in Ref. [4]. The work lacks a new proposal to deal with end-to-end security of IoT. The authors in Ref. [13] have evaluated secure communication mechanisms and compare them in terms of resource consumption. The work concludes with the most effective secure communication mechanism.

10.4   CONCLUSION

In this chapter, we have categorized and discussed the state-of-the-art work done in ensuring security in the IoT network. Efforts in privacy provisioning and light-weight cryptographic framework. Privacy is crucial in IoT especially as the characteristics of such a network is different than the typical Internet network. Such issues and requirements are identified and discussed in this paper. Besides privacy for ensuring security in the IoT network, lightweight cryptographic primitives are required which are suited for IoT network. All the efforts in this direction are discussed.

REFERENCES

1. Kanuparthi, A., R. Karri, and S. Addepalli. 2013. Hardware and embedded security in the context of internet of things. In Proceedings of the 2013 ACM workshop on Security, privacy & dependability for cyber vehicles, Berlin, Germany. ACM.
2. Aleisa, N., and K. Renaud. 2017. Privacy of the internet of things: A systematic literature review. In Proceedings of 50th Hawaii International Conference on System Sciences, Waikoloa, HI.
3. Chen, H. C. 2012. Secure multicast key protocol for electronic mail systems with providing perfect forward secrecy. *Security and Communication Networks*, 6(1), pp. 100–107.
4. D. Christin, A. Reinhardt, and M. Hollick. 2013. On the efficiency of privacy-preserving path hiding for mobile sensing applications. In Proceedings of IEEE LCN, Sydney, NSW. IEEE.
5. D. Christin, A. Reinhardt, S. S. Kanhere., and M. Hollick. 2011. A survey on privacy in mobile participatory sensing applications. *Journal of Systems and Software*, 84(11), pp. 1928–1946.

6. Dinu, D., A. Biryukov, and J. Großsch 2015. "FELICS fair evaluation of lightweight cryptographic systems," in Proceedings of NIST Workshop on Lightweight Cryptography, Gaithersburg, MD, USA, April 2015.

7. Evans, D., D. M. Eyers. 2012. Efficient data tagging for managing privacy in the internet of things. In Proceedings of 2012 IEEE International Conference on Green Computing and Communications, Besancon, France. IEEE.

8. Meca, F. V., J. H. Ziegeldorf, P. M. Sanchez, O. G. Morchon, S. S. Kumar, and S. L. Keoh. 2013. HIP security architecture for the IP-based internet of things. In Proceedings of IEEE Advanced Information Networking and Applications Workshops (WAINA), Barcelona, Spain.IEEE.

9. Piro, G., G. Boggia, and L. A. Grieco.2014. A standard compliant security frame work for IEEE 802.15.4 networks. In 2014 IEEE World Forum on Internet of Things (WF-IoT), Seoul, South Korea. IEEE.

10. Garcia-Morchon, O., and K. Wehrle. 2010. Modular context-aware access control for medical sensor networks. In Proceedings of 15th ACM Symposium on Access Control Models and Technologies, Pittsburgh, PA. ACM.

11. Yang, H., H. Luo, F. Ye, S. Lu, and L. Zhang. 2004. Security in mobile ad hoc networks: Challenges and solutions. *IEEE Wireless Communications*, 11(1), pp. 38–47.

12. Lin, H., and N. W. Bergmann. 2016. IoT privacy and security challenges for smart home environments. *Information*, 7(3), p. 44.

13. Granjal, J., E. Monteiro, and J. S. Silva. 2012. On the effectiveness of end-to-end security for internet-integrated sensing applications. In Proceedings of 2012 IEEE International Conference on Green Computing and Communications (pp. 87–93). IEEE.

14. Hernandez-Ramos, J. L., M. P. Pawlowski, A. J. Jara, A. F. Skarmeta, and L. Ladid. 2015. Toward a lightweight authentication and authorization framework for smart objects. *IEEE Journal on Selected Areas in Communications*, 33(4), pp.690–702.

15. Veijalainen, J., D. Kozlov, and Y. Ali. 2012. Security and privacy threats in IoT architectures. In Proceedings of 7th International Conference on Body Area Networks, Oslo, Norway.

16. Zhou, J., Z. Cao, X. Dong, and A. V. Vasilakos. 2017. Security and privacy for cloud-based IoT: Challenges. *IEEE Communications Magazine*, 55(1), pp. 26–33.

17. Khoo, B. 2011. RFID as an enabler of the internet of things: Issues of security and privacy. In Proceedings of 4th International Conference on Cyber, Physical and S ocial Computing, Dalian, China. IEEE.

18. Seitz, L., G. Selander, and C. Gehrmann. 2013. Authorization framework for the internet-of-things. In Proceedings of World of Wireless, Mobile and Multimedia Networks (pp. 1–6). IEEE.

19. Garcia-Morchon, O., L. Tolhuizen, D. Gomez, and J. Gutierrez. 2012. Towards fully collusion-resistant ID-based es- tablishment of pairwise keys. In Proceedings of Extended Abstracts of the Third Workshop on Mathematical Cryptology (WMC 2012) and the Third International Conference on Symbolic Computation and Cryptography (SCC 2012), pp. 30–36, Castro Urdiales, Spain.

20. Garcia-Morchon, O., D. Gomez-Perez, J. Gutierrez, R. Rietman, B. Schoenmakers, and L. Tolhuizen. (2015). HIMMO-a lightweight collusion resistant key predistribution scheme. In Proceedings of IACR 2015, Mumbai, India.

21. Garcia-Morchon, O., R. Rietman, L. Tolhuizen, D. Gomez, and J. Gutierrez. 2014. The MMO problem. In Proceedings of the 39th International Symposium on Symbolic and Algebraic Computation, New York, NY, USA.

22. Garcia-morchon, O., R. Rietman, I. E. Shparlinski, and L. Tolhuizen. Interpolation and approximation of polynomials in finite fields over a short interval from noisy values. *Experimental Mathematics*, 23(3), pp. 241–260.

23. Garcia-Morchon, O., R. Rietman, S. Sharma, L. Tolhuizen, and J. L. Torre-Arce. DTLS-HIMMO: Efficiently securing a post-quantum world with a fully collusion resistant KPS. In *IACR Cryptology*. IACR.

24. Morchon, O., H. Baldus, and D. Sanchez. Resource-efficient security for medical body sensor networks. In Proceedings of Wearable and Implantable Body Sensor Networks (p. 4). IEEE.

25. Singh, S., P. K. Sharma, S. Y. Moon, and J. H. Park. Advanced lightweight encryption algorithms for IoT devices: survey, challenges and solutions. *Journal of Ambient Intelligence and Humanized Computing.*

26. Szczechowiak, P., L. B. Oliveira, M. Scott, M. Collier, and R. Dahab. 2008. NanoECC: Testing the limits of elliptic curve cryptography in sensor networks. In European conference on Wireless Sensor Networks. Springer.

27. Heer, T, O. Garcia-Morchon, R. Hummen, S. L. Keoh, S. S. Kumar, and K. Wehrle. 2011. Security challenges in the IP-based internet of things. *Wireless Personal Communications*, 61(3), pp. 527–542.

28. Kothmayr, T., C. Schmitt, W. Hu, M. Brunig, and G. Carle. 2012. A DTLS based end-to-end security architecture for the Internet of Things with two-way authentication. In Proceedings of Local Computer Networks, LCN (2012), pp. 956–963, Clear- water Beach, FL, USA.

29. Huang, X, P. Craig, H. Lin, and Z. Yan. 2015. SecIoT: A security framework for the internet of things. *Security and Communication Networks*, 9(16), pp.3083–3094.

30. Xiaohui, X. 2013. Study on security problems and key technologies of the internet of things. In Proceedings of IEEE 5th International Conference Computational and Information Sciences (ICCIS), Hubei, China. IEEE

11 5G Security and the Internet of Things

Athan Biamis and Kevin Curran

CONTENTS

11.1 INTRODUCTION

5G is the state-of-the-art and latest cellular network technology, only beginning its rollout. Statistics from the Global Mobile Suppliers Association (GSA) show that there are 224 operators currently investing in 5G. These 224 operators are stationed in 88 different countries and are currently investing in the form of tests, trials, pilots and deployments (GSA, 2019). As these statistics are from April 2019, we can have no doubt that these numbers would have increased significantly since then and the next GSA report should show that. All countries are still in the rollout phase of the technology, which means that a minority of networks offer it and the availability is usually quite limited to specific large cities and areas. The only network in Ireland to offer 5G thus far is Vodafone who rolled it out in August 2019 in Cork, Dublin, Galway, Limerick and Waterford (Vodafone, 2019). While Eir and Three plan to rollout before the end of 2019 (Maguire, 2019). The availability of 5G is more widespread in the UK with EE, Vodafone, Three and O2 all offering the service but just like in Ireland, only in certain areas. In total there are 17 cities and towns in the UK where 5G is available. The only network to offer 5G in Belfast is EE as of October 2019, while some cities such as London have the choice of all four networks (5G. co.uk, 2019).

The main improvement of 5G is the massive difference in both average speed and maximum speed. While the average speed of 5G will be in the range of 130Mbps–240Mbps, obviously depending on proximity to station and peak times, the maximum speed that will be possible is 10Gbps. The average 4G speed is around 42Mbps, with the absolute maximum being 300Mbps. That makes 5G 100 times faster than 4G. On top of this, the latency of 5G has also improved from previous generations: From 40–50ms with 4G to a target of 1–4ms for 5G. While this is the intended target in the upcoming years, currently most devices average around 8–12ms. This means instead of taking 50 milliseconds for a command being issued and to receive a response, it will only take 12ms.

The wavelength of 5G radio signals will be very short, in the 30–300GHz range, meaning it will have a very high frequency. These wavelengths will be so short that they will be measured in millimetres and are known as "millimetre waves". The problem with millimetre waves is that they cannot travel very well as they are stopped by buildings and absorbed by trees and rain. To combat this problem networks will use "small cells". These are small base stations that will be scattered around every 250m throughout cities. This should stop the signal being dropped due to obstructions as when one small cell is blocked, there will likely be another nearby to utilise. This will require a much larger investment than ever before as you cannot just install a single base station to cover miles and miles of coverage, like was the case with 4G. However, these small cells that will be scattered throughout are miniscule, use very little power and can be placed anywhere, for example on top of lights or buildings. This can be quite easy in a city but will prove very difficult in rural areas (Nordrum and Clark, 2017).

5G is also much more suited to the development of the IoT (Internet of Things), which is the system of billions of devices around the world that will all be interconnected via the Internet (see Figure 11.1). This includes smart TVs, cars, houses,

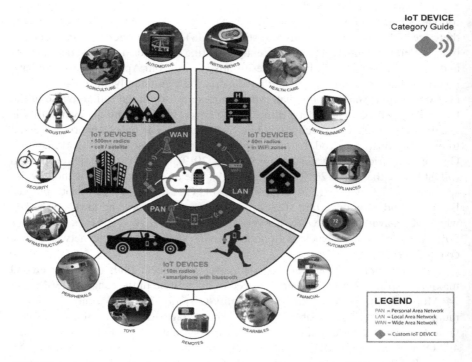

FIGURE 11.1   The Interconnectivity of IoT Technologies (Design 1st, 2018)

thermostats and basically anything with a computer within it. The lower latency and the fact that 5G can handle 10–100x more devices than previous technologies is a perfect remedy for the implementation of the IoT. 5G has the capacity to handle a completely interconnected world in which everything is communicating with everything else via the Internet. While this new age of IoT may seem all positive, it also increases the risk and size of possible damage done. A hacker could gain access to not only your phone, but also to multiple home appliances and your car (Stacey, 2019).

5G has yet to become widely available in most countries and its rollout phase is only beginning. The specifications discussed in this chapter can vary from network to network and country to country. Some networks may be able to reach sub 200Mbps speeds while others will be significantly less. The placement of small cells will also vary, depending on the infrastructure of the specific area. Even taking these factors into account, there is still no doubt that 5G will be capable of these new use cases and be the backbone of the IoT as the basis of 5G cellular networks remains the same.

11.2   SECURITY RISKS

The main new technologies that 5G will be utilising for the first time will incur new types of security risks, and as a result require new types of security methods. They are:

- Software Defined Networks (SDN) and Network Functions Virtualisation (NFV) – These technologies provide networks with the ability of transforming previous network architecture of 3G and 4G where functions were built on specialised hardware and software to solely software oriented. This, in theory, could help improve security as problems could be patched through software updates as opposed to physical replacements. But simultaneously software also has its own associated risks. If software is not developed properly and tested thoroughly then bugs can be discovered which could be exploited. Networks based on software also are much more susceptible to malware attacks which could be even more damaging.
- Network Slicing – This technology allows different virtual networks to run on top of the same physical network. One network will be split up into several different mini networks that each support different radio access networks (RANs). An autonomous car could be using the V2X (vehicle to anything) communication, which uses a low latency with a low throughput. While simultaneously a video can be streamed from within the car with a high throughput but a low latency. Both the autonomous car and the video can be received from the same physical network but on separate virtual network slices within that physical network. The segmentation of network slicing means the network is more reliable as one slice encountering a problem or being attacked will not affect other slices.
- A less centralised architecture – the small cells scattered around will be able to handle data and resources a lot closer to the end user to provide

lower response times, as opposed to a tower several miles away. This is a form of Mobile Edge Technology, which is a network architecture that allows computing capabilities at the edge of the network. A less centralised architecture results in a need for less centralised security. Each small cell must have security so signals cannot be intercepted, whereas before only the towers would have needed to be secure. These small cells would not have the capacity to power large security methods, like towers. That means small cells could be 5G's weak point, compared to 4G (Kavanagh, 2018).

The EU has already begun researching the possible cybersecurity risks with 5G networks and has identified several possible scenarios of exploitation by potential threats, these include:

- Network disruption – either locally among a small number of small cells or even on a global scale. In addition, because of IoT and the number of devices expected to be utilising 5G and becoming reliant on it, even a small disruption could be catastrophic.
- Data being spied on from within the network infrastructure – whether it be from the end-user to the small cell or the small cell to the base station.
- Modification or rerouting of traffic and data from within the network infrastructure. Again, either from the end-user to the small cell or from the small cell to the base station.

These three scenarios are not all of the possible security risks but simply the most likely and damaging to the network and country. A toolbox of mitigating measures has been compiled by the Network and Information Systems Cooperation Group, and by October 2020 EU member states individually and with assistance from the Commission will assess the possible security risks and plan further action to mitigate them (EU Commission, 2019).

In the USA, the National Highway Traffic Safety Administration (NHTSA) has come up with research regarding the security of autonomous vehicles. These are vehicles with features such as driver assistance, collision warning, automatic braking and safety communication. It is believed that with the capabilities of 5G and its enabling of the IoT, a multi-layered approach to cybersecurity is necessary to ensure its safety. These layers would consist of the formation of an industry focussed on cybersecurity in automobiles to facilitate intelligence and information sharing, called Auto-ISAC, the quick detection and immediate response to any possible cyber risks and incidents discovered and a standardised procedure for detecting risks and protecting those vehicles at risk. This research and these findings came to fruition after the first cybersecurity related vehicle recall happened in July 2015 where 1.4 million Chrysler vehicles were recalled in the USA because of the discovery of a software vulnerability in the vehicle's computer (NHTSA, 2016).

Moving onto the health service, 5G has the capacity to facilitate things like remote surgery and remote patient monitoring because of the IoT. The security risk here is massive as an attack could lead to the loss of life, especially when it is considered that

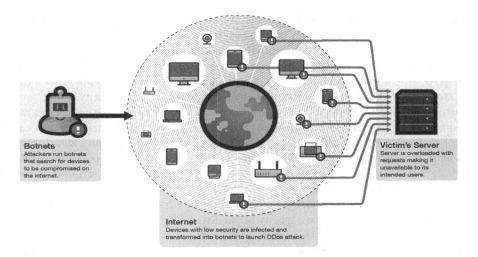

Botnets
Attackers run botnets
that search for devices
to be compromised on
the internet.

Victim's Server
Server is overloaded with
requests making it
unavailable to its
intended users.

Internet
Devices with low security are infected and
transformed into botnets to launch DDos attack.

FIGURE 11.2   DDoS Utilising IoT Devices (Trend Micro, 2016)

the healthcare industry already fell victim to 40% of total data breaches worldwide in 2017 (SDxCentral, 2017). Some devices, especially those on the cheaper side, cut a lot of corners in their security in order to cut costs. Because of the low-grade security, attackers like to target these items. IoT devices with weak or default passwords are extremely common and attackers can use special technology to scan en masse for devices with those weak and default passwords. This was evident in October of 2016 when a massive Distributed Denial of Service (DDoS) attack left the east coast of the USA without the Internet for a day. Known as the "Mirai Botnet", the attacker took control of hundreds of thousands of IoT devices such as cameras, routers and digital video recorders to overwhelm the network (Huber, 2019). See Figure 11.2.

There are already flaws that have been discovered affecting simple communications, such as calls and texts on 5G. Academics discovered several security issues that affected both 5G and 4G in which someone could make multiple phone calls and cancel them in quick succession resulting in a paging message being triggered without notifying the user of a call. This paging protocol is what networks use to notify a mobile device that a call or text is coming through. This attack known as "Torpedo" then opens the device to two other forms of attack: "Piercer", that the attacker can use to find out the victim's International Mobile Subscriber Identity (IMSI); and IMSI-Cracking, in which the attacker brute forces the IMSI number to decrypt it when required. This, ultimately, means that the use of "StingRay" devices that governments use to intercept calls and eavesdrop can exploit this vulnerability and continue their use, even though 5G was supposed to eliminate the use of StingRay completely (Hussain et al., 2019).

Industry is becoming aware of the risks associated with 5G and using it for the IoT. 74% of organisations have made security assessment controls in relation to IoT thus far. These controls would usually consist of procedures such as security assessment, secure passwords, certificate authentication, encryption and security log monitoring of devices (Wipro Ltd, 2018). While it may be true that 5G involves a lot of new technology and features, the underlying security controls that have worked for years in previous generations will also work for 5G. Furthermore, security protocols will even be improved upon, such as the Authentication & Key Agreement (AKA), which has existed since 3G, which in 5G will now be combined with the Extensible Authentication Protocol (EAP) for an extra layer of security. These protocols are what networks use to ensure the phone connecting to the network is the authentic user and not an eavesdropper. The AKA protocol is the main authentication method in 3 & 4G and it works by the end-user and the network provider sharing a long-term secret key. As this key is stored on the SIM card, its encryption is limited by the SIM's low processing power and because of this it only uses symmetric key cryptography (Koutsos, 2019).

The problem with 5G is not the actual technology but instead the new use cases (Elgan, 2018). Because of the capacity of 5G it will mean that industries like healthcare and automotive, and governments will, for the first time, be able to fully rely on its services. These industries will utilise new technologies and devices, whether it be an autonomous car being driven by a computer in the cloud or a patient undergoing surgery by a surgeon in another country. As this scale increases, the security risks also increase, as more devices that never connected before connect for the first time and the sheer amount of them also gets larger. This is where the main security concerns come from. With the new possibilities of functions under the umbrella of IoT, it also directly correlates with the possibility of attacks. Thus, it is not the new technology that is the problem, but the new functions the technology has the power to provide (see Figure 11.3).

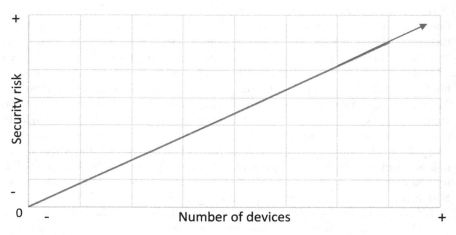

FIGURE 11.3 The Security Risk Rises as the Number of 5G-enabled Technologies iIncreases

11.3   SECURING 5G

The foundation for upkeeping a secure 5G network will be very similar to what was used previously for 3 & 4G. This foundation of simple security relies on several layers that have been tried and tested for years. Networks should have firewalls installed that monitor and take control of all network traffic going in and out. Rules should be installed into the firewall that only allow certain traffic from certain, trusted sources and are able to detect malicious data. This effectively provides a buffer zone or barrier between the network and the Internet. Routine malware scans that are incorporated into a person or organization's schedule in which special software will scan the network and its internal devices looking for possible malicious files. DNS monitoring tools which constantly watch DNS requests. These requests are the foundation of the Internet as they retrieve the IP addresses of websites using the domain name. Malicious attackers could intercept these requests and provide false IP addresses, redirecting users to false websites. Monitoring DNS requests would be a vital element to eliminating that risk (Miller et al., 2020).

The most important new security layer for 5G will be automation. As the range and scale of attacks possible on 5G increases, so will the capabilities and technological advances of Artificial Intelligence (AI), machine learning and automation. As 5G is so decentralised and utilises Mobile Edge Technology, it is believed that the network's end-points, such as the small cells, can be used as "detection spots" which send data to a Centralised Control Plane (CCP). This CCP can have the computing power to analyse all the data coming through and scan for threats (Scialabba, 2018). This form of cloud computing that is made possible because of the new technologies such as Software Defined Networking (SDN) and Network Function Virtualisation (NFV) may have its share of risks; it also has a fortunate upside. This powerful cloud-computing creates the possibility of placing security measures such as, but not limited to: firewalls, DNS monitoring, malware scanning and even powerful encryption or authentication methods within these servers. This frees up the responsibility of the end-user or organisation for detecting risks and replaces it with a much more reliable AI system, eliminating human error. It would also increase the end-user's computing power as they will not have to use as much resources in threat detection locally (Baldoni et al., 2018).

5G, like previous generations, uses the 3rd Generation Partnership Project (3GPP) specifications. These standards and specifications are followed worldwide in order to keep cellular data connections as secure as possible, no matter where the end user is located. The main features of 3GPP are:

- Mutual authentication – this process involves authenticating the end user to make sure they are the correct user of that IP address. This helps support networks charging for access and being able to see who and what the connection was for. It also helps the end user ensure they are connected to the genuine network.
- Encryption – data that is being transmitted and received is encrypted in order to prevent ungenuine eavesdropping.

- Confidentiality – End users' User Identifiers are kept private. This mechanism allows the user to enjoy a private and anonymous connection.
- Eavesdropping with false base stations – Unlike previous generations the International Mobile Subscriber Identity (IMSI) is kept private. This means that devices like StingRays should not be able to eavesdrop on conversations by masquerading as a base station and receiving data not meant for it. On top of that, IMSI numbers are also more frequently refreshed/updated. However, as discussed before, bugs have been discovered that allow the detection of the IMSI number.
- Compartmentalisation – This idea helps isolate possible problems or attacks to certain areas of the network. The Radio Access Network (RAN) is a separate entity to the core network. Network slicing also utilises this idea as different frequencies are in different slices. While one slice may be attacked, the others will not (Ericsson, 2019).

To upkeep the security of SDN, NFV, network slicing and the applications that will be running on it each aspect of the technology will need to have its own security. This consists of securing the SDN layer, which includes the Application Programming Interface (API) and Controller, the infrastructure layer for both physical and virtual, secure network services, secure applications running on the network, secure communication (encryption) and mainstream secure technologies for the end-user, such as threat intelligence and web and email security (Public, Geller and Nair, 2018).

There are several areas in which 5G improves upon previous security. These new security features are outside the scope of 3GPP but are fully implemented into the foundation of 5G anyway. As a result of the vast variety of devices that would be connecting to 5G, a new idea of authentication for access to the network had to be developed. To solve this, instead of using a SIM card to hold the end user's unique identifier, it is stored in the device itself. This means that to connect to 5G, you will technically not require a SIM card. However, most networks will still be requiring the use of a SIM card to connect to their network in order to have a link to your account and credit but even then, this SIM card will not be used in the authentication process like previous generations. Removing the SIM card from the network authentication process moves responsibility from the end user to the individual service providers. A much safer method, under the assumption that these service providers would have sufficient security. 5G also has the upper hand when it comes to roaming encryption. When the user connects to the base station the device and the station must communicate with each other in order to authenticate the identity both ways. This authentication communication is fully encrypted in 5G with 256-bit asymmetric encryption. This is the added layer of the Extensible Authentication Protocol (EAP) mentioned in the previous chapter. Previous generations, including 4G, did not encrypt the authentication process to this degree. In the real world, this means that it is impossible to geo-locate or get the identity of the end user (Purdy, 2019).

There are endless possibilities in which 5G can be implemented by a network. The network architecture is the most important aspect of ensuring its security and robustness. One such defined architecture for securing 5G could look like as follows:

implement top-level physical and logical domains. Each network slice would have its own domain and that domain should be well defined and controlled to keep it secure. In the event that one domain or slice is attacked, only that slice would go down. Others would be unaffected. For these separate domains to communicate with each other, reference points should be installed. These reference points will handle all interactions between the domains. All data transferred through the reference points from different domains should have strictly defined data parameters. A TVRA (Threat Vulnerability Risk Assessment) should be completed to come up with a risk treatment plan. This TVRA should look at the domain structure, data and security between these entities while they are communicating. Security controls should be in accordance with well-established design principles and best practices and these security controls should be well defined (Arfaoui et al., 2018).

The IP layer will also be an important aspect of 5G security. With the new development and rollout of IPv6, alongside 5G, new protocols and features come with it. These are defined by the Internet Engineering Task Force (IETF) and known as IPSec (IP Security). IPSec embeds high quality security provisions and cryptography and was developed to be something within the network layer that is transparent to applications using it and also separate to the link layer, which is the lowest layer in the Internet Protocol Suite. This layer provides the methods and communication protocols for the Internet. The IPSec security features consist of confidential and integral communications with relay protection (Faheem and Rafique, 2015).

To secure the 5G connection to the cloud, virtualisation technologies will be utilised. Each end-node will connect to an independent virtual instance in the cloud through a Virtual Machine. As a result, each user's connection will be isolated and separate from another. 5G possesses the speed and capacity to run each connection in a separate Virtual Machine instance, whereas with previous technologies this idea would have been unrealistic. This procedure is in accordance with many other aspects of 5G that utilise segmentation or isolation such as network slicing (Ahmad et al., 2017).

The general security of 5G has been debated intensely throughout the last few years and as it is only a new technology and its rollout is not even complete; it is difficult to see if any of these security measures will be sufficient. Much of the security protocols from 4G will be the same for 5G. There are also several improvements on previous protocols. However, the problem is these security protocols, including even the improvements, may not be able to match the massive new set of use cases that come with 5G. The security must come from both ends – the end user and the network itself. The network should follow the well-established protocols from previous generations and use the new technologies such as slicing and encryption. The end-user must also keep up standards, for example, changing passwords, having security software on devices and routine malware scans.

11.4   FUTURE OF 5G

5G is expected to become integrated into endless possibilities of technology. The type of technology that becomes a part of the average person's every-day life. There are plans being invested into already by Qualcomm to develop "smart transportation". This would involve traffic lights that communicate with the vehicles on the road so they know what's coming and prepare for it. Other vehicles would also be in constant communication with each other. Their locations will be computerised and the chance of an accident will be reduced as braking distances will be automatically kept. This is done under the belief that it could reduce traffic congestion and improve safety. A V2X (Vehicle 2 Everything) chipset solution has already been developed and is in the testing phase (Altavilla, 2019). Another proposed possibility are "smart drones". These drones would work with both the mobile networks and emergency services to locate the scene of an accident and dispatch a drone with a first aid kit. It is also proposed that remote surgery could take place anywhere by a remote controlled robot, being administered by a surgeon at the hospital. Ambulances could be completely autonomous, calculating in real-time the fastest and safest manouvers and routes (Sanz, 2018). Moving into the Virtual Reality (VR) and Augmented Reality (AR) sphere, it is believed that 5G has the power to revolutionise VR and AR technology. The amount of data that 5G is able to process will mean that it will be able to update in real time without any lag whatsoever. AR technology could involve children chasing virtual characters through real places, exploring a new city and seeing how it used to look, having online calls in which the other person is digitised as if they were there. This could all be done by a slimline pair of glasses utilising 5G (Qualcomm Technologies, Inc., 2018). 5G's capacity to handle multiple devices at one time makes it perfect for enabling smart-home technology. It will allow people to completely connect every device in their home to each other and support them communicating with one another to achieve an aim. For example a service meeter would be connected to a central network which could help energy suppliers respond to sudden flunctiations in use, akin to a gas leak or a doorbell being rung which automatically triggers a separate camera to point at the door. This creates a type of unified system of devices for a completely autonomous home (Jarman, 2019). This perpetuates the importance of cybersecurity, gaining access to a single device can reveal passwords for one whole network, allowing access for all devices, one weak link can be all it takes. A house could be brought under the complete control of an attacker a thousand miles away. A DDoS attack, just like the "Mirai" botenet could cripple every device in the network. Experts in the IoT industry believe that biometric authentication is the main remedy against these attacks as it is virtually impossible for biometric data to be identical. Any smart home devices should also come from a reputable brand, be kept up to date with latest software, never be left with default passwords but most of all – be connected to a completely secure 5G network (Soare, 2019).

Alongside the development of these 5G technologies is a correlating development of cybersecurity ideas and software to protect these technologies. It is possible to create virtual security environments that stay with the same user, no matter what device they use. This is done through virtualisation and cloud technology. 5G would lead to the replacement of the network perimeter with the cloud, and the cloud is where these security feaures would be located. The vast mobile data capacity of 5G also enables extensive machine learning and Artificial

Intelligence to power cybersecurity software centralised in the cloud. This automated threat detection would spot anomalies and deal with them without the need of any human interaction. For example, this software would be going through every connection request as they come and be able to detect thousands of requests at the same time, signalling a possible DDoS attempt and automatically denying them (CPO, 2019).

The risks associated with the massive increases in cloud technology come with a focus on the cybersecurity of the cloud. The money spent on cybersecurity of the cloud worldwide has risen from $185 million in 2017 to $459 million in 2019. This rise can be partially but significantly attributed to the expected growth of 5G technologies (Gartner, 2018). However, many organisations can choose to pay third-party companies with experience to take care of their cloud data. These contracts are outsourced to massive companies with very extensive security; these cloud companies are called Managed Service Providers (MSPs). Amazon Web Services (AWS) has began hosting the USA Department of Defence (Gregg, 2018) and CIA government data after a $10 billion contract was signed in August 2018 (Konkel, 2014). On top of that, another MSP, Microsoft Azure, currently hosts 95% of Fortune 500 companies and is the biggest cloud provider of all (Microsoft, 2019). It is believed that, just like these MSPs have done, the future of all software will be developed with the process of "DevSpecOps", this is the idea of developing security for software as the software itself is being developed. All security checks are coded and are already part of the automated unit testing so any new additions to code written is secure by default. As opposed to adding security at the end of the development process, keeping it as just an afterthought, it will be a part of the development process the whole way through (Shkoda, 2018).

The future of 5G can be predicted differently from place to place and person to person. However, it is widely believed that 5G will become very integral to future technologies, as most new technologies under IoT will have the ability to connect to and utilise it. This means that for the first time on such a massive scale, 5G moves outside the sphere of smartphones and it will be the foundational connectivity for just about everything that needs to communicate. As a result the importance of cybersecurity increases and new technologies such as cloud-based security become more widespread.

11.5 CONCLUSION

5G has the capacity to power much more devices simultaneously and it also has the ability to reach speeds that dwarf any technology before it. This will undoubtedly increase significantly the number of devices connected to the Internet and also their use cases. 5G can duplicate and utilise just about all security features of previous generations of cellular networks and even improve upon them such as NFV, network slicing and private authentication. This means that the real security risk does not come from the foundation or architecture of 5G itself but the expected massive increase in devices connected to the network and their new, sometimes very important functions, autonomous vehicles, ambulances and homes. As the umbrella of

IoT gets bigger, then so do the possibilities for attack. It is expected that the future will have 5G integrated into every aspect of life, whether it be Smart Cities, smart homes, smart cars and automation. It is also expected to utilise cloud computing to power these services in ways never seen before. With these new use cases comes the need for cloud-based cybersecurity which could be completely autonomous and machine learning AI that go through massive amounts of data, detecting and mitigating threats, completely eliminating human error. 5G will be the foundation that all these new technologies communicate and send data through. So, an insecure 5G network is akin to building a house without a foundation.

REFERENCES

5G.co.uk. 2019. 5G coverage: Where is 5G available and when will it come to area? [online] 5g.co.uk. Available at: https://5g.co.uk/coverage/ [Accessed 13 Oct. 2019].

Ahmad, I., T. Kumar, M. Liyanage, J. Okwuibe, M. Ylianttila, and A. Gurtov. 2017. 5G security: Analysis of threats and solutions. In 2017 IEEE Conference on Standards for Communications and Networking (CSCN) (pp. 44–52). New York.

Altavilla, D. 2019. What is 5G today and what the future holds. [online] Computer world. Available at: https://www.computerworld.com/article/3445370/what-is-5g-today-and-what-the-future-holds.html [Accessed 5 Nov. 2019].

Arfaoui, G., P. Bisson, R. Blom, R. Borgaonkar, H. Englund, E. Felix, F. Klaedtke, P. K. Nakarmi, M. Naslund, P. O'Hanlon, J. Papay, J. Suomalainen, M. Surridge, J.-P. Wary, and A. Zahariev. 2018. A security architecture for 5G networks. *IEEE Access*, 6(1), pp. 22466–22479.

Baldoni, G., P. Cruschelli, M. Paolino, C. C. Meixner, A. Albanese, A. Papageorgiou, H. Khalili, S. Siddiqui, and D. Simeonidou. 2018. Edge computing enhancements in an NFV-based ecosystem for 5G neutral hosts. In 2018 IEEE Conference on Network Function Virtualization and Software Defined Networks (NFV-SDN). IEEE.

CPO. 20195G and the future of cybersecurity. [online] CPO Magazine. Available at: https://www.cpomagazine.com/cyber-security/5g-and-the-future-of-cybersecurity/ [Accessed 5 Nov. 2019].

Design 1st. 2018. How will 5G impact IoT product development? [online] Design 1st I Product Design Company. Available at: https://www.design1st.com/impact-5g-on-iot-product-development/ [Accessed 13 Oct. 2019].

Elgan, M. 2018. How to prepare for the coming 5G security threats. [online] Security Intelligence. Available at: https://securityintelligence.com/how-to-prepare-for-the-coming-5g-security-threats/ [Accessed 3 Nov. 2019].

Ericsson. 2019. A guide to 5G network security. [online] Ericsson.com. Available at: https://www.ericsson.com/en/security/a-guide-to-5g-network-security [Accessed 3 Nov. 2019].

EU Commission. 2019. EU-wide coordinated risk assessment of 5G networks security. [online] European Commission. Available at: https://ec.europa.eu/digital-single-market/en/news/eu-wide-coordinated-risk-assessment-5g-networks-security [Accessed 2 Nov. 2019].

Faheem, K., and K. Rafique. 2015.Securing 4G/5G wireless networks. *Computer Fraud & Security*, 5(1), pp. 8–12.

Gartner. 2018. Gartner forecasts worldwide information security spending to exceed $124 billion in 2019. [online] Gartner Newsroom. Available at: https://www.gartner.com/en/newsroom/press-releases/2018-08-15-gartner-forecasts-worldwide-information-security-spending-to-exceed-124-billion-in-2019 [Accessed 6 Nov. 2019].

Gregg, A. 2018. Pentagon doubles down on 'single-cloud' strategy for $10 billion contract. [online] The Washington Post. Available at: https://www.washingtonpost.com/business/capitalbusiness/pentagon-doubles-down-on-single-cloud-strategy-for-10-billion-contract/2018/08/05/352cfee8-972b-11e8-810c-5fa705927d54_story.html [Accessed 14 Nov. 2019].

GSA. 2019. LTE and 5G market statistics—8 April 2019—GSA. [online] GSA. Available at: https://gsacom.com/paper/lte-5g-market-statistics-8-april-2019/?utm=reports4g [Accessed 13 Oct. 2019].

Huber, N. 2019. A hacker's paradise?5G and cyber security. [online] Financial Times. Available at: https://www.ft.com/content/74edc076-ca6f-11e9-af46-b09e8bfe60c0 [Accessed 2 Nov. 2019].

Hussain, S. R., M. Echeverria, O. Chowdhury, N. Li, and E. Bertino. 2019. Privacy attacks to the 4G and 5G cellular paging protocols using side channel information. In Proceedings 2019 Network and Distributed System Security Symposium. [online] Available at: https://assets.documentcloud.org/documents/5749002/4G-5G-paper-at-NDSS-2019.pdf [Accessed 2 Nov. 2019].

Jarman, B. 2019. 5G and smart homes: What you need to know. [online] Iotevolutionworld. com. Available at: https://www.iotevolutionworld.com/smart-home/articles/442986-5g-smart-homes-what-need-know.htm [Accessed 5 Nov. 2019].

Kavanagh, S. 2018. What is network slicing? [online] 5g.co.uk. Available at: https://5g.co.uk/guides/what-is-network-slicing/ [Accessed 2 Nov. 2019].

Konkel, F. 2014.The details about the CIA's deal with amazon. [online] The Atlantic. Available at: https://www.theatlantic.com/technology/archive/2014/07/the-details-about-the-cias-deal-with-amazon/374632/ [Accessed 14 Nov. 2019].

Koutsos, A. 2019. The 5G-AKA authentication protocol privacy. In 2019 IEEE European Symposium on Security and Privacy (EuroS&P). IEEE.

Maguire, A. 2019. High speed mobile comes to Ireland: 5G explained. [online] RTE.ie. Available at: https://www.rte.ie/news/business/2019/0813/1068574-5g-explainer-mobile/ [Accessed 13 Oct. 2019].

Microsoft. 2019. Microsoft azure cloud computing platform & services. [online] Microsoft. com. Available at: https://azure.microsoft.com/en-us/?v=18.40&v=18.40 [Accessed 6 Nov. 2019].

Miller, S., K. Curran, and T. Lunney. 2020. Detection of Virtual Private Network Traffic Using Machine Learning. *International Journal of Wireless Networks and Broadband Technologies (IJWNBT)*, 9(2), pp. 60–81. DOI: 10.4018/IJWNBT.2020070104

NHTSA. 2016. NHTSA. [online] nhtsa.gov. Available at: https://www.nhtsa.gov/technology-innovation/vehicle-cybersecurity [Accessed 2 Nov. 2019].

Nordrum, A., and K. Clark. 2017. Everything you need to know about 5G. [online] IEEE Spectrum: Technology, Engineering, and Science News. Available at: https://spectrum.ieee.org/video/telecom/wireless/everything-you-need-to-know-about-5g [Accessed 13 Oct. 2019].

Public, C., M. Geller, and P. Nair. 2018. 5G security innovation with cisco. In *Netsync*. [online] Cisco. Available at: https://www.netsyncnetwork.com/wp-content/uploads/2019/05/5g-security-innov-wp.pdf.

Purdy, A. 2019. Why 5G can be more secure than 4G. [online] Forbes. Available at: https://www.forbes.com/sites/forbestechcouncil/2019/09/23/why-5g-can-be-more-secure-than-4g/#39253e3057b2 [Accessed 5 Nov. 2019].

Qualcomm Technologies, Inc. 2018. VR and AR pushing connectivity limits. [online] Qualcomm.com. Qualcomm Technologies, Inc. Available at: https://www.qualcomm.com/media/documents/files/vr-and-ar-pushing-connectivity-limits.pdf [Accessed 5 Nov. 2019].

Sanz, J. 2018. 5 ways 5G will change the way you currently live | Smart Mobile Labs. [online] Smart Mobile Labs. Available at: http://smartmobilelabs.com/blog/5-ways-5g-will-cha nge-the-way-you-currently-live/ [Accessed 5 Nov. 2019].

Scialabba, L. 2018. IoT, 5G networks and cybersecurity: Safeguarding 5G networks with automation and AI. [online] Radware Blog. Available at: https://blog.radware.com/ security/2018/09/iot-5g-networks-and-cybersecurity-safeguarding-5g-networks-with -automation-and-ai/ [Accessed 3 Nov. 2019].

SDxCentral. 2017. What are the top 5G security challenges?—SDxCentral. [online] SDxCentral. Available at: https://www.sdxcentral.com/5g/definitions/top-5g-securi ty-challenges/ [Accessed 2 Nov. 2019].

Shkoda, D. 2018. The current state of cybersecurity in the cloud. [online] Medium. Available at: https://medium.com/faun/the-current-state-of-cybersecurity-in-the-cloud-cf996b69 c31a [Accessed 6 Nov. 2019].

Soare, B. 2019. Your smart home is vulnerable to cyber attacks. [online] Heimdal Security Blog. Available at: https://heimdalsecurity.com/blog/smart-home-vulnerable-hacking/ [Accessed 5 Nov. 2019].

Stacey, L. 2019. Will 5G be a miracle worker for IoT connectivity? [online] ITProPortal. Available at: https://www.itproportal.com/features/will-5g-be-a-miracle-worker-for-i ot-connectivity/ [Accessed 1st Nov. 2019].

Trend Micro. 2016. The internet of things ecosystem is broken. How do we fix it?–TrendLabs security intelligence blog. [online] Trendmicro.com. Available at: https://blog.tr endmicro.com/trendlabs-security-intelligence/internet-things-ecosystem-broken-fix/ [Accessed 2 Nov. 2019].

Vodafone. 2019. 5G on Vodafone: The fifth generation of mobile networking. [online] Vodafone.ie. Available at: https://n.vodafone.ie/network/5g.html [Accessed 13 Oct. 2019].

Wipro Limited. 2018. State of cybersecurity report 2018 foresight for the global cybersecu rity community. [online] Wipro. Available at: https://www.wipro.com/content/dam/n exus/en/service-lines/applications/latest-thinking/state-of-cybersecurity-report-2018 .pdf [Accessed 2 Nov. 2019].

12 The Problem of Deepfake Videos and How to Counteract Them in Smart Cities

Samuel McCammon, Claudia Tweedie and Kevin Curran

CONTENTS

12.1 INTRODUCTION

In recent times, the use of "Deepfake" and video altering technology has become an issue, with many individuals using this rising technology for nefarious purposes. The term "Deepfake" is Internet slang used to describe a video based on the internet where the face of at least one of the individuals recorded has been "swapped" with another individual entirely. This means that these videos have the capacity to mislead the public into seeing an individual say or do something which they would otherwise not. Of course, while Deepfakes can have many problematic effects within the Internet and further society, they are not inherently destructive. Many content creators on the Internet have used this technology in the production of comedy videos, and the technology has even proved useful in the creation of Hollywood movies for when an actor is unable to fulfil their role and recasting is not an option.

According to Wagner and Blewer (2019), the term comes from a "portmanteau of deep learning and fake". The term originated from a user of the social media website Reddit, who created and spread a pornographic video with the face of the Hollywood

FIGURE 12.1 Hitler removing Goebbels from a Picture (Source: https://weburbanist.com/2 010/10/27/politics-of-photoshop-15-shady-edits-for-political-purposes/)

actress Gal Gadot spliced onto the face of the original actress (Cole, 2017). While looking at the origin of the media, it is very clear to see the capability of how shadowy the results of the creation of these videos are.

Throughout history, people have used tricks and ways to influence what people see in photos. Several politicians have removed other politicians in photos to show that they no longer align with them. An example of this was when Adolph Hitler had Joseph Goebbels removed from a photograph that was taken in 1937 as shown in Figure 12.1 or when Stalin removed a commissar in another (Figure 12.2). As technology developed, photo manipulation tactics became more advanced, and recently there has been an emergence of creating videos that did not really happen. This can be done in many ways, one of which is a Deepfake.

Deepfakes are mostly videos where someone's face is swapped with someone else's. Although this may seem harmless, the videos can ruin people's lives or careers, or perhaps even start wars. It is also possible to create a Deepfake of someone's voice using similar technologies. It is therefore very important to be able to detect and, if possible, prevent Deepfakes from being created for illegal activities. Depending on the motivations of the creator, they have the potential to alter the public perception on a massive scale. The two most problematic uses of these Deepfake videos, which will be further developed upon in the future,

FIGURE 12.2 Stalin Removing a Commissar from a Picture (Source: https://weburbanist. com/2010/10/27/politics-of-photoshop-15-shady-edits-for-political-purposes/)

are in the creation of Deepfake and revenge pornography and in the creation of "Fake News" and political propaganda, which may have the potential to drastically effect the front of geo-politics.

In the past couple of years Deepfake technology has been used to create pornography and other sexually explicit videos of individuals without their permission or knowledge. Most of these incidents are created for a heterosexual male audience with female actors being Deepfaked into the video. As the use of this technology rises, this sort of content will become much more commonplace on the Internet with celebrities being edited to be present in other pornographic content. Deepfake pornography may also create a crisis with regard to the current extortion and revenge pornography epidemic. An instigator would be able to create a Deepfaked video of an innocent individual and threaten to spread it to the public unless either a monetary value or service is exchanged.

Debatably, an even greater threat of Deepfake videos is their potential to alter public discourse with regard to domestic and foreign politics. In the wake of the 2016 EU referendum in the UK and the election of Donald Trump in the US presidential election, it was clear that English-speaking social media platforms had an epidemic of "Fake News" misleading its users. The term "Fake News" can be defined as "news articles that are intentionally and verifiably false, and could mislead users" (Allcot and Gentzkow, 2017). These Fake News articles were created and spread by outside forces to mislead readers into believing their contents and sow discontent, which could easily manipulate members of society.

Deepfaked videos of political figures could result in widespread disinformation and manipulation. A skilled political agitator would have the ability to do certain actions, such as editing a political opponent to be in a compromising situation to decrease their share of votes in an election, or editing a politician to say things they have not in order to manufacture distrust and resentment. According to Chesney and Citron (2019), as the quality of the Deepfake technology increases, the near future will have Deepfakes "be more vivid and realistic and thus more sharable than the fake news of 2016". It is currently unknown just how much of an effect the emerging Deepfake technology will have on social media in future democratic elections, with some thinking that the creation of Deepfaked videos is too expensive to be used in any wide scale campaign. As Hwang (2018) explains, using Artificial Intelligence is a "relatively costly tool for generating hoaxes".

The future might also hold other nefarious uses for Deepfake technology, with regards to crimes such as fraud and scamming. In September 2019, it was reported that Artificial Intelligence was used to scam the chief executive of a British energy company out of €200,000 (Statt, 2019). The scammers used this Deepfake technology to mimic the voice of the executive's boss and ordered the money to be wired into a Hungarian shell company. As the technology evolves and becomes more widespread, businesses and corporations will have to take security measures to counteract the chance of getting scammed out of substantial amounts of money. However, it seems again that because the technology remains currently costly and time-exhaustive, the entities most at risk for this sort of crime are the high-level corporations who have the resources to make the criminal pay-out worth it.

One of the many uses, seen as legal and ethical by the general public, for Deepfake technology comes in the medium of cinematic movie making. Deepfakes may be used within certain movies to replace actors who cannot otherwise perform in that role, and the director chooses against recasting. A famous example of this technology being used is within the 2016 Disney movie *Rogue One: A Star Wars Story*. Within this movie, Deepfake technology was used to recreate the actor Peter Cushing reprising the role of Grand Moff Tarkin, despite having died in 1994. Using Deepfake technology to replace deceased actors carries some controversy, however. The journalist Dave Itzkoff (2016) stated that "In doing so, they also waded into a postmodern debate about the ethics of prolonging the life span of a character and his likeness beyond that of the actor who originated the role". The use of Deepfakes further blurs the line between actors and the characters they once portrayed for the audience. There are also concerns that at some stage in the future, Deepfake technology may make the acting profession obsolete with special effects being used instead of the actor themselves. Journalist Luke Kemp (2019) asks whether we could "one day see aesthetically convincing digital humans combined with the AI-driven virtual humans to produce entirely artificial actors?"

12.2   HOW DEEPFAKES ARE MADE

There are many different components and technologies which may be involved in the making of Deepfakes. Recreational face swap technology has become a common place feature within the current technological climate, with mobile applications such as Snapchat offering the ability to switch their face with another individual. In 2015, Snapchat bought the Ukrainian startup company 'Looksery' for $159 million dollars, in order to claim the face swap technology which they had developed. According to James Le (2018) of Medium, the three main steps behind this technology are the detection of all the human faces in an image or frame, the detection of the "facial landmarks" upon these faces, and the processing of the image to create a final altered image as an output. The Snapchat application is able to detect the face from an image by going through the low level code behind an image to find any colours which would define the features of a face (Syed, 2019). For example, the area around an eye socket is darker than the rest of the face, while the forehead will be paler.

While Deepfake materials would seem to work similarly to face swapping technology, a key difference between the two, however, is that the creation of Deepfakes relies heavily on Artificial Intelligence, or AI. The field of AI is massive in scope and growing, but has been succinctly described as "the study of mental faculties through the use of computational models" (Charniak and McDermott, 1985). "Machine Learning" is a subset in the field of AI which relies on "computation algorithms that are designed to emulate human intelligence by learning from the surrounding environment" and have been extremely useful in a number of fields including "pattern recognition, computer vision, spacecraft engineering, finance, entertainment, and computational biology" (El Naqa and Murphy, 2015). In other words, machine learning is a form of AI wherein a program uses data and information to make decision for itself. Another term which is used when describing AI is neural network, which can be described as "a series of algorithms that endeavors to recognise underlying relationships in a set of data through a process that mimics the way the human brain operates" (Chen, 2019).

Technology that is capable of facial recognition is a vital component in the creation of Deepfake videos, as the Artificial Intelligence has to single out the face of the character in the original video and splice the secondary face onto it. An effective tool behind face recognition software is the use of a Generative Adversarial Network, or GAN. GAN is another machine learning technique which was created in 2015. As one of its creators, Ian Goodfellow et al. (2014) describes, this technique uses two neural networks to "compete" against one another. When given a training set, such as a video or image, the use of GAN can create original data with the same characteristics as the training set.

Figure 12.3 illustrates the steps taken when a training set in input into the network. The *Generator* is responsible for creating instances of data, while the *Discriminator* authenticates whether the data originates from the training set. Autoencoders are another machine learning technique used in the creation of Deep Fakes. The purpose of an autoencoder is to learn how to "efficiently compress and encode data then learns how to reconstruct the data back from the reduced encoded representation **to** a representation that is as close to the original input as possible" (Badr, 2019). As shown in Figure 12.4, the steps involved in this process are laid out. At the *Encoder* stage the data is compressed into a reduced representation, while at the *Decoder* stage the data is reconstructed to be as close to the input as the machine can.

The autoencoder is used to extract the most important features to recreate the original input. In order to Deepfake an image two separate decoders are used for two different images, with the face of the person pictured being fed into their particular encoder. However, instead of going into their own decoder, the image is swapped to go to the other images decoder. Upon doing this, the decoded image will reconstruct the person in the image to have the features of the person in the second image.

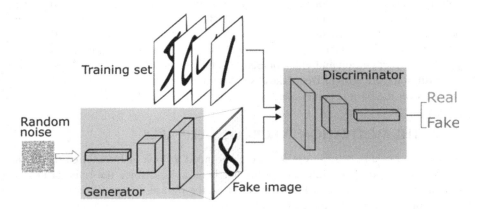

FIGURE 12.3   Generative Adversarial Network (Silva, 2018).

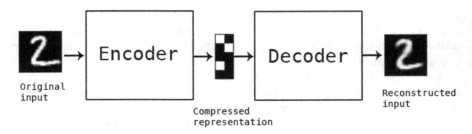

FIGURE 12.4   Autoencoders (Chollet, 2016).

An example of AI which is being used alongside the development of Deepfakes is the "Google Duplex" system. This technology allows users to recreate what sounds like a human voice via telephone calls. Duplex is based around a Recurrent Neural Network, a neural network which is mainly used for speech recognition. The data for which the network learns its information from will be "Google's automatic speech recognition (ASR) technology, as well as features from the audio, the history of the conversation, the parameters of the conversation (e.g. the desired service for an appointment, or the current time of day) and more" (Leviathan, 2018). The program and developers learn from thousands of different voices and conversations stored by Google, even picking up intonations and speech disfluencies in order to sound passably natural.

While the intended use of this software is to create a new interface for the manipulation of computers, focusing on spoken word instructions to contact others via the telephone, the use of Duplex can be corrupted for Deepfaking another individual's voice. The financial fraud case described earlier used AI-based speech imitation software similar to Google Duplex to trick the company into hand over money to the scammers. Open-source machine learning tools such as TensorFlow by Google are also often used in the creation of Deepfakes and their AI. TensorFlow is a "machine learning system that operates at large scale an in heterogeneous environments" with the purpose of supporting "a variety of applications with a focus on training and inference on deep neural networks" (Abadi et al., 2016). In other words, it can be described as an open source AI library. On the whole, TensorFlow has the data stored relevant to and is used for applications which use voice recognition, text analysis, image recognition and video detecting. The data provided through TensorFlow is useful in the creation of Deepfakes as it has the ability to provide the relevant data on whatever medium is being faked, such as an individual's face or voice.

12.3   THE MOTIVATION TO CREATE DEEPFAKES

In order to evaluate why Deepfakes exist, we need to look at Internet culture as a whole. The trope of the "Internet Troll" has been around since the Internet began to gain popularity. The first known mention of the phrase was in 1992 in a Usenet group for debunking myths and legends (Brown, 2016). The group invented their own glossary after a while and listed a troll as someone who would post responses to "attract predictable responses or flames". "Trolls" are people that not only rouse other Internet users with harmless debates or comments, but nowadays they also do things that are much more menacing – for example, creating fake videos of female celebrities in pornographic material. Pornographic content is not just limited to females, nor celebrities. As long as the creator has enough training content for the subject, they can create realistic enough depictions of ordinary people. In 2012, Noelle Martin fell victim to Deepfakes where people found her non-sexual pictures on her social media and used them to create fake pornographic videos. Some of the photos were taken when she was under 18 (Curtis, 2018). This is potentially even worse than those created with celebrity faces – people do not know if it has been faked or not.

There is also a certain sense of a community around Deepfakes. The subreddit *r/deepfakes* would not have developed to the point that it did if there was no community around it. Many of the people participating in the distribution of Deepfakes on *r/SFWdeepfakes* felt angry when the subreddit was taken down, with the users stating that they did not understand why it was different to people Photoshopping faces onto nude models (with one user saying "as long as it's not video it's OK right?") (RedCow1, 2017). Another reason would be for political reasons. As discussed before, in the past, political leaders have doctored images to push a particular agenda. Due to the introduction of Deepfakes, this can now be applied to videos. Shallowfakes are videos that although the content has not changed, they have been manipulated to put across a different point of view than what was previously intended. The day following Nancy Pelosi claiming that Donald Trump was "engaged in a cover up", Trump tweeted a shallowfake that was edited to make it look like she was stuttering through a speech and was therefore incompetent and did not know what she was talking about (Trump, 2019). There have been no detrimental effects to Deepfakes in the political sphere as of yet, but if someone created one, they could sway voters in favour of the other candidate.

12.4   THE SECURITY CONCERNS AROUND DEEPFAKES

Some people may dispute that Deepfakes are nothing more than harmless, or, at the very most, the consequences as a result of Deepfakes are not anything major. However, others would argue that they can have very dangerous consequences. Politically, they could potentially start wars. The United States' relationship with North Korea is unstable, to say the least, and there is a possibility that someone could develop a deepfake where one of the leaders declares war on the other. Currently, Deepfakes can be quite easy to detect using the human eye, but technology advances quickly. Therefore, within the next five years, this scenario could be possible. On a less severe (but still major) scale, people could use Deepfakes as a way to further influence people's political views. Deepfakes have the potential of spreading untrue information about candidates and other political leaders (for example, the tweet that Trump posted of the Shallowfake of Nancy Pelosi). Even if the video is proven false, it could still stick in voters' minds and change their view on the people depicted in them. The security concerns for celebrities are also quite severe. Not only can they be used to generate pornographic content, but they can also be used to smear a celebrity's status by, for example, creating a Deepfake of them using a slur or committing a crime. This can then ruin their career, as much like political smear campaigns, it can leave a lasting impact on people's opinions of them, even if the video is proven to be fake.

Political leaders and other public figures are not the only possible victims of Deepfakes. As a society, we have become accustomed to uploading images that represent our lives on that day. These could be downloaded and used in a Deepfake video without the subject knowing about it. Our digital footprint is so vast, and it will be hard to remove everything, even if we try. Predators can therefore prey on this vulnerability and use the pictures to develop Deepfakes, sometimes for revenge or sometimes for no reason at all. People could use Deepfakes as a way to impersonate someone who works at a company and they could further develop spear phishing strategies. According to the Wall Street Journal, a Deepfake was created to demand a transfer of more than €200,000 by using it to impersonate a chief executive's voice. The CEO of the company believed he was speaking to his manager, and he was told it was urgent (Stupp, 2019). With people becoming more aware of phishing emails, this is a new and dangerous way for fraudsters to scam people. As the Deepfake technology progresses, the likelihood that they could be implicated in legal battles also increases. If the Deepfakes are convincing enough, there is a potential that people could use them to convict others for a crime they did not commit. Alternatively, public figures could claim that an incriminating or offensive video is not them, but a Deepfake. People could also create videos that cause panic using Deepfakes, such as emergency broadcasts and terrorist threats (Townsend, 2019). Overall, the concerns in terms of personal and public security for Deepfakes are massive. People's lives could be put in jeopardy and careers can crumble as a result of being a victim to one. What could be interpreted as harmless fun by one person could be catastrophic to someone else's life.

12.5   HOW ORGANISATIONS ARE COUNTERACTING THE USE OF DEEP FAKE TECHNOLOGY

With the risks and dangers that the emerging Deepfake technologies are bringing to businesses, organisations, society and individuals, the number of security measures and techniques which can be used to detect Deepfake mediums have been growing at a great pace in order to combat Deepfakes. For many of the instances of financial fraud using Deepfakes, basic security precautions can be used to combat the scammer. A password or security question may be appropriate to use when an individual within an organisation is dealing with a large amount of data. This will create an extra barrier for any scammer who uses a Deepfake to impersonate being a high level member of the company demanding the transfer of money. However, this is not a perfect solution as it, like every security solution which uses passwords, is only as strong as the user makes it. A weak password or security question could be easily tackled by a competent scammer. This solution may also lead to an atmosphere of distrust and paranoia within the organisation as there would be no strong way to verify whether the orders of a higher-up individual are legitimate or not. Instead, it may be better to use a technological solution to tackle the Deepfake issue. While Deepfaked images and videos can work well enough to pass to the human eye, the effect they create is not perfect. Technology can be used to detect these imperfections, and thus determine whether the input media is a fake or real. An example of one of these imperfections is that often times, a Deepfake image or video will feature a head pose inconsistent with the face. According to the research conducted by Yang et al. (2019), "Deep Fakes are created by splicing synthesized face region into the original image, and in doing so, introducing errors that can be revealed when 3D head poses are estimated from the face images". The solution for which they suggest is to use a support-vector machine to evaluate the features and landmarks of a face within an image or video, to see if it corresponds with the angle which the head is tilted and determine whether the presented image is real or not.

Another solution similar to analysing an image for "head tilts" is the analysing of an image to detect whether the image contains any distinctive artifacts, generated from the limited resolution that occur from the Deepfake algorithm. According to Li and Lyu (2018), this limitation of Deepfake technology occurs as the algorithm "can only synthesize face images of a fixed size, and they must undergo an affine warping to match the configuration of the source's face". A deep learning method may be used to detect these distinctive artifacts in the image by "comparing the generated face areas and their surrounding region with a dedicated Convolutional Neural Network (CNN) model". This solution carries the advantage of saving more time and resources compared to other solutions, as there is no need to feed it another Deepfaked image as a comparison.

The "PRNU" of an image can also be analysed to determine whether it is a Deep fake. The acronym PRNU stands for Photo Response Non-Uniformity and is used to describe a noise pattern produced by the light sensors on a digital camera. The researchers Koopman et al. (2018) speculate that as each PRNU is unique to a camera, it can be used to detect whether a video is a Deepfake or not. The analysis of PRNU is said to be important as "it is expected that the manipulation of the facial area will affect the local PRNU pattern in the video frames", whereas this will not happen in videos in which the contents are faked (Hui 2018). There are multiple other methods of detecting Deepfake features, with Agarwal and Varshney (2019) listing "visual artifacts, image quality, lipsync, blinking, or warping for classifaction" as features which can be used to discern the real from the fake. Another method of tackling Deepfake videos is through tracking the video back to its original source to see if it is legitimate. According to the research provided by Hasan and Salah (2019), one method of doing this is to use "Blockchain" and "Smart Contract" technologies. This research describes Blockchain as having "the ability to provide immutable and tamper-proof data and transactions in a decentralized distributed ledger" which can then be used to "present a decentralized Proof Authenticity (PoA) system".

The term Smart Contract is used to describe a protocol within a Blockchain, which allows secure transactions without any third party involvement. The chapter also describes how a Smart Contract will utilise "the hashes of the interplanetary file system (IPFS) used to store digital content and its metadata". The chapter summarizes its solution to the Deep Fake problem by stating that it "relies on the principle that if the content can be credibly traced to a trusted or reputable source, the content can then be real and authentic".

12.6   DEEPFAKES AND THE LAW

With the potential and threats of Deepfake technology rising quickly since the technology's development, countries and courts around the world have enacted laws to prevent Deepfake technologies to be used in nefarious activity, before it has a chance to make too much traction. The US state of California has banned the creation and distribution of Deepfake videos, images or other recordings within 60 days of an election (Paul, 2019). This measure is an attempt to protect potential voters from succumbing to malicious misinformation and fake news from an unscrupulous source, so that proper elections can be held for every candidate involved. Otherwise in America, introducing legislation to prohibit the creation and distribution of deep fake videos as there is an argument that this may conflict with the state's constitutional First Amendment, the protection of free speech for people and the press. According to Harris (2018), while Deepfake videos are not necessarily covered by the First Amendment, due to the fact that they are often false and obscene, the fact is that many courts "are still hesitant when dealing with false speech to avoid chilling otherwise protected or worthy speech". Harris also states that Deepfake videos will often fall into "Fair Use" categories and thus would be protected against potential copyright infringement.

In the UK, there is currently no laws which prohibit the manufacture and distribution of Deepfake pornography or political videos. In October of 2018, the Women and Equalities Committee called for parliament to implement criminalize the "nonconsensual and distribution of intimate sexual images, on the basis of the victim's lack of consent" (Parliament, House of Commons, 2018). This law would cover the outlawing of the creation and distribution of Deep Fake pornography throughout the UK. While there are currently no significant laws that can be used to combat Deepfakes and the new problems they are creating, many websites and social media platforms have taken action based on their own ethics. Gallagher of the Huffington Post (2019) has noted that the websites PornHub, Twitter and GIF-hosting website Gfycat have all placed bans on content which utilizes Deepfake technology to create pornographic content. The community which was the origin of the rise of pornographic Deepfake content, r/deepfake of the social media website Reddit, was also banned by the website's administrators in 2018 with Deepfake pornography also being banned from the website entirely (Lutkin, 2018). As Deepfake mediums are such a new technology and are rapidly developing alongside the growth of AI software, it may be very difficult for courts and website administrators to develop a plan on how to tackle these problems, especially with the Deepfake technology improving to make the effect increasingly unnoticeable. As such, it is hard to know just what the future has in store for Deepfakes and the ways in which they will be tackled.

12.7   THE FUTURE OF DEEPFAKES

No one really knows what the future of Deepfakes holds. Deepfakes are so new and are getting so lifelike so quickly, and there is no doubt that this trend will continue. Not only will the technology to make them will become more accurate, but also more data will be able to be collected by AI and added to the learning set to make it more realistic. The potential of using them in legal cases only increases the more realistic the Deepfakes become. People could therefore get away with crimes they committed or could accuse others of crimes they did not commit. Phishing scams could continue to get more complex, as less people would expect someone's voice to be fake than an email. Detecting Deepfakes will get harder the more lifelike it appears, and that could bring about its own problems.

On the other hand, it could also bring numerous advantages. The technology will continue to get easier to use, and although this can be a bad thing, it opens exploration for developers to create virtual assistants and for independent video creators to be able to edit their movies or sketches. Companies and government will most likely continue to fight against the illegal use of Deepfakes. There are no plans to introduce laws other than the laws already introduced in California for 2020, but the implications of Deepfakes can be life-altering, as well as they could easily be used to sway voters. Therefore, some would argue that the videos are against democracy, which does not even consider the cybersecurity dangers to.

12.8   CONCLUSION

The potential of Deepfake technology for use in nefarious practices is great in number at the current time, and will only expand as the technology grows and the Deepfake effect becomes much more subtle to human eyes and to technical detection programs. At the moment the main issues Deepfake technology seem to be used for are pornography, political subterfuge, extortion and financial scamming. It is highly important for businesses and organisations to find a way to tackle the technology as it arises, considering the security risks it may pose to a business's finance, a government's credibility and individuals' freedoms. The creation of Deepfake content is highly linked to Artificial Intelligence and Machine Learning. AI software created by technology companies such as Google has been taken and used in the framework of the development of these Deepfakes. Examples of this are in the Google Duplex and TensorFlow being used to increase the effectiveness of the content being created.

The two main technological components used to create Deepfakes are the *Generative Adversarial Network* and *Autoencoder*. The term "GAN" is used to refer to a machine learning technique wherein two neural networks are used to compete with each other in order to create original data from an original dataset. The term Autoencoder is used to define a method of encoding an input in a compressed representation, before being decoded into a reconstructed version of the original input. As Deepfake technology is closely linked to AI, itself a rapidly developing field of research, the methods of combatting it are significantly limited at this point in time. Cybersecurity professionals are currently engaging in a form of an "arms race" with the bad actors to find a solution to determine whether images, videos and voices are genuine before the technology develops to a point where it would be extremely difficult to do so. The main method being used to detect Deepfakes is to use technology to find minor irregularities and differences that the human eye cannot typically see.

Examples of these irregularities in Deepfakes are head angles, facial resolution and visual artifacts.

Due to the relatively short time span between the first development of Deepfakes and the present, there has been very little change with regard to legislation and laws of courts around the world. Many countries already have laws against sexual harassment and non-consensual pornography, under which the creation and distribution of Deepfake pornography would fall. Likewise, many countries also have laws against financial fraud and extortion, so that using Deepfakes to these ends would also end up being illegal. However, most countries and courts do not have any laws put in place with regard to the distribution of Deepfakes that intend to spread misinformation and discontent, with some countries even debating whether making these unlawful would violate their free speech laws. The subsequent days and years ahead will see a further effort to quell and combat the issues of Deepfake, from legislators and judicial figures, to software developers and security consultants. Whether the Deepfake problem can be completely overcome and extinguished from the Internet will remain to be seen, however, as the technology and field of AI develops beyond what is possible at this time.

REFERENCES

Abadi, M., et al., 2016. TensorFlow: A system for large-scale machine learning. In: 12th USENIX Symposium on Operating Systems Design and Implementation, 2–4 November 2016, Savannah, Georgia. Available: https://www.usenix.org/system/files/conference/osdi16/osdi16-abadi.pdf[Accessed 11 Nov. 2019].

Agarwal, S., and L. Varshney. 2019. Limits of deepfake detection: A robust estimation viewpoint. arXiv:1905.03493.

Allcott, H., and M. Gentzkow. 2017. Social media and fake news in the 2016 election. *Journal of Economic Perspectives*, 31(2), pp. 211–236.

Badr, W. 2019. Auto-encoder: What is it? And what is it used for? (Part 1). Available: https://towardsdatascience.com/auto-encoder-what-is-it-and-what-is-it-used-for-part-1-3e5c6f017726 [Accessed 11 Nov. 2019].

Brown, K. 2016. From LOL to LULZ, the evolution of the internet troll over 24 years. Splinter News, 1 Jun 2016. Available at: https://splinternews.com/from-lol-to-lulz-the-evolution-of-the-internet-troll-o-1793855652 [Accessed 1 Nov. 2019].

Charniak, E., and D. McDermott. 1985. *Introduction to Artificial Intelligence* (p. 6). Reading, MA: Addison-Wesley.

Chollet, F. 2016. Building autoencoders in keras, *what are autoencoders?*, The Keras Blog Available: https://blog.keras.io/building-autoencoders-in-keras.html [Accessed 11 Nov. 2019].

Cole, S. 2017. AI-assisted fake porn is here and we're all f*cked. Available: https://www.vice.com/en_us/article/gydydm/gal-gadot-fake-ai-porn [Accessed 07 Nov. 2019].

Curtis, C. 2018. Deepfakes are being weaponized to silence women: But this woman is fighting back. The Next Web, 1 Sept 2018, Available at: https://thenextweb.com/tech/2018/10/05/deepfakes-are-being-weaponized-to-silence-women-but-this-woman-is-fighting-back/

El Naqa, I., and M. J. Murphy. 2015. What is machine learning? In *Machine Learning in Radiation Oncology*, I. El Naqa, R. Li, and M. Murphy (Eds.) (p. 3–11). Switzerland: Springer.

Gallagher, S. 2019. What are deepfakes, are they illegal and can they be stopped? Available: https://www.huffingtonpost.co.uk/entry/what-is-deep-fake-pornography-and-is-it-illegal-in-the-uk_uk_5bf4197ce4b0376c9e68f8c5?guccounter=1&guce_referrer=aHR0cHM6Ly93d3cuZ29vZ2xlLmNvbS8&guce_referrer_si [Accessed 13 Nov. 2019].

Goodfellow, I., J. Pouget-Abadie, M. Mirza, B. Xu, D. Warde-Farley, S. Ozair, A. Courville, and Y. Bengio. 2014. *Generative Adversarial Nets*. Montreal: Universite de Montreal.

Harris, D. 2018. DeepFakes: false pornography is here and the law cannot help you. *Duke Law & Tech Review*, 99(4), pp. 99–129.

Hasan, H., and K. Salah. 2019. Combating deepfake videos using blockchain and smart contracts. *IEEE Access*, 7, pp. 41596–41606.

Hui, J. 2018. How deep learning fakes videos (Deepfake) and how to detect it? Available: https://medium.com/@jonathan_hui/how-deep-learning-fakes-videos-deepfakes-and-how-to-detect-it-c0b50fbf7cb9 [Accessed 11 Nov. 2019].

Hwang, T. 2018. A vote against deepfakes. *NewScientist*, 239, pp. 22–23.

Itzkoff, D. 2016. How 'rogue one' brought back familiar faces. Available: https://www.nytimes.com/2016/12/27/movies/how-rogue-one-brought-back-grand-moff-tarkin.html [Accessed 11 Nov. 2019].

Kemp, L. 2019. In the age of deepfakes, could virtual actors put humans out of business? Available: https://www.theguardian.com/film/2019/jul/03/in-the-age-of-deepfakes-could-virtual-actors-put-humans-out-of-business [Accessed 11 Nov. 2019].

Koopman, M., A. Macarulla Rodriguez, and Z. Geradts. 2018. Detection of Deepfake Video Manipulation, IMVIP 2018, Belfast, UK, pp. 84–96.

Le, J. 2018. Snapchat's Filters: How computer vision recognizes your face. Available: https://medium.com/cracking-the-data-science-interview/snapchats-filters-how-computer-vision-recognizes-your-face-9907d6904b91 [Accessed 11 Nov. 2019].

Leviathan, Y. 2018. Google duplex: An AI system for accomplishing real-world tasks over the phone. Available: https://ai.googleblog.com/2018/05/duplex-ai-system-for-natural-conversation.html [Accessed 11 Nov. 2019].

Li, Y., and S. Lyu. 2018. Exposing deepfake videos by detecting face warping artifacts. https://arxiv.org/abs/1811.00656.

Lutkin, A. 2018. 'Deepfake' pornography has been banned from reddit. Jezebel. Available: https://jezebel.com/deepfake-pornography-has-been-banned-from-reddit-1822838301 [Accessed 13 Nov. 2019].

Parliament. House of Commons. 2018. *Sexual Harassment of Women and Girls in Public Places* (HC 2017-2019 (5)). London: Women and Equalities Committee.

Paul, K. 2019. California makes 'deepfake' videos illegal, but law may be hard to enforce. Available: https://www.theguardian.com/us-news/2019/oct/07/california-makes-deepfake-videos-illegal-but-law-may-be-hard-to-enforce [Accessed 13 Nov. 2019].

RedCowl. 2017. /r/Deepfakes has been banned. Reddit, 4 July 2017, Available at: https://www.reddit.com/r/SFWdeepfakes/comments/7vy36n/rdeepfakes_has_been_banned/ [Accessed 13 Nov. 2019].

Silva, T. 2018. An intuitive introduction to geneative adversarial networks (GANs). FreeCodeCamp, Available: https://www.freecodecamp.org/news/an-intuitive-introduction-to-generative-adversarial-networks-gans-7a2264a81394/ [Accessed 11 Nov. 2019].

Statt, N. 2019. Thieves are now using AI deepfakes to trick companies into sending them money. The Verge, 5th Sept. 2019, Available: https://www.theverge.com/2019/9/5/20851248/deepfakes-ai-fake-audio-phone-calls-thieves-trick-companies-stealing-money [Accessed 11 Nov. 2019].

Stupp, C. 2019. Fraudsters used AI to mimic CEO's voice in unusual cybercrime case. *Wall Street Journal*, 30 August 2019. Available: https://www.wsj.com/articles/fraudsters-use-ai-to-mimic-ceos-voice-in-unusual-cybercrime-case-11567157402.

Syed, A. 2019. How do snapchat filters work? Available: https://www.technobyte.org/how -snapchat-filters-work/ [Accessed 11 Nov. 2019].

Townsend, C. 2019. Deepfake technology: Implications for the future. US Cybersecurity Magazine, June 2019, Available: https://www.uscybersecurity.net/deepfake/ [Accessed 12 Nov. 2019].

Trump, D. 2019. Pelosi stammers through news conference. Twitter, August 2019, Available: https://twitter.com/realDonaldTrump/status/1131728912835383300 [Accessed 3 Nov. 2019].

Wagner, T., and A. Blewer. 2019.The word real is no longer real: Deepfakes, gender, and the challenges of AI-altered video. *Open Information Science*, 3(3), pp. 32–46.

Yang, X., Y. Li, & S. Lyu. 2019. *Exposing Deep Fakes Using Inconsistent Head Poses*. Brighton, UK: IEEE.

BIBLIOGRAPHY

Ding, L. 2019. Deepfake technology: A paradox of economic and political possibilities. Masters of Media.

Iperov. 2019. DeepFaceLab. Available: https://github.com/iperov/DeepFaceLab [Accessed 20 Oct. 2019].

Giles, M. 2018. The GANfather: The man who's given machines the gift of imagination. Available: https://www.technologyreview.com/s/610253/the-ganfather-the-man-w hos-given-machines-the-gift-of-imagination/ [Accessed 5 Nov. 2019].

Nicholson, C. 2019. A beginner's guide to generative adversarial networks (GANs). Available: https://skymind.ai/wiki/generative-adversarial-network-gan [Accessed 27 Oct. 2019]. (Accessed: November 3rd 2019).

BBC. 2019. Google makes deepfakes to fight deepfakes. Available: https://www.bbc.co.uk/ news/technology-49837927 [Accessed 5 Nov. 2019].

Fingas, J. 2019. Amazon joins Facebook's fight against deepfakes. Available: https://www.eng adget.com/2019/10/21/amazon-joins-facebook-deepfake-challenge/ [Accessed 5 Nov. 2019].

Patrini, G. 2019. Mapping the deepfake landscape. Available: https://deeptracelabs.com/ mapping-the-deepfake-landscape/ [Accessed 5 Nov. 2019].

Thornhill, J. 2019. New tools are evolving in the fight against deepfakes. Available: https://ww w.ft.com/content/4183b400-f960-11e9-98fd-4d6c20050229 [Accessed 5 Nov. 2019].

Fischer, W. 2019. California's governer signed new deepfake laws for politics and porn, but experts say they threaten free speech. Available: https://www.businessinsider.com/cal ifornia-deepfake-laws-politics-porn-free-speech-privacy-experts-2019-10?r=US&IR= T [Accessed 9 Nov. 2019].

Goggin, B. 2019. From porn to 'game of thrones': How deepfakes and realistic-looking fake videos hit it big. Available: https://www.businessinsider.com/deepfakes-explained-the -rise-of-fake-realistic-videos-online-2019-6?r=US&IR=T [Accessed 13 Nov. 2019).

O'Sullivan, D. 2019. Deepfake videos: Inside the pentagon's race against disinformation. Available: https://edition.cnn.com/interactive/2019/01/business/pentagons-race-ag ainst-deepfakes/ [Accessed 13 Nov. 2019].

Martinez, A. 2018. The blockchain solution to our deepfake problems. Available: https://ww w.wired.com/story/the-blockchain-solution-to-our-deepfake-problems/ [Accessed 13 Nov. 2019].

Centre of International Governance Innovation. 2018. What is blockchain? Available: https:// www.cigionline.org/multimedia/what-blockchain [Accessed 13 Nov. 2019]. (Accessed: 13th November 2019).

Charleer, S. 2018. Why deepfakes are a good thing. Available: https://towardsdatascienc e.com/why-deepfakes-are-a-good-thing-10ceb86deaed [Accessed 14 Nov. 2019)

Dhillon, S. 2019. An optimistic view of deepfakes. Available: https://techcrunch.com/2019/07 /04/an-optimistic-view-of-deepfakes/ [Accessed 14 Nov. 2019).

Malaria Must Die. 2019. David Beckham speaks nine languages to launch malaria must die voice petition. Available: https://www.youtube.com/watch?v=QiiSAvKJIHo [Accessed 14 Nov. 2019].

13 The Rise of Ransomware Aided by Vulnerable IoT Devices

David McElhinney and Kevin Curran

CONTENTS

13.1 INTRODUCTION

When ransomware first appeared, security teams seldom saw it as a threat (Des, 2018). Victims were generally home computer users who did not pay attention to suspicious websites or cryptic email attachments (Des, 2018). Early ransomware from the late 90s to 2010 were mainly just pranks and vandalism where the goal of the hacker was to gain notoriety (Des, 2018). Generally, ransom demands would show a message on-screen to offer spyware removal (Des, 2018). A fee was required to repair the non-existent problems of the victim's computer, but in reality, the computer was working fine (Des, 2018). During mid-2011, because of anonymous payment services, the first major outbreaks in ransomware occurred (Sjouwerman, 2016). In the first two quarters of 2011, about 30,000 ransomware samples were detected, and in the third quarter, detections were doubled to 60,000 (Sjouwerman, 2016). Since 2011 ransomware has risen sharply.

Ransomware has become appealing to hackers who seek an alternative to the banker Trojan due to its offering many advantages to developers (Kettering, 2016). This is because it is more straightforward to develop, provides easy access to funds and does not need to always be connected to a command and control centre to execute (Kettering, 2016). Cryptocurrencies such as Bitcoin provide excellent anonymity and also give the edge of allowing payments with a very small transaction fee (VanillaPlus, 2017). This makes ransomware a very lucrative business for criminals. Nowadays, ransomware is much more deadly. Currently, ransomware attacks are being targeted at enterprise, cloud and data infrastructures, because these are more profitable against organisations (Palmer, 2019). Files on PCs and servers are not the only targets of criminals, their aim is to also lockdown full network environments to prevent organisations recovering from a backup which ensures that victims do not have a choice when it comes to paying (Palmer, 2019). In May 2017, the WannaCry ransomware struck Britain's National Health Service (NHS) (Fruhlinger, 2018). This cost the NHS £92 million and the NHS was found guilty of using out of date systems such as Windows XP (Field, 2018). The minimum annual global revenue for ransomware is $1 billion and the cost for businesses because of this is $8 billion per year with the average cost being $133,000 (Bera, 2019).

Ransomware attackers are now being a lot more selective when it comes to choosing who to attack (Cabrera, 2019). This is because the attackers are looking at organisations who will most likely fall for an attack and those who will likely pay a higher ransom (Cabrera, 2019). Figure 13.1 shows the industries targeted in the first half of 2019.

Nobody would like to pay a ransom as doing so funds criminals and motivates them to create better ransomware to target even more victims (Curran, 2017). Victims cannot be guaranteed that paying the ransom will result in the files being decrypted which has been the case on numerous occasions (Curran, 2017). If the files are worth the ransom, more often than not people will pay. Usually, the ransom is much cheaper than losing the files (Curran, 2017). This is why organisations are a big target of ransomware as losing access to their data would be devastating.

There are two main types of ransomware which are crypto ransomware and locker ransomware (Kaspersky, 2019). Crypto ransomware is used to encrypt all of the victim's files and demand a ransom in order to decrypt the files (Kaspersky, 2019). Locker ransomware operates differently, it does not encrypt files (Kaspersky, 2019). Instead, the victim is locked from using their device while the criminals demand a ransom in order to unlock the device (Kaspersky, 2019). Figure 13.2 gives a high-level overview of how ransomware works. Steps 4 and 5 show how files are searched for and encrypted, with locker ransomware files not encrypted.

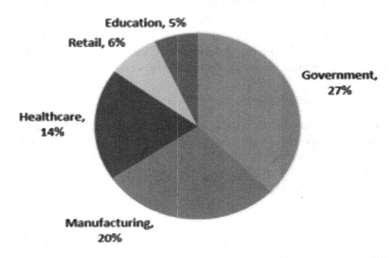

FIGURE 13.1 Ransomware Targets the First Half of 2019 (Cabrera, 2019).

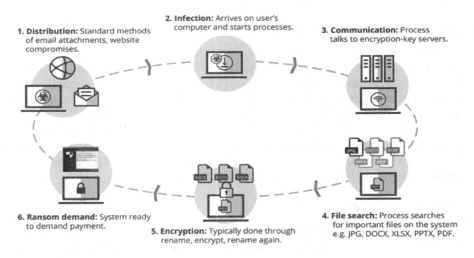

FIGURE 13.2 How Ransomware Works (McAfee, 2017).

13.2 ATTACK VECTORS

There are many ways in which ransomware can infect your PC which will be discussed below. For one to protect themselves from ransomware they must understand how it spreads.

13.2.1 EMAIL ATTACHMENTS AND LINKS

This is the most common attack vector for criminals, mainly due to the fact it requires little effort, and lots of people are still not concerned when clicking email links (Betternet, 2017). This method functions by a criminal sending a legitimate looking email that looks like it is from a reputable company; the recipient is asked to open an attached file or click a link (Betternet, 2017). The attached file could be a word document that is laced with a malicious macro, or the link could be to a drive-by download site. By opening the attachment or clicking the link the recipient will get infected with the ransomware and have their files encrypted.

13.2.2 ONLINE ADVERTISEMENTS

This is usually called malvertising, this attack vector is deployed through advertisements that you see pop up on websites (Betternet, 2017). Accidentally clicking on one of these advertisements will infect the user with ransomware. Criminals to reach a wider range of targets purchase these ads to deploy on legitimate sites such as social media and online shopping (Betternet, 2017).

13.2.3 DOWNLOADS

Criminals attract users with free downloads – this could be from illegal torrent sites or legitimate platforms like the Google Play Store – once the file is opened the user gets infected with the ransomware (Betternet, 2017).

13.2.4 WATER HOLE ATTACKS

Another method for distributing ransomware is through waterhole attacks. The hacker learns which website the targets visit (Rankin, 2017). The attack will then look for vulnerabilities on these websites. If any vulnerabilities are present then the hacker will use techniques to exploit these vulnerabilities, commonly hackers will inject JavaScript or HTML code to redirect the victim to a vulnerable website which hosts the code (Rankin, 2017). Once the victim clicks the infected object they are redirected to the malicious site to install or update software (O'Kane et al., 2018). For example, it could be an offer for a free anti-virus update or a Java update. Once downloaded the user is infected with the ransomware.

13.2.5 EXPLOIT KITS

Exploit kits are software packages which are designed to locate security vulnerabilities in the victim's computer (Comodo, 2018a). For example, vulnerabilities in Adobe Flash Player, Java, Microsoft Silverlight, etc. Criminals inject code into a legitimate website to redirect users to the malicious website. No additional actions are required by the victim (Comodo, 2018a). Once the file downloads the weakness is automatically exploited in the victim's computer in order to execute the ransomware. These are commonly called drive-by-downloads.

13.2.6 BOTNETS

Botnets can also be used to distribute ransomware. Botnets are a network of infected computers that are under the control of the bot-herder (Cloudflare, 2019). The bot herder can command every single computer on the botnet to carry out criminal activities (Cloudflare, 2019). Botnets can be used for things such as email spam, distributed denial of service (DDOS) attacks, and also ransomware (Cloudflare, 2019). For example, the bot herder can command every computer on the botnet to install ransomware. For large botnets, this is extremely profitable. A great example is the Gameover ZeuS Botnet which was used to distribute the CrytpLocker ransomware, CryptoLocker was estimated to have infected more than 234,000 computers worldwide (Leinwand, 2014).

13.3 EVOLUTION OF RANSOMWARE

This section will discuss how ransomware has risen over the last 30 years from when it was first sighted in 1989. Encryption is meant to bring privacy to users in order to keep their data safe, but instead, hackers have been using ransomware as a type of blackmail and only decrypting the data when the ransom is paid (Brunau, 2018). Windows has been a popular target for ransomware due to its security loopholes and wide market share. Nearly all pieces of ransomware discussed below are targeted at Windows unless stated otherwise.

13.3.1 1989

The first ransomware virus that was ever documented was the Aids Trojan in 1989 (KnowBe4, 2019a). The trojan was developed by Joseph Popp in 1989 who gave 20,000 infected floppy disks to the people who attended the AIDS conference for the World Health Organisation (KnowBe4, 2019a). Each of the floppy disks was labelled "AIDS Information – Introductory Diskettes" and contained the virus (Kraft Business Systems, 2019). After the 90th reboot of the virus being installed the virus ran and hid important directories along with encrypting user files (Kraft Business Systems, 2019). Victims were displayed a message asking for $189 to be sent to a PO Box in Panama (KnowBe4, 2019a). Figure 13.3 shows the screen that victims saw once infected (KnowBe4, 2014b).

13.3.2 2005

Sixteen years later in 2005 ransomware resurfaced. GPCoder was targeted at a variety of file extensions on Windows systems (Fawkes, 2017). Once found, a copy of the files is made in encrypted form and the originals are deleted from the system (Fawkes, 2017). The files were encrypted using RSA-1024-bit encryption making it difficult to decrypt the files (Fawkes, 2017). Users were then displayed a message directing them to a txt file on their desktop that contained the details on how to pay the ransom and unlock the files which were affected (Fawkes, 2017).

13.3.3 2006

Then the Archievus Trojan was identified. Archievus used 1024-bit RSA encryption and encrypted the My Documents folder (Fawkes, 2017). The victim could still use

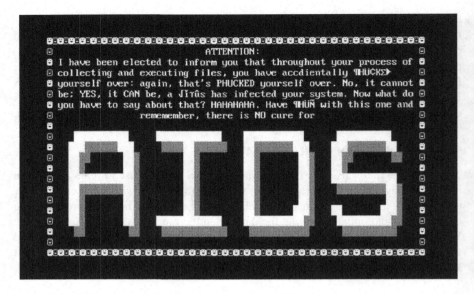

FIGURE 13.3   Aids Trojan Infection Message (KnowBe4, 2019a).

their computer, but many people store their working documents in this folder so the effect was quite large (Fawkes, 2017). To remove the virus, victims were sent to a website to purchase a 30 digit password (Fawkes, 2017).

13.3.4   2007

The year 2007 brought a different type of ransomware: one which did not use encryption (MalwareFox, 2016). Instead, victims were locked out of their system and made pay a ransom in order to access their system again (MalwareFox, 2016). The WinLock ransomware displayed pornographic images on the victims PC until the victim sent an SMS to a premium number which charged $10 (MalwareFox, 2016). Reportedly the criminals behind this ransomware earned as much as $16m in one month (Leydon, 2010).

13.3.5   2012

Ransomware called the Reveton worm appeared in 2012; the worm locks the victim out of their computer and displays a screen from a law enforcement agency (KnowBe4, 2012). The worm is used to scared victims by saying that they committed a crime such as downloading child pornography or pirated software (KnowBe4, 2012). Some cases of Reveton displayed webcam footage to scare the victim into thinking they are a criminal (O'Kane et al., 2018). Reveton was mainly spread through the BlackHole exploit kit (KrebsonSecurity, 2012). In order for the victim to regain computer access, payment had to be made using a prepaid voucher service (O'Kane et al., 2018). Figure 13.4 shows what the lock screen looked like.

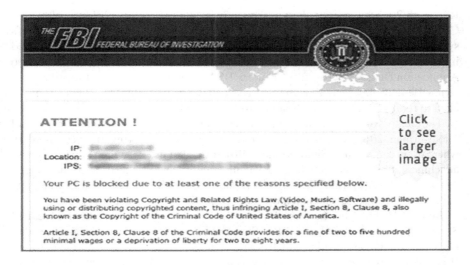

FIGURE 13.4   Reventon Worm Lock Screen (KnowBe4, 2012).

13.3.6   2013

In 2013, CryptoLocker opened ransomware on the grand scale (Fruhlinger, 2017b). This ransomware was spread in many different ways such as through email message attachments, links or drive-by download sites (Nachreiner, 2013). Upon execution, CryptoLocker contacts the command and control server to generate a public/private key for the victim's computer with the use of RSA and Advanced Encryption Standard (AES) 2048-bit encryption (Nachreiner, 2013). The private key was stored on the attacker's command and control server, but the public key was stored in a registry entry on the victim's computer (Nachreiner, 2013). The ransomware encrypted files with certain extensions while deleting the originals (Sjouwerman, 2016). Victims are threatened to pay within three days or else the private key will be deleted (Sjouwerman, 2016). Payments could be received via bitcoin or prepaid cash vouchers (Sjouwerman, 2016).

Android ransomware was discovered in mid-2013 and appeared as a fake antivirus program (Lipovský et al., 2016). The ransomware's background service makes the phone basically impractical to use as it keeps displaying malware warning popups whenever the victim tries to launch an application (Lipovský et al., 2016). The pop-ups are perpetual each time you ignore one another one pops up, after six hours it gets more aggressive and starts showing pornographic images which the victim cannot close (Lipovský et al., 2016). The victim will be made pay $89.99 to remove the ransomware and the credit card details are now in the hands of the hacker and sent over the network unencrypted (Lipovský et al., 2016).

13.3.7   2014

CryptoDefense was discovered in February 2014 and was mainly spread through spear phishing email campaigns (KnowBe4, 2014a). Just like CryptoLocker, it uses

RSA with 2048-bit keys to encrypt the victim's data (KnowBe4, 2014a) – although, CryptoDefense used the Windows CryptoAPI to create the key pair on the victim's system (KnowBe4, 2014a). The issue with this is that the private key was stored in plaintext on the victim's computer (KnowBe4, 2014a). Victims just had to go to Application Data > Microsoft > Crypto > RSA folder on their PC for the private key (KnowBe4, 2014a). Even though there was a flaw, CryptoDefense hackers still managed to return $34,000 in the first month (KnowBe4, 2014a).

The creators of CryptoDefense then released an enhanced version called CryptoWall (Sjouwerman, 2016). This had a few differences, such as not storing the encryption key where users can reach it (Sjouwerman, 2016). Instead of users having to open an email attachment, Cryptowall exploited a Java vulnerability and was distributed via dangerous advertisements on websites such as Disney, Facebook and The Guardian newspaper where infected users had their drives encrypted (Sjouwerman, 2016).

May 2014 brought the first file-encrypting ransomware for Android called SimpLocker (Lipovský et al., 2016). SimpLocker fools the victim through the disguise of a popular application which is a popular technique used for Android malware (Lipovský et al., 2016). SimpLocker was also distributed via a trojan downloader; these are applications with the purpose of downloading other malware (Lipovský et al., 2016). Once installed the victim sees a fake FBI message asking for a ransom anywhere between $200 and $500, and accuses the victim of viewing illegal content (Lipovský et al., 2016). The victim's SD card files are then encrypted using the AES cypher (Lipovský et al., 2016). The encryption key was hardcoded inside the binary as plain text which made it complicated to decipher (Lipovský et al., 2016). SimpLocker also used the Extensible Messaging and Presence Protocol (XMPP) to communicate with the command and control server; this made it increasingly difficult to trace the command and control server than if HTTP was used (Lipovský et al., 2016). Synolocker was discovered first in August 2014 (KnowBe4, 2014a). This ransomware encrypted files saved on the NAS and also changes the admin web page to ask for a ransom (OpenDNS Security Research, 2014). Servers who have port 5000 and port 5001 are vulnerable to this ransomware (Super User, 2016). Payment must be made of 0.6 bitcoin to a website on the Tor network to decrypt the data (Super User, 2016). Synolocker disables the victim from accessing the system through SSH and Telnet (OpenDNS Security Research, 2014).

13.3.8   2015

TeslaCrypt appeared in early February 2015 and was administered by the Angler and Nuclear browser exploit kits (SecureWorks, 2015). In the beginning, the ransomware targeted computer gamers and infected their game files, but later versions targeted a wide range of files such as docx, pdf, etc. (360 Total Security, 2016). Files were encrypted via the AES-256-bit encryption (SecureWorks, 2015). TeslaCrypt used the Tor network for command and control; this did not require network connectivity in order to encrypt files which made prevention and recovery much more complex (SecureWorks, 2015). TeslaCrypt shut down in May 2016 and released the master decryption key allowing victims to decrypt their files (360 Total Security, 2016).

Chimera also appeared in 2015, the ransomware is distributed via email campaigns which target certain employees with job offers or business proposals (KnowBe4, 2019b). The email contains a further information link to a dangerous download hosted on Dropbox (KnowBe4, 2019b). Upon clicking the Dropbox link the ransomware is automatically downloaded and then immediately starts encrypting data on local and connected network drives (KnowBe4, 2019b). This seems like any other ransomware that encrypts the victim's files and demands a ransom, but it also threatens that if the ransom is not paid then the victim's files will be published online (Malwarebytes, 2015). Chimera did not actually upload any files; instead, it was just a bogus threat (Malwarebytes, 2015). Victims were asked to pay 2.5 Bitcoins in order to decrypt their files; now free decryption software is available for Chimera (KnowBe4, 2019b).

The Android ransomware called Lockerpin was found in August 2015 and spread via an app masked for watching adult videos (Lipovský et al., 2016). Once installed, the victim sees a fake FBI message requesting a $500 ransom which accuses the victim of viewing illegal material. The victim's pin is also changed to a random four-digit number (Lipovský, Štefanko and Braniša, 2016). Previous Android ransomware locked the screen via the fake message constantly looping which was not as difficult to remove as this could be done by using the Android Debug Bridge (ADB) (Lipovský et al., 2016). Lockerpin was more complex and the only way to remove the pin lock screen was to factory reset the device and lose all your data or else use a mobile device management (MDM) system to reset the pin (Lipovský et al., 2016). In late 2015, SamSam ransomware appeared (Boyd, 2018). SamSam was not delivered through standard distribution methods like emails or drive-by-downloads (Symantec, 2015). Instead, SamSam uses tools like Jexboss which can identify unpatched servers that run Red Hat's JBoss enterprise products (Symantec, 2015). Upon gaining access to an unpatched server, the hacker then uses other tools to gather credentials and information on networked computers (Symantec, 2015). The hacker then deploys the ransomware on these systems to encrypt the files and demand a ransom (Symantec, 2015). What sets SamSam apart from other types of ransomware is how it targets unpatched servers (Symantec, 2015). This shows how criminals are directly targeting organisations in ransomware attacks (Symantec, 2015). In 2018, SamSam is using vulnerabilities in remote desktop protocol (RDP), Java-based web servers or file transfer protocol (FTP) in order to get access to the victim's network (Boyd, 2018).

2015 also saw the beginning of Ransomware-as-a-service (Raas) this allows the non-technical criminals to distribute ransomware for a low membership fee (Aguilan, 2019). Cybercriminals simply have to sign up to the ransomware service and then the service provider gives the ransomware (Aguilan, 2019). The cybercriminal will spread the ransomware and get payments from the victims (Aguilan, 2019). This payment is then shared at an agreed proportion between the distributor and provider (Aguilan, 2019). Tox was the first Raa in 2015; it affects Windows and encrypts all of the victim's files (Aguilan, 2019). Tox was available via the dark web (Aguilan, 2019). There are many pieces of ransomware that are now available as a service; some notable ones include Encrypter, Satan, Yatron, Petya, Jokeroo and CryptoLocker (Aguilan, 2019).

13.3.9 2016

January 2016 brought new ransomware called 7ev3n, which encrypts your data and charges 13 Bitcoins for decryption, at the time this was the largest ransom seen (Abrams, 2016a). 7ev3n was spread by spam emails that included it as an attachment (NJCCIC, 2016). The ransomware also tampers with Windows modifying system settings and boot options to disable keyboard and keys and system recovery options (Abrams, 2016a). Due to this victims cannot bypass the lock screen which creates a nightmare for the user (Abrams, 2016a). Free decryptors are available today for this ransomware. CryptXXX was found in April 2016 and administered through the Angler exploit kit (Thomson, 2016). The ransomware encrypts over 40 file formats and steals any Bitcoins on the victim's PC (Thomson, 2016). The earliest versions of CryptXXX used weak encryption and Kasperky released software to reverse the encryption. The third version was much tougher and included a StillerX credential-stealing module that scanned port number 445 for email, VPN, and online poker logins (Thomson, 2016). The third version was cracked and recovered users files, but unfortunately not their Bitcoins (Thomson, 2016).

KeRanger was the first piece of ransomware discovered for Mac inside the installer for Transmission 2.90 which encrypts certain file extensions in the /Users and /Volumes folder using AES encryption (Abrams, 2016b). KeRanger infected Transmission which is a popular BitTorrent client and the ransomware was signed with a valid certificate for a Turkish company (Abrams, 2016b). KeRanger demanded the payment of one Bitcoin in order to decrypt the files (Abrams, 2016b).

Jigsaw is a piece of ransomware that threatens to delete files but actually does it (KnowBe4, 2019c). Jigsaw spreads through malicious email attachments (2-spyware, 2019). When the victim becomes infected with Jigsaw their files are encrypted via the AES algorithm and a countdown timer starts (KnowBe4, 2019c). Victims have to pay a $150 ransom in order to get their files decrypted (KnowBe4, 2019c). If the ransom is not paid within an hour, one file, as each hour passes more than one file is deleted with the number increasing each time the one-hour timer resets (KnowBe4, 2019c). If the program is restarted as many as 1,000 files are deleted (KnowBe4, 2019c). A decryptor is currently available online to decrypt files infected by the Jigsaw ransomware (KnowBe4, 2019c).

Locky was discovered at the beginning of 2016 and encrypts files on Windows (Avast Academy Team, 2017). Locky was distributed through email spam and exploit kits (Avast Academy Team, 2017). Locky could encrypt more than 160 file types and used RSA-2048 and AES 128-bit cypher with electronic cookbook (ECB) mode to encrypt the victim's files (Avast Academy Team, 2017). Payment varied between 0.5 and one bitcoin. A decryptor is now available for Locky. Petya spread in March of 2016 through email spam by pretending to be a job applicant's resume (Fruhlinger, 2017a). The package contained two files, one of a young man and the other of an executable file that had PDF in the file name (Fruhlinger, 2017a). Once clicked you will be accessed to grant Windows User Access Control to tell you that that the file will make changes to your computer (Fruhlinger, 2017a). Many people won't hesitate to accept this warning at all. Once executed, Petya will reboot your computer and you will see the Windows CHKDSK screen that you would see after a crash (Fruhlinger, 2017a). In the background, the ransomware is performing tasks to restrict your access to your files (Fruhlinger, 2017a). Petya is different to other ransomware in the way it encrypts your files instead of targeting specific files to encrypt, a boot loader is installed instead which overwrites the victim's master boot record, then the master file table is encrypted which is a database to every file on the volume (Fruhlinger, 2017a). The victim's files are still there, but the computer does not know where the files are located, a bitcoin is demanded as payment for decryption (Fruhlinger, 2017a). A decryptor tool is available for the original versions of Petya.

13.3.10   2017

NonPetya appeared in 2017 and is similar to Petya in a few ways, one NonPetya encrypts the master file table and still asks for bitcoin as payment (Fruhlinger, 2017a). There are a few differences though in which NonPetya is more malicious (Fruhlinger, 2017a). For example, NonPetya can spread without the need for user interaction; it started by a backdoor sowed in an account software package, which nearly every company in Ukraine uses (Fruhlinger, 2017a). NotPetya then used a number of methods to spread to other computers which include the EternalBlue and EternalRomance exploits (Fruhlinger, 2017a). These two exploits were developed by the US National Security Agency (NSA) to exploit a flaw in the Windows SMB protocol (Fruhlinger, 2017a). NonPetya can also be spread by using a tool called Mimi Katz to find network administration credentials in the victim's computer's memory, then the PsEcex and WMIC tools already installed on Windows can gain remote access to other Windows clients on the local area network to infect (Fruhlinger, 2017a). NotPetya also encrypts the victim's whole hard drive and it turns out not to even be ransomware but instead is a wiper (Fruhlinger, 2017a). With Petya, an identification code is sent when a victim pays so the criminals know the victim's machine to provide the decryption key (Fruhlinger, 2017a). Computers infected with NotPetya instead have a randomly generated number that would not identify the user's machine which means the data would not be decrypted (Fruhlinger, 2017a). NotPetya also damages the victim's data to the state that it cannot be repaired (Fruhlinger, 2017a).

The ransomware worm called WannaCry appeared in May 2017. WannaCry affected Windows computers; it encrypted the files on the hard drive and then demanded payment in bitcoin in order to decrypt the files (Fruhlinger, 2018). WannaCry exploited a vulnerability in the Server Message Block (SMB) protocol (Fruhlinger, 2018). SMB assists with clients communicating with each other on a network (Fruhlinger, 2018). Microsoft's implementation was fooled by specially crafted packets that were used to execute arbitrary code (Fruhlinger, 2018). The US (NSA) was believed to have found this vulnerability and rather than reporting it, the NSA created code called EternalBlue to exploit the vulnerability in the SMB protocol (Fruhlinger, 2018). Microsoft discovered the vulnerability and released a patch a month before the release of WannaCry, but a lot of systems remained vulnerable (Fruhlinger, 2018). WannaCry was released on May 12 and spread quickly using the

EternalBlue exploit to infect computers (Fruhlinger, 2018). WannaCry could self-spread because of the External Blue exploit (Cooper, 2018). Microsoft hit out at the US government for not providing knowledge of the vulnerability earlier (Fruhlinger, 2018). WannaCry does not start encrypting files once it infects your computer (Fruhlinger, 2018). First, the ransomware tries to access a URL before executing; if it can contact the URL WannaCry will shut itself down (Fruhlinger, 2018). British security research March Hutchins discovered this and registered the domain to set up a site which stopped the spread of the ransomware (Fruhlinger, 2018). WannaCry demanded a $300 bitcoin payment method for decryption and infected over 200,000 computers in 150 different countries (Clickatell, 2016). WannaCry disabled the likes of hospitals, automobile manufacturers, banks, warehouses, universities, mobile operators and banks (Clickatell, 2016). Figure 13.5 shows the WannaCry ransomware note screen.

13.3.11   2018

Ryuk was discovered in 2018 and is designed for targeted attacks (Cohen and Herzog, 2019). The ransomware hit organisations in the US and worldwide severely and the ransom amount for victims is between 15 and 50 Bitcoins (Cohen and Herzog, 2019). Ryuk is distributed by botnets like Trickbot and Emotet which are mainly used as banking trojans (Dodia and Kumar, 2019). Ryuk uses both RSA-4096-bit and AES-256-bit in order to encrypt victims' files; it will also try to encrypt network drives

FIGURE 13.5   WannaCry Ransomware Note Screen (Mathews, 2017).

first and then local drives (Cohen and Herzog, 2019). This ransomware drops a text document in every directory asking for the ransom and providing the bitcoin address (Cohen and Herzog, 2019). Spotted in January 2018 was GandCrab; the ransomware targeted consumers and businesses using Windows (Malwarebytes, 2019). GandCrab uses the RaaS model so other criminals find ways to distribute the software (Malwarebytes, 2019). GandCrab was primarily distributed through exploit kits (Malwarebytes, 2019). Upon being hit with the ransomware the victim receives notes on their computer which directs them to a website on the dark web (Malwarebytes, 2019). The website explains that all of the victim's files were encrypted; victims can decrypt one file of their choice for free (Malwarebytes, 2019). The ransom is paid in a cryptocurrency called Dash due to the currency's focus on privacy (Malwarebytes, 2019). The ransom falls anywhere between $600 and $600,000. A decryptor is available for earlier versions 1, 5, 5.01, and 5.02 (Malwarebytes, 2019). This section has displayed how ransomware has evolved since it began. Decryption tools are available for particularly weak pieces of ransomware, but with recent ransomware, the encryption has become more robust and virtually unbreakable.

13.4   HOW TO SECURE AGAINST RANSOMWARE

Protecting oneself against ransomware is extremely important (Savage et al., 2015). Doing so will save the business or individual a lot of time, stress and money. This section will discuss ways to protect individuals and businesses from ransomware to save the headache. The most important thing to do is ensure a good backup system is in place. This is why the 3-2-1 rule should be followed which means at least three copies of files should be kept (Emsisoft Malware Lab, 2019). The copies should be stored on at least two different types of storage media, and one copy should be stored offline (Emsisoft Malware Lab, 2019). The more backups a company has the less chance of losing data (Emsisoft Malware Lab, 2019). All devices eventually fail and this is why at least two types of storage media should be used (Emsisoft Malware Lab, 2019). For example, one copy stored on a local drive and another on a file server. One of the backup copies needs to be stored offline so even if a ransomware attack occurs the backup will not be affected (Emsisoft Malware Lab, 2019). Backup drives also should be set as read-only, the drive should only switch to write mode when it is time to back up and then back to read-only mode when the backup has completed.

Installing an adblocker will help to keep one safe as ransomware is administered through malicious advertisements online. Disabling macros in Microsoft Office is another prevention method as spam emails that contain ransomware will usually come with an office document attachment that has a malicious macro (McAfee, 2017). If a document asks you to turn on macros do not do it (McAfee, 2017). Only give users the privileges they need when working. For example, if the user only needs to edit documents and browse the web, then they do not need administrator privileges. Keep your software up to date on your computer; lots of ransomware take advantage of vulnerabilities in outdated software. By ensuring to keep your software and operating system up to date as this lessens the chance of being infected by ransomware. Organisations should configure computers to not load memory pens as this is another form of ransomware distribution. Installing a good anti-virus system can scan links to ensure the website is not malicious and also prevent ransomware from running.

Emails should be scanned and filtered before reaching users. The easiest way to stop the ransomware link in an email is to prevent it from arriving. Content scanning and email filtering will be a huge aid in preventing ransomware scams reaching users (Ranger, 2019). A web filter should be incorporated to protect users from visiting dangerous websites where ransomware lurks (TitanHQ, 2016). Plugins that are not required do not need to be installed, if the user does not need Java then do not install it (TitanHQ, 2016). Computers should be configured to show file extensions, this way if all the file extensions are displayed identifying malicious files with a double extension is easier (TitanHQ, 2016).

Staff should be trained to recognise suspicious emails. Last year more than 99% of the attacks to gain access relied on human error (Sanders, 2019). Employees should be educated about how dangerous clicking on links can be. Only a fraction of employees will listen and people usually make a mistake before they learn, however this can be too late (Curran and Curran, 2020). Security teams are taking part in a new movement where phishing emails with fake malware are sent to employees and when activated tell employees about the mistake they just made and the dangers of it (Curran and Curran, 2020).

Certain types of ransomware such as Cryptolocker and Filecoder target computers with Windows RDP (Comodo, 2018b). RDP is a Windows utility that gives remote access to another computer (Comodo, 2018b). If you do not need to use RDP then turn it off as this is another way for hackers to target your computer.

13.5   FUTURE OF RANSOMWARE

With the increasing number of Internet of Things (IoT) devices, these will be and are a target of ransomware. It is forecasted by 2022 that there will be 29 billion IoT devices connected to the Internet (Ericsson, 2018). There are now smart fridges, washing machines, thermostats, light bulbs, etc, that can be controlled over the Internet. For example, imagine ransomware taking over your smart thermostat and increasing your temperature until the victim pays the ransom. This would be heaven for cybercriminals being able to control victims' devices like this. Ransomware is predicted to target IoT devices in 2020; to prevent hackers from attacking IoT devices, designers need to work closely with security teams in the company or else hire experts who can incorporate risk-mitigating techniques (Bayern, 2019). Companies must also put remediation plans in place for when an attack occurs. WannaCry allowed people to see the possibilities of ransomware interfering with IoT devices. In 2017, 55 speed cameras in Victoria, Australia were infected with the WannaCry ransomware (Howe, 2018). The cameras were not targeted directly; instead, it was because a technician connected them to an infected piece of hardware (Howe, 2018). This just shows the possibilities out there already.

Taking control of a thermostat control system with ransomware has already been demonstrated. Two white hat hackers have demoed the first ransomware to work against a smart device which in this case happens to be a thermostat control system (Franceschi-Bicchierai, 2016). The hackers did not have malicious intentions but just wanted to make a point that some IoT devices do not take simple security measures which leaves users in danger (Franceschi-Bicchierai, 2016). The hackers admitted that the attack is not easy to pull off due to requiring the user to download and transfer the ransomware onto their thermostats (Franceschi-Bicchierai, 2016). The idea is not implausible, as lots of Android users in the past have been hacked by installing malicious apps on their phone (Franceschi-Bicchierai, 2016). Hackers, for example, could disguise this and fool people by saying the piece of ransomware is an update and many people who are not aware of this would proceed to install this and become infected. Figure 13.6 shows what the screen looked like on the thermostat control system.

There is even ransomware available for Android-based Smart TVs (Security Affairs, 2017). A software engineer called Darren Cauthon had his LG Smart TV infected on Christmas day and was asked to pay a ransom of $500 (Security Affairs, 2017). Cauthon's wife downloaded an app on the TV that promised to provide free movies but instead, the app was ransomware which locked the device (Security Affairs, 2017). The ransomware looked to be a version of Frantic Locker (Security Affairs, 2017). The factory reset settings on the TV did not work so Cauthon called LG and was offered to visit a service centre to pay $340 for assistance (Security Affairs, 2017). In the end up LG provided hidden reset instructions to factory reset the TV to remove the ransomware (Security Affairs, 2017).

Healthcare IoT devices will be a target for ransomware in the future. During 2017, two hospitals in the USA were using a medical device to improve the quality of magnetic resonance imaging (MRI) images and then all of a sudden the WannaCry ransomware screen displayed itself on the LCD readouts and typically demanded a ransom (Enzoic, 2019). The devices ran a version of Windows that was unpatched (Enzoic, 2019). Patients were not in danger and the vendor provided a patch to

FIGURE 13.6   Thermostat Control System Message (Franceschi-Bicchierai, 2016).

prevent any further damage (Enzoic, 2019). This was significant due to being the first known event of a successful attack via ransomware on a medical device (Enzoic, 2019). Ransomware threats on medical devices are occurring because of changes in medical device manufacturing (Enzoic, 2019). Originally medical devices used proprietary firmware, which prevented them from being a target in cyber attacks (Enzoic, 2019). Now manufacturers build medical devices running Windows, the benefit being operating system patches are easier to apply, but the major drawback is that ransomware can now infect medical devices (Enzoic, 2019). Mitigating these attacks is critical in healthcare as attacks on medical devices could put lives at risk (Enzoic, 2019).

Internet-connected cars in the future will also be a target for ransomware. A study conducted by the Future of Automotive Security Technology Research (FASTR) explained that connected cars might be the next target for ransomware developers (Naveen Goud, 2017). FASTR found out through research that once a car is connected to the Internet the whole vehicle is exposed to the threat surface (Naveen Goud, 2017). Automobile manufacturers are interested in creating computerised cars that operate on processor intelligence (Naveen Goud, 2017). The Executive Director of FASTR Craig Hurst said that manufacturers are displaying lots of passion when presenting cars driven by processors to their customers (Naveen Goud, 2017). He also said because of this car manufacturers are dismissing the basics related to security that are found as default in different modern devices such as smartphones and laptops (Naveen Goud, 2017). In 2016, the Federal Bureau of Investigation distributed a warning to the automobile industry (Naveen Goud, 2017). The warning was advice from law enforcement to manufacture cars that have enough cybersecurity features to be isolated from cyber attacks (Naveen Goud, 2017). For example, there is a possibility that a car could be hacked by ransomware and the victim is forced to pay a ransom or else the hacker would lock the user from their car or crash it. These are all possibilities in the future if cars are not properly protected when connected to the Internet. IoT devices must be built with security in mind, if not this could lead to a disaster in the future.

13.6 CONCLUSION

Ransomware has massively evolved since 1989: what started off as something small has now erupted into a lucrative business for cybercriminals. With an ever-growing number of devices connected to the Internet along with anonymous payment methods ransomware sees no signs of disappearing. More devices means more targets for criminals. RaaS even allows the script kiddies to use ransomware to make money. Encryption techniques in ransomware are getting better as the years progress; much of the well-written ransomware is nearly unbreakable. The annual global revenue for ransomware is $1 billion and the cost for businesses is $8 billion. Security needs to be majorly improved to reduce the impact of ransomware. Nobody wants to have to pay ransoms to fund criminals. This is why it is crucial that IT departments keep systems up to date and monitor the network for unusual activity. For example, WannaCry, which infected the NHS, showed how crucial patching is as the ransomware could self-propagate on the network to computers which were not patched. Employees should also be educated on how to spot malicious content. The 3-2-1 backup process must be employed so that data is not lost. Users should only be given the computer privileges that they need in order to work. Remediation plans should be in place to get back online swiftly. IT departments should use Microsoft's Windows Preparation Tool so if recovering from a backup all the settings of the PC do not have to be reconfigured again. This would save businesses a lot of time and money.

IoT devices are going to continuously grow and with 29 billion IoT devices forecasted by the end of 2022 manufacturers must ensure they are designed with security in mind. Ransomware to IoT devices is even more dangerous than to desktop computers, which is why hackers will target these devices. It has already been proven as thermostats, medical devices and smart TVs have already been victims of ransomware. In the future, ransomware could target IoT devices such as your car or smart home control system and lock them down. Hackers could potentially stop your car from starting or turn your home's temperature up or down until the victim pays the ransom. The Federal Bureau of Investigation has already warned the automobile industry to ensure cars are isolated from cyber attacks. IoT devices must have security mechanisms built in to mitigate cyber attacks. If this is not done then ransomware attacks will become even more dangerous in the future.

REFERENCES

2-spyware. 2019. Remove jigsaw ransomware / virus (removal instructions). [online] 2-spyware.com. Available at: https://www.2-spyware.com/remove-jigsaw-ransomware-virus.html [Accessed 12 Nov. 2019].

360 Total Security. 2016. 360 Total security blog. [online] 360 Total Security Blog. Available at: https://blog.360totalsecurity.com/en/remove-teslacrypt-ransomware/ [Accessed 8 Nov. 2019].

Abrams, L. 2016a. 7ev3n Ransomware trashes your PC and then demands 13 bitcoins. [online] BleepingComputer. Available at: https://www.bleepingcomputer.com/news/security/7ev3n-ransomware-trashes-your-pc-and-then-demands-13-bitcoins/ [Accessed 8 Nov. 2019].

Abrams, L. 2016b. Information about the KeRanger OS X ransomware and how to remove it. [online] BleepingComputer. Available at: https://www.bleepingcomputer.com/news/security/information-about-the-keranger-os-x-ransomware-and-how-to-remove-it-/ [Accessed 10 Nov. 2019].

Aguilan, J. 2019. How does ransomware-as-a-service work? [online] Qa.com. Available at: https://www.qa.com/resources/our-thinking/ransomware-as-a-service/ [Accessed 13 Nov. 2019].

Avast Academy Team. 2017. What is locky ransomware? How it works and how to remove it. [online] Avast. Available at: https://www.avast.com/c-locky#topic-4 [Accessed 10 Nov. 2019].

Bayern, M. 2019. Forrester: The 5 IoT predictions paving the way for 2020. [online] TechRepublic. Available at: https://www.techrepublic.com/article/forrester-the-5-iot-predictions-paving-the-way-for-2020/ [Accessed 10 Nov. 2019].

Bera, A. 2019. 34 Shocking ransomware statistics (2019): SafeAtLast.co. [online] SafeAtLast.co. Available at: https://safeatlast.co/blog/ransomware-statistics/ [Accessed 11 Nov. 2019].

Betternet. 2017. 4 Common ransomware attack vectors. [online] Free VPN for Online Security & Privacy News and Updates | Betternet Blog. Available at: https://www.bet ternet.co/blog/4-common-ransomware-attack-vectors/ [Accessed 8 Nov. 2019].

Boyd, C. 2018. SamSam ransomware: What you need to know. [online] Malwarebytes Labs. Available at: https://blog.malwarebytes.com/cybercrime/2018/05/samsam-ransomwar e-need-know/.

Brunau, C. 2018. Datto. [online] Datto.com. Available at: https://www.datto.com/au/blog/ how-to-protect-against-ransomware [Accessed 7 Nov. 2019].

Cabrera, E. 2019. Where will ransomware go in the second half of 2019? [online] Trendmicro. com. Available at: https://blog.trendmicro.com/where-will-ransomware-go-in-the-second-half-of-2019/ [Accessed 11 Nov. 2019].

Clickatell. 2016. WannaCry ransomware attack: Everything you need to know. [online] Clickatell. Available at: https://www.clickatell.com/articles/information-security/wan nacry-ransomware-attack/ [Accessed 10 Nov. 2019].

Cloudflare. 2019. What is a DDoS botnet? [online] Cloudflare. Available at: https://www.clo udflare.com/learning/ddos/what-is-a-ddos-botnet/ [Accessed 9 Nov. 2019].

Cohen, I., and B. Herzog. 2019. Ryuk ransomware: A targeted campaign break-down. [online] Check Point Research. Available at: https://research.checkpoint.com/ryuk-ransomwa re-targeted-campaign-break/ [Accessed 11 Nov. 2019].

Comodo. 2018a. How is ransomware delivered? | Stop ransomware attacks. [online] Comodo Enterprise. Available at: https://enterprise.comodo.com/how-is-ransomware-deliver ed.php [Accessed 8 Nov. 2019].

Comodo. 2018b. How to protect yourself against ransomware? [online] Comodo Enterprise. Available at: https://enterprise.comodo.com/forensic-analysis/how-to-protect-yoursel f-against-ransomware.php [Accessed 9 Nov. 2019].

Cooper, C. 2018. WannaCry: Lessons learned 1 year later. [online] Symantec.com. Available at: https://www.symantec.com/blogs/feature-stories/wannacry-lessons-learned-1-y ear-later [Accessed 12 Nov. 2019].

Curran, K. 2017. Hacking. In *The SAGE Encyclopedia of the Internet* (3rd ed), SAGE.

Curran, K., and J. Curran. 2020. Blockchain security and potential future use cases.In Blockchain for cybersecurity and privacy: Architectures, challenges and applications. CRC Press.

Des, J. 2018. Trends in ransomware and attacks on high-value targets: Exabeam. [online] Exabeam. Available at: https://www.exabeam.com/information-security/ransomware -trends/ [Accessed 11 Nov. 2019].

Dodia, R., and A. Kumar. 2019. Examining the ryuk ransomware. [online] Zscaler. Available at: https://www.zscaler.com/blogs/research/examining-ryuk-ransomware [Accessed 11 Nov. 2019].

Emsisoft Malware Lab. 2019. Seasonal ransomware highlights the need for better report-ing and information sharing. [online] Emsisoft | Security Blog. Available at: https:// blog.emsisoft.com/en/34083/how-to-protect-your-companys-backups-from-ransomwa re/ [Accessed 12 Nov. 2019].

Enzoic. 2019. Top cybersecurity threats and how SIEM protects against them. [online] Security Boulevard. Available at: https://securityboulevard.com/2019/09/ransomware-implication s-for-medical-devices-and-the-healthcare-industry/ [Accessed 10 Nov. 2019].

Ericsson. 2018. Internet of things forecast: Ericsson mobility report. [online] Ericsson.com. Available at: https://www.ericsson.com/en/mobility-report/internet-of-things-forecast [Accessed 13 Nov. 2019].

Fawkes, G. 2017. A history of the ransomware threat: Past, present and future. [online] VpnMentor. Available at: https://www.vpnmentor.com/blog/history-ransomware-threa t-past-present-and-future/ [Accessed 6 Nov. 2019].

Field, M. 2018. WannaCry cyber sttack cost the NHS £92m as 19,000 appointments cancelled. [online] The Telegraph. Available at: https://www.telegraph.co.uk/technology/2018/10/11/wannacry-cyber-attack-cost-nhs-92m-19000-appointments-cancelled/ [Accessed 13 Nov. 2019].

Franceschi-Bicchierai, L. 2016. Hackers make the first-ever ransomware for smart thermostats. [online] Vice. Available at: https://www.vice.com/en_us/article/aekj9j/internet-of-things-ransomware-smart-thermostat [Accessed 10 Nov. 2019].

Fruhlinger, J. 2017a. Petya ransomware and NotPetya malware: What you need to know now. [online] CSO Online. Available at: https://www.csoonline.com/article/3233210/petya-ransomware-and-notpetya-malware-what-you-need-to-know-now.html [Accessed 10 Nov. 2019].

Fruhlinger, J. 2017b. The 5 biggest ransomware attacks of the last 5 years. [online] CSO Online. Available at: https://www.csoonline.com/article/3212260/the-5-biggest-ransomware-attacks-of-the-last-5-years.html [Accessed 7 Nov. 2019].

Fruhlinger, J. 2018. What is wannacry ransomware, how does it infect, and who was responsible? [online] CSO Online. Available at: https://www.csoonline.com/article/3227906/what-is-wannacry-ransomware-how-does-it-infect-and-who-was-responsible.html [Accessed 10 Nov. 2019].

Howe, S. 2018. Why IoT could be the next ransomware target. [online] Cso.com.au. Available at: https://www.cso.com.au/article/645755/why-iot-could-next-ransomware-target/ [Accessed 12 Nov. 2019].

Kaspersky. 2019. What are the different types of ransomware? [online] Kaspersky.co.uk. Available at: https://www.kaspersky.co.uk/resource-center/threats/ransomware-examples [Accessed 11 Nov. 2019].

Kettering, C. 2016. Ransomware: attack trends, prevention, and response. [online] Check Point. Available at: https://www.checkpoint.com/downloads/products/ransomware-trends-prevention-and-response-whitepaper.pdf [Accessed 11 Nov. 2019].

KnowBe4. 2012. Reveton worm ransomware. [online] Knowbe4.com. Available at: https://www.knowbe4.com/reveton-worm [Accessed 8 Nov. 2019].

KnowBe4. 2014a. CryptoDefense ransomware. [online] Knowbe4.com. Available at: https://www.knowbe4.com/cryptodefense-ransomware [Accessed 8 Nov. 2019].

KnowBe4. 2014b. SynoLocker ransomware | KnowBe4. [online] Knowbe4.com. Available at: https://www.knowbe4.com/synolocker [Accessed 8 Nov. 2019].

KnowBe4. 2019a. AIDS trojan | PC cyborg | Original ransomware | KnowBe4. [online] Knowbe4.com. Available at: https://www.knowbe4.com/aids-trojan [Accessed 6 Nov. 2019].

KnowBe4. 2019b. Chimera ransomware | KnowBe4. [online] Knowbe4.com. Available at: https://www.knowbe4.com/chimera-ransomware [Accessed 8 Nov. 2019].

KnowBe4. 2019c. Jigsaw ransomware | KnowBe4. [online] Knowbe4.com. Available at: https://www.knowbe4.com/jigsaw-ransomware [Accessed 10 Nov. 2019].

Kraft Business Systems. 2019. The evolution of ransomware: 2019 brings the 30 year anniversary. [online] Kraft Business Systems. Available at: https://kraftbusiness.com/cyber-security/evolution-of-ransomware-2019-brings-30-year-anniversary/ [Accessed 6 Nov. 2019].

Krebs on Security. 2012. Inside a 'reveton' ransomware operation: Krebs on security. [online] Krebsonsecurity.com. Available at: https://krebsonsecurity.com/2012/08/inside-a-reveton-ransomware-operation/ [Accessed 12 Nov. 2019].

Leinwand, D. 2014. Federal agents knock down zeus botnet, cryptolocker. [online] USA Today. Available at: https://eu.usatoday.com/story/news/nation/2014/06/02/global-cyber-fraud/9863977/ [Accessed 9 Nov. 2019].

Leydon, J. 2010. Russian cops cuff 10 ransomware Trojan suspects. [online] Theregister.co.uk. Available at: https://www.theregister.co.uk/2010/09/01/ransomware_trojan_suspects_cuffed/ [Accessed 7 Nov. 2019].

Lipovský, R., L. Štefanko, and G. Braniša. 2016. The rise of android ransomware. [online] Welivesecurity. Available at: https://www.welivesecurity.com/wp-content/uploads/2016/02/Rise_of_Android_Ransomware.pdf [Accessed 11 Nov. 2019].

Malwarebytes. 2015. Inside chimera ransomware: The first 'doxingware' in wild. [online] Malwarebytes Labs. Available at: https://blog.malwarebytes.com/threat-analysis/2015/12/inside-chimera-ransomware-the-first-doxingware-in-wild/ [Accessed 8 Nov. 2019].

Malwarebytes. 2019. GandCrab ransomware: Removal and prevention guide. [online] Malwarebytes. Available at: https://www.malwarebytes.com/gandcrab/ [Accessed 11 Nov. 2019].

MalwareFox. 2016. What is ransomware? [online] MalwareFox. Available at: https://www.malwarefox.com/ransomware/ [Accessed 6 Nov. 2019].

Mathews, L. 2017. How wannacry went from a windows bug to an international incident. Forbes. [online] 17 May. Available at: https://www.forbes.com/sites/leemathews/2017/05/16/wannacry-ransomware-ms17-010/ [Accessed 12 Nov. 2019].

McAfee. 2017. Understanding ransomware and strategies to defeat it McAfee labs. [online] McAfee. Available at: https://www.mcafee.com/enterprise/en-us/assets/white-papers/wp-understanding-ransomware-strategies-defeat.pdf [Accessed 12 Nov. 2019].

Nachreiner, C. 2013. Everything you wanted to know about. [online] Secplicity: Security Simplified. Available at: https://www.secplicity.org/2013/11/04/everything-you-wanted-to-know-about-cryptolocker/ [Accessed 7 Nov. 2019].

Naveen Goud. 2017. Connected cars are vulnerable to ransomware attacks: Cybersecurity insiders. [online] Cybersecurity Insiders. Available at: https://www.cybersecurity-insiders.com/connected-cars-are-vulnerable-to-ransomware-attacks/ [Accessed 12 Nov. 2019].

NJCCIC (New Jersey Cybersecurity & Communications Integration Cell). 2016. 7ev3n. [online] NJCCIC. Available at: https://www.cyber.nj.gov/threat-profiles/ransomware-variants/7ev3n [Accessed 12 Nov. 2019].

O'Kane, P., S. Sezer, and D. Carlin. 2018. Evolution of ransomware. *IET Networks*, 7(5), pp.321–327.

OpenDNS Security Research. 2014. Synolocker, a new ransomware targeting synology NAS. [online] OpenDNS Umbrella Blog. Available at: https://umbrella.cisco.com/blog/2014/08/04/synolocker-new-ransomware-targeting-synology-devices/ [Accessed 8 Nov. 2019].

Palmer, D. 2019. Ransomware attacks are getting more ambitious as crooks target shared files. [online] ZDNet. Available at: https://www.zdnet.com/article/ransomware-attacks-are-getting-more-ambitious-as-crooks-target-shared-files/ [Accessed 6 Nov. 2019].

Ranger, S. 2019. Ransomware: 11 steps you should take to protect against disaster. [online] ZDNet. Available at: https://www.zdnet.com/article/ransomware-11-steps-you-should-take-to-protect-against-disaster/ [Accessed 9 Nov. 2019].

Rankin, B. 2017. Network security and watering hole attacks. [online] Lastline. Available at: https://www.lastline.com/blog/network-security-and-watering-hole-attacks/ [Accessed 9 Nov. 2019].

Sanders, J. 2019. More than 99% of attacks in the past year relied on human error to gain access. [online] TechRepublic. Available at: https://www.techrepublic.com/article/more-than-99-of-attacks-in-the-past-year-relied-on-human-error-to-gain-access/ [Accessed 9 Nov. 2019].

Savage, K., P. Coogan, and H. Lau. 2015.The evolution of ransomware. [online] Available at: https://www.symantec.com/content/en/us/enterprise/media/security_response/whitepapers/the-evolution-of-ransomware.pdf [Accessed 7 Nov. 2019].

SecureWorks, D. 2015. TeslaCrypt ransomware threat analysis. [online] Secureworks.com. Available at: https://www.secureworks.com/research/teslacrypt-ransomware-threat-analysis [Accessed 8 Nov. 2019].

Security Affairs. 2017. It has happened again,ransomware infected an LG smart TV. [online] Security Affairs. Available at: https://securityaffairs.co/wordpress/54991/malware/lg-smart-tv-ransomware.html [Accessed 10 Nov. 2019].

Sjouwerman, S. 2016. Ransomware on the rise: The evolution of a cyberattack. [online] TechBeacon. Available at: https://techbeacon.com/security/ransomware-rise-evoluti on-cyberattack [Accessed 6 Nov. 2019].

Super User. 2016. Synolocker ransomware: infomation, encryption type, symptoms, distribu- tion method: VinRansomware. [online] vinransomware. Available at: http://www.vinr ansomware.com/synolocker-ransomware [Accessed 8 Nov. 2019].

Symantec. 2015. Samsam may signal a new trend of targeted ransomware. [online] Symantec Security Response. Available at: https://www.symantec.com/connect/blogs/samsam -may-signal-new-trend-targeted-ransomware [Accessed 12 Nov. 2019].

Thomson, I. 2016. Don't pay up to decrypt: Cure found for CryptXXX ransomware, again. [online] Theregister.co.uk. Available at: https://www.theregister.co.uk/2016/12/21/cure _found_for_cryptxxx_ransomware_again/ [Accessed 8 Nov. 2019].

TitanHQ. 2016. How to prevent ransomware attacks: Web filtering. [online] TitanHQ. Available at: https://www.spamtitan.com/web-filtering/how-to-prevent-ransomware -attacks/ [Accessed 12 Nov. 2019].

VanillaPlus. 2017. How cryptocurrencies have aided cyber-criminals using ransomware. [online] VanillaPlus: The global voice of telecoms IT. Available at: https://www.van illaplus.com/2017/03/23/26146-cryptocurrencies-aided-cyber-criminals-using-ranso mware/ [Accessed 6 Nov. 2019].

14 Security Issues in Self-Driving Cars within Smart Cities

Conor Woodrow and Kevin Curran

CONTENTS

14.1 INTRODUCTION

Once thought to be held to the realms of science fiction such as *Back to the Future*, self-driving cars, or more broadly known as Connected and Autonomous Vehicles (CAVs), are growing ever closer to becoming our present reality. Companies across the tech and automobile industry, including the likes of Google, Uber, Tesla, Waymo and Volkswagen, are furthering the development of fully automated vehicles, claiming 2019 as the year of the Level 4 autonomous vehicle. As multiple companies develop technology independently, it is unlikely any two CAVs will be identical in design. As such, the Society of Automotive Engineers (SAE) has defined six levels of automation in cars to classify a system's level of sophistication as shown in Figure 14.1.

Level 0 – No Automation

Level 0 represents a standard car with no additional features or system capabilities. Every aspect of operating the vehicle requires driver involvement (Car and Driver, 2017).

Level 1 – Driver Assistance

At level 1 system capabilities such as adaptive cruise control become available, allowing the car to control either steering or speed under certain circumstances. The driver must still perform all other responsibilities while driving the vehicle (Car and Driver, 2017).

Level 2 – Partial Automation

System capabilities now include the ability to steer, accelerate and brake in certain circumstances, thanks to systems such as Traffic Jam Assist,

SAE AUTOMATION LEVELS

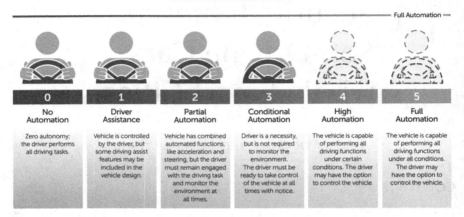

FIGURE 14.1   SAE Levels of Automation (NHTSA, 2017)

Volvo Pilot Assist, or Tesla Autopilot. These systems still require the driver to respond to traffic signals, change lanes and scan for hazards (Car and Driver, 2017).

Level 3 – Conditional Automation

The car is now capable of handling most aspects of driving without driver input, including monitoring the environment. However, the driver is still necessary if not required, as the system will prompt the driver to intervene in scenarios the system is not capable of overcoming. Level 3 systems such as the Audi Traffic Jam Pilot still require the driver to always be available to take control and so are not fully automatic (Car and Driver, 2017).

Level 4 – High Automation

While certain specified conditions are met, such as the car being limited to exact geographic areas or road types, the vehicle is now capable of operation without the need for driver input or oversight. At this stage, a car that is restricted to a specific area, such as an Uber taxi for a city, may require zero driver input. Meanwhile, a privately-owned car may require the driver to manage all driving duties on surface-level streets and then manage all control when entering a highway (Car and Driver, 2017).

Level 5 – Full Automation

Level 5 autonomous driving requires no human interaction. Vehicles are able to steer, accelerate, brake and monitor road conditions like traffic jams. Essentially, Level 5 automation enables the driver to sit back and relax without having to pay any attention to the car's functions whatsoever.

Vehicles will be driven using Artificial Intelligence (AI) and will respond to real-world data points, generated from sensors.

The function of Automatic Vehicles (AVs) is made possible due to a marriage of various environmental sensors, which retrieve data from the AV's local environment, and embedded computer systems within the AV, which processes the multi-sensor data to compute and implement intelligent control decisions autonomously (Madan et al., 2019). Each CAV manufacturer is currently testing and developing a broad assortment of on-board sensors to capture data from the vehicle's local environment, including multispectral cameras, LiDAR (Light Detection And Ranging), Ultrasonic, Radio Frequency (RF), GPS, and Radar (Garakani et al., 2018). In addition retrieving data through on-board sensors, CAVs are capable of inter-communication, not only between other smart vehicles but also with the Internet and roadside infrastructure.

This ability for CAVs to communicate with other smart devices through the Internet of Things (IoT) is instrumental in obtaining most of the necessary data required to make crucial driving decisions. Most of the communication between the CAV and other smart devices can be separated into Vehicle-to-Vehicle communication (V2V) and Vehicle-to-Everything communication (V2X), which includes communication to infrastructure (V2I), network (V2N) and device (V2D). This form of communication is facilitated by Vehicular Ad Hoc Networks (VANET), utilising Dedicated Short-Range Communication System (DSRC) based protocols. The significance of the high-speed communication these protocols allow for cannot be understated; due to the high speed of motor vehicles, any loss or delay in relevant data can result in severe consequences during the embedded computer system's decision-making process (Mohd et al., 2018). See Figure 14.2.

Connected and Autonomous Vehicles have the potential to be greatly beneficial towards society, both economically and socially. In a study commissioned by the Society of Motor Manufacturers and Traders Ltd (SMMT) and prepared by KPMG (SMMT, 2015), it was estimated that CAVs could add £51 billion per year to the UK economy by 2030, in addition to creating more than 320,000 jobs, of which only 25,000 would be in the automotive industry. In addition to this economic boost, 25,000 serious accidents could be avoided thanks to a reduction in driver error through autonomous decision making, saving an estimated 2,500 lives. Furthermore,

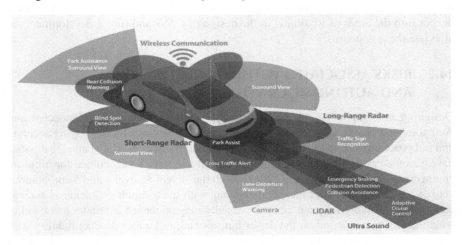

FIGURE 14.2   CAV Internet of Things Sensors (Mast Technologies, 2011)

in research performed by the SMMT (SMMT, 2017), it was discussed how self-driving cars can help the most disadvantaged of society, including the young, elderly and disabled, through greater freedom of mobility. The benefits of CAVs involved lower insurance costs, reduced stress of driving with the freedom to travel where you want, fewer accidents and the ability to rest while on long journeys. It has also been suggested that this increased freedom of movement will help reduce loneliness and isolation in the elderly as they have greater freedom to leave the home without intense walking or driving and allow individuals with disabilities a better chance of finding a job that is not restricted by location.

The future fleet of connected and autonomous vehicles may soon be upon us as technology continues to advance and far outpace public perceptions. Soon automated trucks will reduce delivery times of cross country travel across North America as they lack the human need to eat or sleep, long stressful car rides will become relaxing rests as the need to remain constantly aware for several hours is removed, and a reduction in traffic congestion, accidents, and loss of life as connected vehicles will be able to communicate with one another near instantly. Although this future may appear closer than it is, public perception is not entirely in favor of self-driving cars, raising concerns about public safety. As consumer trust is key in an economic market, lacking in positive public perception and failing to address valid concerns for personal health and cybersecurity in CAVs may lead to a delay or possible failure in their adoption. In this chapter, we will discuss the potential benefits presented by CAVs, the dangers and weaknesses found within their design, and developments for the future to help alleviate concerns for these flaws.

This brief introduction into the concept of Connected and Autonomous Vehicles discussed the defined levels of automation and the current technology implemented in modern designs to achieve a high level of automation in today's self-driving cars. However, several risks and vulnerabilities can be exposed and exploited, not only in high-level automated cars that require little driver input but also in models where the only features included consist of driver assistance. The following sections will delve deeper into the areas of weakness in the design of CAVs and future developments to alleviate these concerns.

14.2   RISKS ASSOCIATED WITH CONNECTED AND AUTONOMOUS VEHICLES

Designing and implementing ethical and cyber-secure systems for Connected and Autonomous Vehicles cannot begin and end for manufacturers by developing accurate and fail proof sensors and decision-making technology. Social, ethical and legal issues have become pervasive within automotive design and must be accounted for in future engineering methods (Skipp et al., 2019). With the advent of level 4 and 5 autonomous vehicles, legal liability laws must update along with the technology. Incidents such as car crashes involving fully autonomous vehicles may no longer fall under tort liability where negligence is found on the driver but, instead, fall under product liability with the manufacturer, who failed to exercise reasonable care in designing a safe product under multiple use cases. This legal responsibility extends further into cyber liability,

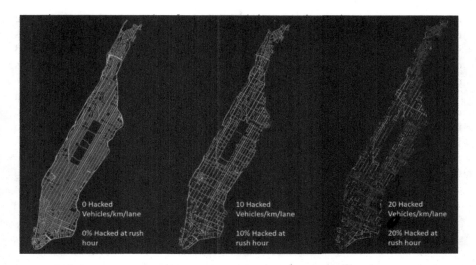

FIGURE 14.3   Simulation of Manhattan Traffic Flow & Congestion (Vivek et al., 2019)

whereby CAV users have the right to data protection and privacy under data protection acts such as the General Data Protection Regulation (GDPR). However, as cars become further interconnected, the potential for malicious cyber-crimes and hacking of personal data rises and poses a serious risk, not only for the personal security of CAV users but also posing a threat to the physical safety of the public.

A small-scale hack affecting only 10% of vehicles in Manhattan could result in a city-wide gridlock capable of hindering emergency services (Vivek et al., 2019). See Figure 14.3. Collisions as a result of compromised vehicles present a physical danger to occupants and pedestrians, and have negative effects on the overall traffic flow (American Physical Society, 2019). Any connected device can potentially be compromised by malicious actors. Therefore, as driverless cars become more prevalent, the number of vulnerabilities that can be exploited by the pool of increasingly sophisticated malicious actors will also continue to grow. Moreover, there is a greater risk when driverless cars interact with third party and cloud service providers. When multiple devices are connected, there is a risk that a weak link in any of them can be exploited to compromise them all (Moysa and Koczerginski, 2016).

The susceptibility of CAVs to malicious hacking and cybercrimes is not a potential threat of the near future when level 4 and 5 autonomous vehicles become more commonplace but is instead the current reality society is faced with today, which will only prove to become an increasingly likely occurrence as smart devices become more abundant and our cars become more interconnected. As an example, in 2015 researchers Charlie Miller and Chris Valasek demonstrated the vulnerability of modern non-automated vehicles by remotely hacking a Jeep Cherokee. Using a laptop while at a 10-mile distance, it was possible to remotely hack the vehicle over the Internet through the cellular connection to the on-board entertainment system. After gaining a foothold into the Electronic Control Unit (ECU) of the vehicle, the researchers were able to move laterally through the system and gain control of the radio, steering and the brake system. In the video (Wired, 2015), malicious attacks were demonstrated such as disabling acceleration while driving on a highway and disabling the car's brakes when attempting to park, among other possibilities such as querying the GPS for location information.

The motivation for criminals to attempt to hack into a vehicle's operating system can range from personal benefit with the intent to steal valuable passenger data, interrupt or disrupt the standard function of the system, or maliciously attempt to jeopardize the safety of either the system, the passenger or the public. Such theoretical attacks can include:

- Hacking cars for ransom before allowing a user to either enter or exit the vehicle, possible when the car is parked or in motion.
- Hacking the car's operating system to remotely destroy it, causing financial harm to the user.
- Remotely hacking a fully autonomous car to hijack the vehicle controls and redirect the vehicle to a more secluded and convenient area for robbery or assault.
- Disabling of the light-detecting and ranging sensors of an automated vehicle could lead to major crashes and large-scale traffic incidents.
- Finally, as the concept of the Internet of Things (IoT) evolves and expands, driverless cars, as well as other smart home devices, will be able to communicate with each other, allowing your phone or car to turn on the heating system at home. A hacker who gains access to one of these smart devices due to weaker defences could gain access to your home and every other smart device through one entry way.

Most modern vehicles of this age are equipped with smart capabilities such as the ability to communicate with other smart vehicles, devices and roadside infrastructure (Mohd et al., 2018). As CAVs can make driving decisions autonomously without driver input, they must gather an increasingly larger amount of data from an array of sensors, other Connected vehicles, and the Internet. The on-board driving model of the CAV is then capable of making necessary driving decisions with this obtained information. Most of the data utilised are obtained from other smart entities such as other CAVs and the roadside infrastructure; as such, communication is paramount to ensuring CAVs are safe for the public. As previously discussed in this report, communication between smart devices is feasible with the aid of VANET, allowing for Vehicle-2-Vehicle (V2V) and Vehicle-2-Infrastructure (V2I) communication. The information provided via VANET needs to be both accurate and precise but must also be transmitted timely and securely as it is vital to passenger safety. Therefore, even a slight delay in the network availability could prove deleterious and demonstrates the disastrous consequences of cybercrimes such as Distributed Denial of Services (DDoS) attacks on the communication channels of CAVs. During a DDoS attack, an attacker or several distributed attackers can spam messages addressed to target CAV, overriding resources in the VANET resulting in a jamming of the communication

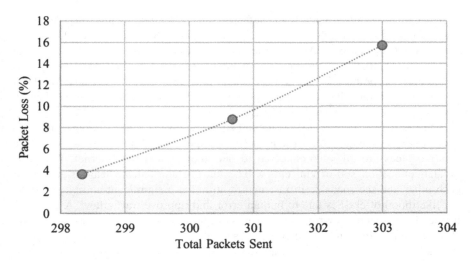

FIGURE 14.4   Percentage of Packet Loss at Node A against Number of Packets Sent (Mohd et al., 2018)

channel. Without the necessary and relevant data obtained from separate smart entities, a failure in the decision-making system of the vehicle could result in a possible loss of life. Other types of attack which could negatively impact the normal function of VANET include false information attacks, ID disclosure and masquerading.

Figure 14.4 displays the results of experiments to simulate a DDoS attack on a host (Mohd et al., 2018). It shows the trend of greater packet loss with increasing total packets sent. The first dot represents the average packet loss when using five attackers, the second is average packet loss when simulating eight attackers, and the third dot represents the average of the experiments done with 12 attackers. A significant percentage of up to 16% of packets sent were either lost or delayed, unable to reach the destination node A, proving the danger of a potential DDoS attack preventing vital information reaching the decision-making system of a CAV (Mohd et al., 2018).

As many different companies and organisations such as Tesla and Mercedes-Benz are each developing autonomous vehicles individually, it is unlikely that any two systems will be identical. Therefore, a cyber attack on any singular proprietary system will not necessarily spread to other systems. As systems become more generic and more commonly use software spreads across platforms, then it becomes increasingly probable that one successful hack could spread across every vehicle which implements the same system (Weimerskirch and Dominic, 2018). Hacks of this kind have previously been seen on a global scale affecting popular systems such as Windows computers. During the WannaCry ransomware attack an estimated total of 300,000 computers in 150 countries were shut down during a four-day period in May of 2017, resulting in damage costs of an estimated $4 billion.

Cyber attacks performed on CAVs are divided into two categories, software attacks and hardware attacks. Software attacks result in false readings from the software or the altering of the values obtained from the sensors. Hardware attacks, rather than attempting to attack the software, are performed against the Electronic Control Unit (ECU) which is found in all smart devices (Garakani et al., 2018).

These intrusions into CAVs can then be further classified into local and remote attacks. Local attacks are the most direct method of intruding the CAV due to physical connection points like RF sensors, CAN port and charging stations. While in remote attacks, intruders attempt to penetrate one of the external communication systems of the CAV, such as the VANET.

The Internet of Things (IoT) is an embedded feature of CAVs, aiding in the systems' ability to navigate busy roads and make split-second decisions as our future smart devices are all interconnected to one another and the Internet. With this greater connection, self-driving cars will be able to communicate near-instantly with each other and the roadside infrastructure, granting a significant ability to reduce the likelihood of crashes due to human error and improve traffic flow. A common traffic phenomenon known as traffic waves or ghost jams occurs at areas where cars abruptly stop in the lane, one driver forces the drivers behind to drastically degrade their acceleration or come to a complete stop, at which point the drivers behind must wait for the lead car to start or accelerate again before they too can accelerate. In long chains of traffic, although the cause of this slowdown may have long passed, the effect remains and several cars further down the chain will be forced to slow down as the effect travels down the line. This phenomenon is simply because each driver must wait for a signal to accelerate as coordination to accelerate simultaneously is impossible between humans. This issue is solved due to communication between connected vehicles; in a situation where several CAVs await a stoplight to signal to turn green, it would be possible for all vehicles to accelerate and begin driving once the signal turns green simultaneously, as each system can send and receive signals indicating their action, reducing traffic congestion as vehicles spend less time waiting (Grey, 2016). All devices connected to the IoT, even the simplest ones, are controlled by Electronic Control Units (ECUs). These ECUs are also present in CAVS and can connect to the vehicle network, mobile phones and the Internet. Although this greater communication can be beneficial such as by providing easier transfer of data and communication without human interaction, it also provides greater risk as a hacker which gains access to driver's mobile phone can then gain access to the connected vehicle network and install malware in every vehicle ECU and take control of every system function from the windshield wipers and radio, to steering and braking (Burzio et al., 2018). Such cyber attacks have been proven successful in penetrating protected environments, like banks, by first penetrating less secure, simple IoT systems such as air condition systems and moving laterally through the interconnected devices. Such insecure devices have given hackers the ability to establish the first foothold within a network which could be considered state-of-the-art and the concept easily transitions to a personal car and the driver's connected home devices.

14.3 FUTURE DEVELOPMENTS

From the development of self-driving cars to the development of IoT connected cars, the automotive industry still has a long way to go before a future where driving may be considered a thing of the past thanks to the introduction of level 5 fully autonomous vehicles. Many challenges lie in the path towards the success of CAVs, including the ever-looming danger of cybersecurity issues. However, future developments are currently being researched and implemented through testing, not only to develop the decision-making system to facilitate driving without user interaction in level 5 autonomy but also to develop a structurally secure system from cyber-attacks, one which can prevent attempted attacks and will not completely fail if an attack occurs.

One possible solution to the threat of criminals attempting to hack the information traded wirelessly between connected vehicles and the roadside infrastructure has been announced by South Korean (SK) Telecom. Previously, it was thought that the information transferred across VANET could not be encrypted due to the necessary speed required for the transfer of information to allow for the on-board decision-making systems to make split-second decisions. This unencrypted data posed a significant security threat should any malevolent entity attempt to steal this valuable data or supply incorrect information, however, Quantum Computing developed by SK Telecom and previously trialled by the US military may remove this issue. The solution is known as a "Quantum Security Gateway" and from the previous testing performed by the US military, is considered unhackable. According to SK Telecom, the solution is an "integrated security device that will be installed inside cars and protect various electronic units and networks in the vehicle" (Griffin, 2019). The gateway will transfer a quantum random-number generator and quantum key along with the vehicle's data ensuring that the vehicle is impossible to hack. Should any attempts to penetrate or intercept the vehicle's communication channels be detected, then the device will notify the driver and a central monitoring system. This technology was initially created to facilitate security in the 5G era but can now also be used to secure all vehicle systems, including Vehicle-2-Everything (V2X), Bluetooth communication systems, radar and driver assistance (Griffin, 2019; Soare, 2019).

Another latest technology which has the potential to provide long-term sustainability and higher operational efficiency, as well as enhancing data security, privacy, and authentication is Blockchain technology. According to a report by Fragma-Lamas and Fernández-Caramés (2019), "blockchain technology can offer a seamless decentralized platform where information about insurance, proof of ownership, patents, repairs, maintenance, and tangible/intangible assets can be securely recorded, tracked and managed". As blockchain is a decentralised storage system it can maintain confidentiality by preventing unauthorized access to vital information, as should one node in the storage system become compromised, the rest of the storage system will maintain normal operations as they are separate and uncompromised. Blockchain also boasts no single point of failure, in the event of a Denial of Service attack a cloud-centred database may become unavailable but, each full blockchain node contains a copy of the entire blockchain and can preserve network performance by blocking updates when a threat against a node is detected. The many advantages blockchain offers for privacy and security to CAVs and many other information storage systems make the architecture appear as an attractive solution to distribute cyber-resilient information, however, an objective evaluation must be made by organisations to determine if investing in blockchain technology is the optimum solution from an economic and cybersecurity standpoint or if alternative solutions are more appropriate (Fraga-Lamas and Fernández-Caramés, 2019).

With the advent of IoT technology, every device and system introduced to a self-driving car with a connection to the Internet or the ability to communicate with other intelligent software presents a possible entryway to malicious hackers. This presents a large constraint on the design and production of CAVs as each component must be certified as cyber-secure to confirm that the entire system is secure from penetration or is prepared to not fail upon a successful intrusion. To ensure such stringent requirements are met and maintained by organizations, especially if certain components are generic across the industry, security design standards must be introduced to keep up with the current level of technology and its modern threats. As of December 2018, the British Standard Institute produced and released a specification on the fundamental principles of automotive cybersecurity to set a marker for those developing in the industry. The aim of this standard should help ensure that systems are designed to be resilient to attacks and respond appropriately when defences fail, as confirmed by the UK Future of Mobility Minister Jesse Norman who stated: "This cybersecurity standard should help to improve the resilience and readiness of the industry and help keep the UK at the forefront of advancing transport technology" (Great Britain. Department for Transport, 2018). This work builds on top of the eight principles set out by the UK Government where it is stressed that cybersecurity must be at the forefront of future CAV design and must be properly considered at all levels, from designers and engineers to senior executives and suppliers (Great Britain. Department for Transport, 2017).

Future developments must be made toward the method of designing and engineering autonomous vehicles as the introduction of connectivity and connected vehicles has brought the need for a major change to the current engineering methods. The current "V" engineering method works well for bounded systems with known interactions and predictable functions, but as Kanr. (2016) have presented in their findings, "connectivity to complex systems within and beyond the vehicle, and the implementation of machine learning, both change the game entirely" as system scopes become unbounded with emergent functions from machine learning decision-making systems and unknowable interactions. As such, the previous method built to optimise the design of unconnected systems cannot readily support systems where it may be impossible to test all failure modules, as failing is now global and unpredictable; instead, we must focus on how best to fail rather than how not to fail at all. A successful attack against a connected system only needs to succeed once, after which point further attacks do not require an equal amount of expertise to exploit further connected systems as the first entry. kant (2016) outline that any new operating method for the design of connected vehicles must include three parameters:

- Monitor current operating state within "Safe Operating Area" versus known "Design Limit";
- Assess possible futures and select "Best Outcome";
- Deploy a "Mitigation Plan" with "Justifiable Confidence" of "Good Outcome".

14.4 CONCLUSION

Connected and Autonomous Vehicles hold great potential benefits for society, providing freedom of movement to the disadvantaged, boosting economies and helping to reduce incidents of severe crashes and loss of life due to human error. However, it is also clear that the more connected vehicles become, and the more systems involved with their function become exposed to the Internet and interconnected with other smart devices, then the opportunities for hacking and loss of data or possible terrorism and loss of life grow exponentially. With increasing investment into the technology, it is now more than ever that organisations must focus their efforts on ensuring cybersecurity as the rest of the world also updates to meet the fleet of the future.

The industry methodology for the development of connected vehicles must adapt as each entity in the chain of development is now responsible for the overall security of the vehicle. An increased level of penetration testing and validation for each component of systems may be necessary to ensure security is maintained and that each component is certified; a collaboration between companies may prove beneficial in this area as a race to be the first to produce a fully automated vehicle cannot be won by releasing an open doorway to your entire home for hackers. This requirement of security also falls into the concept of the Internet of Things and requires solutions such as quantum computing to ensure that our unsecured simple devices also do not present a risk to the function of important systems that should be considered secure. Following this need to certify that all components are cyber secure, the standards should not be left to companies alone, but countries must work in tandem with representatives and experts in the field to lay out regulations and standards for the future which are expected to ensure the safety of the public both physically and digitally.

REFERENCES

American Physical Society. 2019. *The first look at how hacked self-driving cars would affect New York City traffic.* Maryland: ScienceDaily. Available from: https://www.scienced aily.com/releases/2019/03/190304121519.htm [Accessed 14 November 2019].

Burzio, G., G. F. Cordella, M. Colajanni, M. Marchetti, and D. Stabili.2018. Cybersecurity of connected autonomous vehicles : A ranking based approach. In 2018 International Conference of Electrical and Electronic Technologies for Automotive, AUTOMOTIVE 2018, London, UK.

Car and Driver. 2017. *Path to autonomy: Self-driving car levels 0 to 5 explained.* Michigan: Car and Driver. Available from: https://www.caranddriver.com/features/a15079828/au tonomous-self-driving-car-levels-car-levels/ [Accessed 14 November 2019].

Fraga-Lamas, P., and T. M. Fernández-Caramés. 2019. A review on blockchain technologies for an advanced and cyber-resilient automotive industry. *IEEE Access*, 7, pp. 17578–17598.

Garakani, H.G., B. Moshiri, and S. Safavi-Naeini. 2018. Cyber security challenges in autonomous vehicle: Their impact on RF sensor and wireless technologies. In Proceedings—ANTEM 2018: 2018 18th International Symposium on Antenna Technology and Applied Electromagnetics, New York.

Great Britain. Department for Transport. 2017. *The key principles of cyber security for connected and automated vehicles.* London: UKDFT. Available from: https://assets.publishing.serv ice.gov.uk/government/uploads/system/uploads/attachment_data/file/661135/cyber-securi ty-connected-automated-vehicles-key-principles.pdf [Accessed 14 November 2019].

Great Britain. Department for Transport, Centre for Connected and Autonomous Vehicles, The Rt Hon Jesse Norman. 2018. *New cyber security standard for self-driving vehicles.* London: UKDFT. Available from: https://www.gov.uk/government/news/new-cyber-security-standard-for-self-driving-vehicles [Accessed 14 November 2019].

Grey, C. 2016. *The simple solution to traffic.* Available from: https://www.youtube.com/watch?v=iHzzSao6ypE [Accessed 14 November 2019].

Griffin, M. 2019. SK telecom launches quantum encryption gateway "to make self-driving cars unhackable". *Fanatical futurist.* 12 March. Available from: https://www.fanaticalfuturist.com/2019/03/sk-telecom-launches-quantum-encryption-gateway-to-make-self-driving-cars-unhackable/ [Accessed 14 November 2019].

Kant, V. 2019. Cyber-physical systems as sociotechnical systems: a view towards human–technology interaction. *Cyber-Physical Systems,* 2:1–4: 75–109, doi: 10.1080/23335777.2017.1289983 UK.

Madan, B. B., M. Banik, and D. Bein. 2019. Securing unmanned autonomous systems from cyber threats. *Journal of Defense Modeling and Simulation,* 16(2), pp. 119–136.

Mast Technologies. 2011. *MAST Applications automotive*[image]. Available from: http://www.masttechnologies.com/wp-content/uploads/2011/06/MAST-Applications-Automotive.jpg [Accessed 14 November 2019].

Mohd, T.K., S. Majumdar, A. Mathur, and A. Y. Javaid. 2018. Simulation and analysis of DDoS attack on connected autonomous vehicular network using OMNET++. In 2018 9th IEEE Annual Ubiquitous Computing, Electronics and Mobile Communication Conference, UEMCON 2018 (pp. 502–508). [Accessed 15 October 2019].

Moysa, G., and M. Koczerginski. 2016. *The cybersecurity implications of driverless cars.* Toronto: McMillan LLP. Available from: https://www.mcmillan.ca/Files/196067_The_Cybersecurity_Implications_of_Driverless_Cars.pdf [Accessed 14 November 2019].

NHTSA (National Highway Traffic Safety Administration). 2017. *Society of automotive engineers (sae) automation levels* [image]. Washington, DC: NHTSA. Available from: https://www.nhtsa.gov/sites/nhtsa.dot.gov/files/styles/paragraphs_image_crop/public/nhtsa_sae_automation_levels.png?itok=0GsCp1em [Accessed 14 November 2019].

SMMT (The Society of Motor Manufacturers and Traders Ltd). 2015. *Connected and autonomous vehicles: The UK economic opportunity.* London: SMMT. [Accessed 14 November 2019].

SMMT (The Society of Motor Manufacturers and Traders Ltd). 2017. *Connected and autonomous vehicles: Revolutionising mobility in society.* London: SMMT. Available from: https://www.smmt.co.uk/wp-content/uploads/sites/2/Connected-and-Autonomous-Vehicles-Revolutionising-Mobility-in-Society.pdf [Accessed 14 November 2019].

Soare, B. 2019. Are hackers threatening the adoption of self-driving cars? *Heimdal security.* 5 April. Available from: https://heimdalsecurity.com/blog/hackers-self-driving-cars/ [Accessed 14 November 2019].

Vivek, S., D. Yanni, P. Yunker, and J. Silverberg. 2019. Cluster comb[image]. Available from: https://manhattan-hackedvehicles.herokuapp.com/static/img/cluster-comb.png [Accessed 14 November 2019].

Weimerskirch, A., and D. Dominic. 2018. *Assessing risk: Identifying and analyzing cybersecurity threats to automated vehicles.* Michigan: Mcity. Available from: https://mcity.umich.edu/wp-content/uploads/2017/12/Mcity-white-paper_cybersecurity.pdf [Accessed 14 November 2019].

Wired. 2015. *Hackers remotely kill a jeep on a highway | WIRED.* Boone, IA: Wired. Available from: https://www.youtube.com/watch?v=MK0SrxBC1xs&feature=emb_title [Accessed 14 November 2019].

15 Trust-Aware Crowd Associated Network-Based Approach for Optimal Waste Management in Smart Cities

Choy Kok Han, Ali Safaa Sadiq, Seyedali Mirjalili and Mohammed Adam Taheir

CONTENTS

15.1   INTRODUCTION

The Internet of Things (IoT) is a recent communication paradigm that envisions a near future, in which things are commonly used in a daily life. These things are representing sensors that are integrated with microcontrollers, transceivers for digital communication and protocol stack that helps the objects/things to have the ability to communicate with one another as well as with the users, becoming an integral part of the Internet [1]. In short, any thing that can be connected to the Internet and controlled from devices that are lying behind an Internet Protocol (IP) address would be part of the wide network named IoT.

Nowadays, waste management has been an issue for many years especially in cities that are densely populated. Inefficient waste management will cause overflowing garbage bins, which will cause harm to the environment leading human health to deteriorate. An example of inefficient waste management is the current system where the garbage collector follows a fixed route to collect garbage from streets and houses on a fixed time and day based on a predefined schedule [2]. This is not efficient due to the fact that the garbage bin will be eventually left unattended for an amount of time until the garbage collector comes for the collection in the next appointed date and time. During the time, there will be a possibility where more and more garbage accumulated, which will cause the overflowing of the dustbin. Moreover, the conventional collection system is inefficient, since there will be scenarios where some of the garbage bins will not reach a proper collection level, but the garbage collector still collects them, as it is part of their routine. This will cause a waste of fuel and time that will need to be covered by the waste management authorities. This could be avoided when the garbage collector obtains a verified genuine notification from the smart garbage bin only when it gets a proper amount of waste, additionally will be provided with the shortest path to the garbage bin as an application of Smart-City-based-IoT technology.

15.2   RELATED WORK AND PROBLEM DEFINITIONS

Many researchers have proposed several solutions to manage the problems associated with garbage management. For instance, the authors [3] have designed an intelligent solid waste bin that collects data in real time. The intelligent solid waste bin was integrated with various sensors to obtain the actual fill level of the smart bin. The authors have also used a decision algorithm for their monitoring application to sense solid waste data. However, the authors' proposed work only focuses on the design of the bin without including discussion on optimizing the cost of garbage collection.

On the other hand, the authors [4] proposed a system where the Smart Waste M3 platform is adopted for Smart Waste Management. The Smart M3 platform is an open source project that allows different entities to share information and also cooperate in a transparent way to the heterogeneities of different sensory data [4]. By doing so the proposed platform could interconnect heterogeneous devices and sharing data with a large number of people. The authors also integrated two sensors, which is the proximity sensor and the weight sensor attached to the garbage bin for real-time monitoring. The author shows several simulations with a map full and half-full garbage bin, besides the garbage collectors were sent to collect the assigned waste bins within a specified region. Though the system lacks of scheduling and routing facilities that should be available for the garbage collector, which supports the advancement of Smart Cities.

As another attempt by the authors [5], an objective was stated to minimize the total collection's accumulated distance. In the beginning, the authors addressed the issues of solid waste transportation issue in Chennai city at India. Thus, the authors have suggested using the Geographic Information System (GIS) application and Dijkstra algorithm to identify the optimal routes for 13 selected garbage bins out of total 200 garbage bins. By doing so, the proposed solution was able to reduce waste collection distance, thus reducing the time and cost. However, their proposed method did not consider the possibility of fake-shared information that could lead to overwhelming the entire system.

In contrast, another related system has been proposed by [6] where the Radio-frequency identification (RFID) and other communication technologies such as Global Positioning System (GPS), GIS and GSM/GRPS digital cellular are integrated into the garbage bin as well as the truck for real-time tracking and waste monitoring. The RFID tag is attached to the garbage bin while the RFID reader is attached to the garbage collector truck. The reading process converts radio waves emitted by the waste bin into digital information. The garbage bin is also equipped with a camera to detect the level of the garbage bin. The system would capture an image of the garbage when the garbage collector is within the vicinity of the garbage bin. Nevertheless, the proposed system does not obtain in real time the bin's status data, thus it solely depends on the historical data to estimate the actual content of the garbage bin. The authors also did not discuss the scheduling and routing for the garbage collection's process.

While the authors in [7] have proposed a quite similar system to the one in [6], they integrated RFID, GPS and GRPS into the garbage bin and truck. The difference is that the garbage bin is equipped with different sensors and the weighing sensor has been equipped on the vehicle to detect the loaded waste so that they could detect the available capacity of the vehicle instantly. The authors introduced a new heuristic routing model, which consists of Saving methods, Sweep algorithm, Nearest neighbor and tabu search.

On the other hand, [8] authors proposed a solution that developed a wireless sensor network, which consists of three-tier architectures. The garbage bin in this system is integrated with several sensors such as temperature, weight and humidity sensors. The data collected by the sensors would be delivered to the servers by using GSM / GRPS. The control station will continuously analyse the received data and update the garbage bin's information. A web-based program is run on the server to manage the data and also monitor the status of the garbage bin, the program allows users to monitor the bin status. The authors considered the minimum energy consumption and less operation cost by avoiding GRPS in every bin. Yet, the authors did not consider any third-party involvement, which could help in reporting or passing on information of waste's location and quantity from areas where network coverage does not exist within a Smart City.

In order to address the aforementioned challenge of the availability of network infrastructure, authors [9] proposed an efficient infrastructure-less network called crowd-associated network that uses a set of crowds to fill in communication gaps among the components. They have called their crowd volunteer agent while relaying data from a component to others component until it reaches its destination. The author focuses on reducing the cost of deployment and maintenance cost of the infrastructure. The genetic algorithm was applied in this article to find a feasible trade-off between distance and cost. However, the authors did not consider the authenticity of the data sent by the suggested volunteer agent. Since the data is not verified, a malicious volunteer agent might send fake data into the network, which might cause garbage collectors to go a further distance to collect fake reported garbage bins. Table 15.1 shows a list of related work along with their main features.

From the given discussion on the related work within this section, the main objective of our study is to propose a trust-aware crowd associated network-based approach that computes an optimum path for the garbage collector when the garbage bin is filled. In the following section, we will explain the key concept of crowd-associated network to provide the readers with a brief background on its functionality.

15.2.1 CROWD ASSOCIATED NETWORK

A set of crowds that plays a significant role in filling the communication gaps with others associate and becomes an inseparable part in the network is called Crowd Associated Network (CrAN). In CrAN, there are two kinds of components; a dedicated agent and a non-dedicated agent. The dedicated agent is where components are installed in the network to perform a specific task. These types of agents are fixed in a place and would exchange information with the non-dedicated agent to achieve its goal. Whereas, for the crowd that is a non-dedicated agent, agents act as an intermediate relay within proposed network architecture. The non-dedicated agents would retrieve data from the dedicated agents and deliver the data to the other dedicated agents. The non-dedicated agents may also exchange information within themselves to increase the chances of the data reaching the dedicated agents and increase its performance. A side note is that anyone can be part of the crowd if they comply with the network requirement. Those that are interested to be part of the crowd would be given a network component to be installed in their vehicles. We will refer in this chapter to the crowd as volunteer agent (VA) as the crowd is volunteering themselves to be part of the network. In the Crowd Associated Network, there will be five main components: smart garbage bin, volunteer agents, Access Point (AP), control centre and garbage collector. The joint effort of these components will allow necessary data to be delivered and also compute an optimum path.

15.3 PROPOSED METHOD

In this section, the overview of our proposed method will be demonstrated in addition to the network architecture, data transmission method, the waste collection route optimization algorithm, simulation setup and evaluation method.

TABLE 15.1
Related Works with their Features

Related Article	Technique used for Garbage Measurement	Garbage Level Measurement	Weight of the Garbage Measurement	Scheduling and Routing Consideration	Method for Routing Solution	Third Party Involvement
[3]	Ultrasonic sensor	Yes	Yes	No	-	None
[4]	Proximity Sensor	Yes	Yes	No	-	Human
[6]	Image Processing	Yes	No	No	-	None
[7]	Ultrasonic	Yes	No	Yes	A heuristicrouting model consist of (Saving methods, Sweep algorithm, Nearest neighbour and tabu	Human
[5]	-	-	-	Yes	Dijkstra Algorithm	None
[8]	Sensors	Yes	Yes	No	-	None
[9]	Sensors	Yes	-	No	-	Volunteer Agents
My Project	Ultrasonic	Yes	Yes	Yes	Dijkstra Algorithm	Volunteer Agents

15.3.1 Overview

This project requires a smart waste garbage bin (SGB) to be implemented in Smart Cities to monitor the level of rubbish of the garbage bin. The SGB will be embedded with multiple sensors to measure the weight and level of the garbage bin. In the SGB, there will be an IoT device that has the ability to acquire the information of the SGB and transmit the information to nearby associates, which is mainly VA. Once the level and weight of the garbage bin reach a certain threshold, the SGB would generate Data packets that contain the information of the garbage bin and start sending them to VAs that are within the range. VA that receives the data packets will then relay the data to other associates until it reaches its destination, which is the AP. After that, the recipient AP would forward the data packets to the Control Centre (CC) for further processing. Once the CC receives that data, it will process the data packets and store them accordingly. When a certain number of garbage bins is ready to be collected, the CC would compute the shortest path to all the garbage bins then send it to the garbage collector agent to collect the garbage in an efficient manner. At the end of the trip, the garbage collector agent can rate the VAs that have been involved in delivering the information to the CC. The rating system is created to avoid false data being created by a malicious VA. The higher the rating means the more trustable the data is while the lower rating data send by the VA would not be trusted. Thus, when a data packet sent by a VA that has low rating reached the CC it will be discarded instantly and a retrack process will be taken to identify such VA; hence CC would be able to filter out the data that is received by VAs. For an easier understanding of how data is passed, Figure 15.1 displays the scenario of how data flows.

15.3.2 Network Architecture

The network architecture of the proposed system is displayed in Figure 15.2. It is clear that our proposed architecture has been separated into two phases. Phase 1 is

FIGURE 15.1   Scenario of how Data Pass over Proposed Architecture

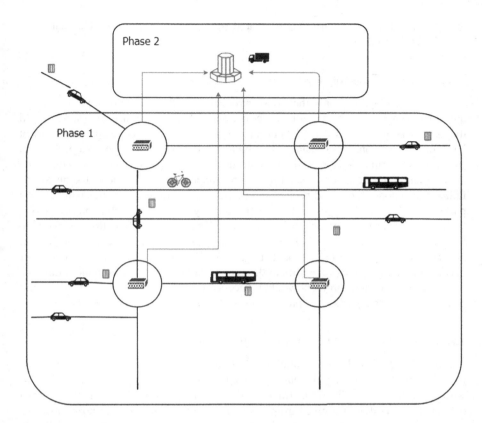

FIGURE 15.2   General Two-tier Architecture Implementation

mostly about collecting data from the access plane of the reported waste spots within a Smart City, while phase 2 is involved in data processing and computing the shortest path for the Garbage Collector. The overviews phase 1 is that the smart garbage bin that is placed on the roadside to ease the collection process. The smart garbage bin that connected to the IoT network would then acquire the status of the garbage bin and generate waste Data packets. Waste data packets would then be gathered by any passing VA. VAs could be a smart public bus, smart cars, a pedestrian or a cyclist holding a connected smart phone. The VAs would keep exchange this data to others VA (as a relay-hop) until one of the VAs could successfully deliver the data packets to the nearest available AP. Eventually, the AP would deliver the received waste data packets to the CC for further processing them to be used by the next phase 2.

Thus, we move to the second phase, which is the data processing. After receiving waste data packets from the recipient AP, the CC would then process the data packet and store them in the buffer; it is worth mentioning that the old data would be overwritten by the new data to maintain data storage. Afterwards, the optimal route as a solution will be computed and would then be sent to the garbage collector to collect garbage in an efficient way. When the garbage collector finishes collecting all the garbage it would then return to the CC and send packets back to the CC that it has finished collecting the garbage.

15.3.3 DATA TRANSMISSION

In the proposed system, only the smart garbage bin will generate data packets while the other component acts as an intermediate relay data points carrying packets until they reach the nearest AP. The data packets would have the garbage bin measurement level and its location. It is crucial to highlight that if sending a single data packet that carries this information there will be a high chance that the data packet would not reach its destination whenever this packet has been dropped by any reason of the network's failure. Therefore, duplicated packets would be sent out to increase the chance of the packet reaching the AP. This will be applied also by all relay VAs that intermediating the transmission process from the SGB to the distained AP. Thus, the VA needs to have a routing capability. As has been suggested by [9] a replication-based protocol will be used. As the name of the protocol suggests, it will replicate data packets whenever needed and increase the probability of the data packet to reach its destination. Lastly, a medium access control protocol would be needed on the entire component to transmit and receive the data packet and provide connectivity to the IoT wide network.

15.3.4 WASTE COLLECTION ROUTE OPTIMIZATION

For optimizing the collection route, the Dijkstra algorithm has been utilised to compute the optimum path for the entire garbage bins that are reported to be collected within a given Smart City. Dijkstra algorithm is an algorithm that finds the shortest path between nodes in a given graph. It is also known as dynamic programming. Dijkstra is known as a greedy algorithm as it will not visit an edge that has already been visited, which is what we want in our case. Figure 15.3 shows the main steps of Dijkstra Algorithm in the form of pseudocode.

```
1 Initialise the cost of each node to infinity;nDistance
2 Initialise the cost of the source to zero;nPrevious
3 While there are still unknown nodes that are left in
the graph:
4     Select the nodes with the lowest cost; b
5     Mark the nodes as taken
6     For each node;a which is adjacent to b
7          dist = nDistance + edge (b,a)'s weight
8          if dist is smaller than a's distance
9               a's distance would be nDistance
10              a's previous would be b
```

FIGURE 15.3 Dijkstra Pseudocode

15.3.4.1 Algorithm Flowchart (Figure 15.4)

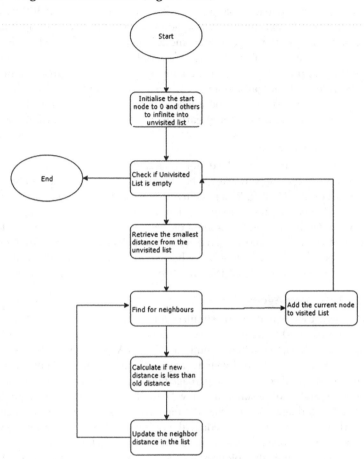

FIGURE 15.4 Waste Collection Flowchart using Dijkstra Algorithm

15.3.5 SIMULATION SETUP

To show a proof of concept, we have conducted a simulation based on our proposed framework. The simulation was carried on using Netlogo a multi-agent programmable modeling environment, for more details of simulated model; readers can refer to Appendixes A1 and A2. The simulation consists of three main agents, which are the garbage bin, garbage truck and volunteer agents. We would first generate a graph with *n* number of vertices. In the graph, each turn in a road is a node while the edge is the roads. Measurements graphs have been generated to show the amount of cost and waste collected for each sequence. An output will also be included for a better view of the collected data. The cost and waste collected by the garbage truck would be extracted into a ".cvs" format from the Netlogo system.

15.3.5.1 Garbage Bin

The garbage bin has a capacity parameter with a maximum level of 100 waste units. In this simulation, 25 bins have been assigned to a city with a random amount of garbage level at the beginning stage of the simulation. When a garbage level is less than or equal to 50, the colour of the garbage bin would be grey, whilst the bin load getting more than 50 the colour will then change to yellow and finally when it is more than 80 the colour of the garbage bin will beset to red; indicating it is ready to be collected. We have annotated all these legends and values on the developed simulation GUI, which shows the amount of garbage bin to be monitored till it reaches full.

15.3.5.2 Garbage Truck

The garbage truck would start at the depot created in the simulation. The garbage truck would follow the optimum path that has been computed to collect the garbage bins that are almost full or already full. When the truck passes a bin with red colour, the colour of the garbage bin will be rested to grey colour and the level of the garbage bin will be set to zero. In our simulation, the amount of load that a truck can carry would be to a constant value of "1". Total cost per trip can be calculated by calculating the distance between all the nodes. The weight links between the garbage bins would act as the distance and we assume it takes 0.15 to reach from one garbage bin to another.

15.3.5.3 Volunteer Agent

A volunteer agent is created in this simulation to relay data to the CC. The VA has a rating percentage of 100; the percentage could change depending on the rating given by garbage truck. In our developed simulation, the VAs are classified into two kinds, genuine and fake agents. The bad volunteer agents would try to send fake data that lead to changing the original colour of the garbage bins to a different colour, which indicates the status of the SGB. For instance, a yellow SGB: the bad VA would change the colour to red. Once the garbage truck reaches the reported SGB and realizes it is actually not full, the garbage truck then would reduce the rating of the VA. Accordingly, when the rating of the volunteer agent is less than 60, the VA will no longer be able to send data packets that would change the colour of the garbage bin, followed by a re-tracking process will be triggered by the CC. Hence, the VA will be no longer trusted, and data sent by the untrusted volunteer agent will not be taken into consideration as the agent will be removed from the crowd associated network. While the good VAs will keep sending genuine data of the SGBs and an incentive reword will be applied after a defined number of trusted reported garbage locations and volume around the Smart City.

In netlogo, an existing library called the *"nw:extension"* has been utilised to integrate Dijkstra algorithm to perform the shortest path calculation. It is important to note that there is a limitation in using *"nw:extension"*, which only computes the shortest path between two nodes. This is insufficient in our case as we have lots of garbage bins, thus some improvising is needed. To begin, we first had to create all possible paths by using a permutation process. From there onwards, we find the shortest path of each node to another node by using *"nw-turtles-weighted-path-to"*. *"Nw-turtles-weighted-path-to"* is a primitive in the *nw* extension; it returns the shortest path between the source and the target turtle. Finally, the path with the least

```
1 List of all possible path in a list
2 while list is not empty
3     Assign the first node in the list to a variable
4     Assign the second node in the list to a variable
5     Get shortest path from first node to second node
      using nw:turtles-on-weighted-path-to
6     Put the path in a list
7      Remove first node from the path list
```

FIGURE 15.5   Improvised Pseudocode for in Netlogo

weight needed will be returned to complete the path calculation. Figure 15.5 shows our improvised pseudocode of "*nw:turtles-on-weighted-path-to*".

15.3.6 EVALUATION

The evaluation will be done by comparing the cost of a collection vehicle and the total amount of garbage collected per sequence with the old setup where the garbage truck would collect every garbage bin at a scheduled time. Moreover, comparison will be done with bad VA, to see how an untrusted agent can affect the distance needed for the garbage truck to collect the reported bins. For simulation purposes, we will not ignore the data sent by untrusted volunteer agents to see how it affects the accumulated cost. The old cost path will be also calculated by assuming the garbage truck will stop at each garbage bin as shown in Figure 15.6, without the existence of the smart setup of SGB.

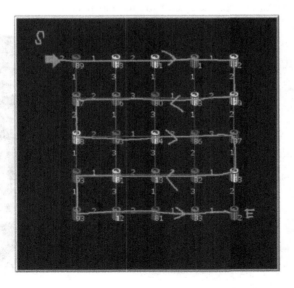

FIGURE 15.6   The Path an Old Garbage Truck Will Take

15.4   RESULTS AND DISCUSSION

The implementation of the simulation with Netlogo for waste monitoring and optimal route selection for waste collection will be verified by running several simulations. The initial setup of the program will have 25 bins located randomly in a city and a volunteer agent placed between two bins. All the bins will have a random level of garbage generated and their colour changes according to the provided condition. The VA can be a good volunteer agent or a bad volunteer agent. The monitor would provide the amount of garbage bin that is full. When the go button is clicked the "*ShortestPathNeeded*" monitor would show the amount of distance and time of the shortest path needed to collect all the red SGBs. Thus, the garbage truck will move towards allocated SGBs until the entire red garbage bins have been collected.

This can be seen in Figure 15.7; after finishing collection, the garbage truck goes back to the depot and waits for six or more garbage bins that are ready for collection. For every tick (minute), a random value within a scale of 0 to 3 will be added into the garbage bin. Each time it finishes collecting the SGBs, the total cost as well as total amount of collected waste during that cycle would be captured and plotted on the respective graph to demonstrate the performance in real time. When it detects that six or more SGBs are full, a new vehicle will be sent out to collect them. This will continue until the "GO" button is pressed again. For the following simulation, this process will continue in three scenarios. Each scenario will run five times, each time the program will run within an average of four to five hours. The total collected data per time is around 1,500–2,000. The data collected during the five runs are exported to excel sheet and a nova single factor is used to find the average of the five data samples. This is to validate and verify the data of our simulation and ensure reliability. Figure 15.7 displays when setup has been clicked, while Figure 15.8 demonstrates the simulation when the "GO" button has been clicked.

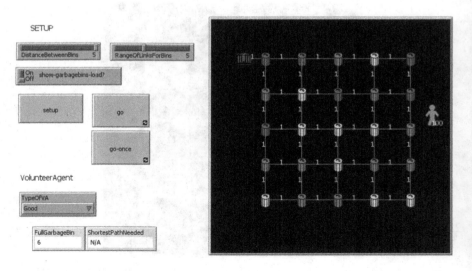

FIGURE 15.7   Initial Setup for Waste Monitoring and Collection in Netlogo

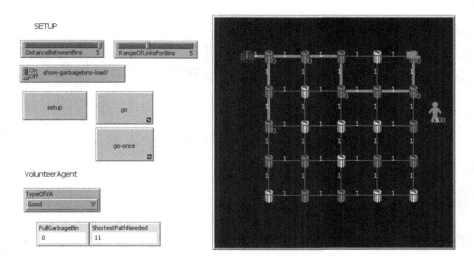

FIGURE 15.8   Optimal Path for Waste Collection to Six Readied Bins and Colour Changes when Collected

The first scenario would represent the most basic initial setup. This can be seen in Figure 15.6.

The next scenario will increase the number of garbage bins in the simulation. This can be seen in Figure 15.13.

The final scenario consists of multiple paths available for the garbage truck to move, which can be seen in Figure 15.18.

From the performance analysis of the three simulated scenarios, it can be observed that our proposed solution could maintain less cost in collecting the entire SGBs, as compare to the old way of collection. Moreover, in terms of the amount of weight that a truck could carry, our proposed solution could maintain the garbage truck with an average weight without overloading the garbage as compared with the old way of collection. This is due to the fact that using Dijkstra algorithm, the garbage truck would obtain the computed shortest path to all SGBs beforehand is send out for collection. Thus, the cost needed to collect the garbage bins is substantially reduced as can be seen from the results collected out of three simulated scenarios in Figures 15.9, 15.10, 15.14, 15.15, 15.19, 15.20 and 15.21, accordingly. The other reason behind this improvement was that our proposed method only sent out the garbage truck when six or more SGBs are full (red colour) within a given segment of the Smart City. By doing so, the amount of garbage within each truck will not be overloaded and this also reduces the time the SGB is left full. From Figures 15.10, 15.15 and 15.20, when data packets sent by VAs are not filtered out, this will contribute negatively in increase the cost of travel of the garbage trucks as they have to go a further distance to collect fake reported SGBs. Thus, the results show how important it is to filter out fake data when a fake VA is discovered, which has been achieved in our proposed method by applying the trust mechanism on each VA.

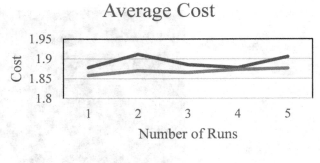

FIGURE 15.9 Average Cost for Scenario 1 in Comparison with Genuine and Fake VAs

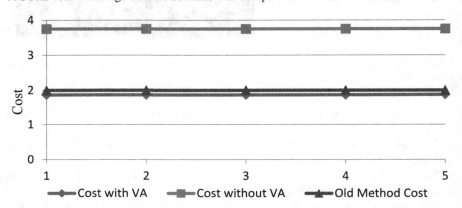

FIGURE 15.10 Average Cost for Scenario 1 in Comparison with Old Method

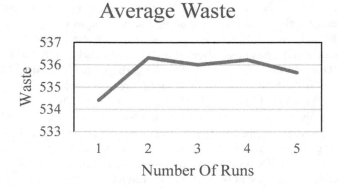

FIGURE 15.11 Average Waste for Scenario 1

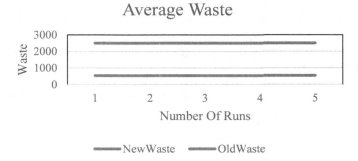

FIGURE 15.12   Average Waste for Scenario 1 in Comparison with Old Method

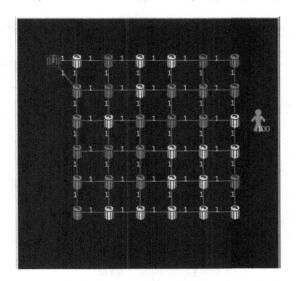

FIGURE 15.13   Scenario 2 with More Garbage Bins

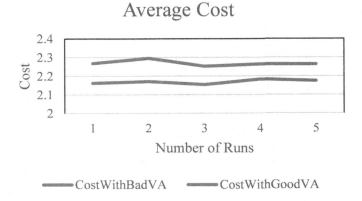

FIGURE 15.14   Average Cost for Scenario 2 in Comparison with Good VA and Bad VA

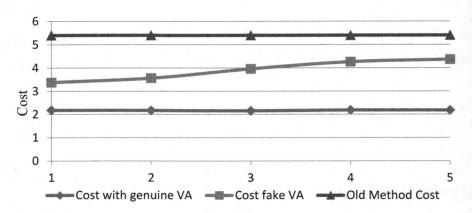

FIGURE 15.15 Average Cost for Scenario 2 in Comparison with Old Method

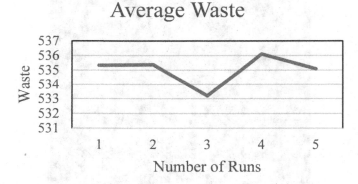

FIGURE 15.16 Average Waste for Scenario 2

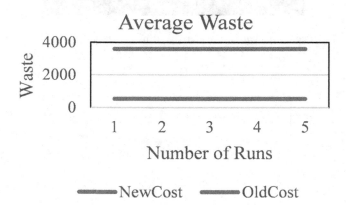

FIGURE 15.17 Average Waste for Scenario 2 in Comparison with Old Method

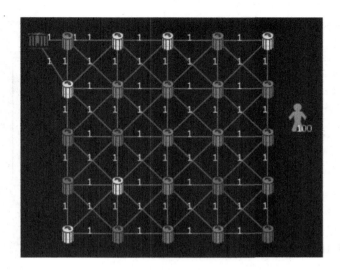

FIGURE 15.18 Scenario 3 with Multiple Paths

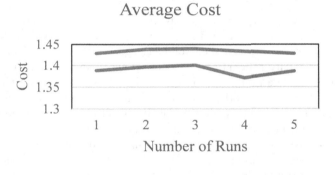

FIGURE 15.19 Average Cost for Scenario 3 in Comparison with Good VA and Bad VA

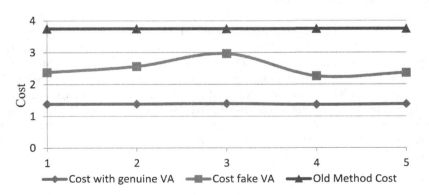

FIGURE 15.20 Average Cost for Scenario 3 in Comparison with Old Method

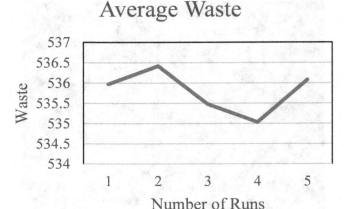

FIGURE 15.21　Average Cost for Scenario 3

15.5　CONCLUSION AND FUTURE WORK

In this chapter, we have proposed a trust mechanism based on crowd associated architecture as it utilizes the crowd as part of the IoT network within the proposed architecture. A set of crowds (called volunteer agents) who collect data from smart garbage bins and deliver them to other volunteer agents in a multi-hope based communication till the data would reach its destination, which is the nearest access point that is connected to the network infrastructure. The access point would then forward the data to the control centre. After receiving the data from various sources, at a later time, the control centre will compute an optimum path for the garbage collector in order to reduce the cost of fuel as well as time in collecting garbage by reducing the travel distance. We have used Dijkstra algorithm to find the shortest path to all the reported SGBs as full. To prove the concept of our proposed architecture, we have conducted an extensive simulation with three scenarios, and it has been shown that the proposed solution could indeed reduce the cost needed to collect SGBs within the simulated Smart City segment.

Many aspects can be improved in the proposed solution, which has been left for future work to be further considered. An option for future work is applying a more developed mathematical model for route optimization such as modern meta-heuristic algorithms for fasting the process of finding more feasible solutions. In future work, we could also apply a decision making algorithm to decide the amount / volume of garbage that each truck could collect based on the amount of garbage a truck can carry and the total amount of garbage that has been reported as full. Lastly, a decision algorithm that will filter out data sent by low-rating volunteer agents, so when computing optimum path, the system will proactively avoid taking the fake data into consideration.

APPENDICES

A1: Internal Design Detail

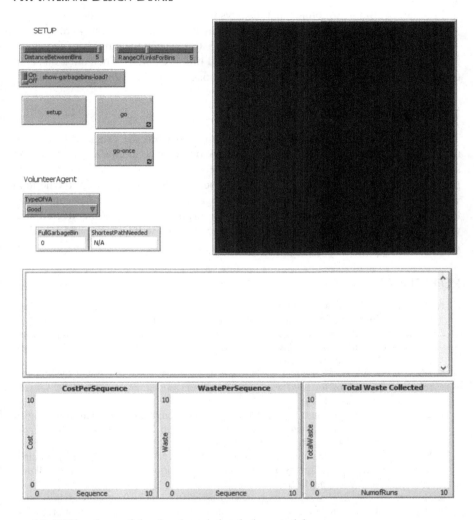

A2: Diffinations of the developed simulation model.

DistanceBetweenBins – To determine the distance between the garbage bins, the lesser the range the more number of garbage bin will appear in the setup

RangeOfLinksForBins – To determine the range of links between bins, which means only bins within range of 5 will form a link.

Show-garbagebins-load? – If on you can see the amount of garbage in the bin if off you can only see colour

Setup – To display the agents in the world

Go – The simulation will loop forever until the go button is press again

Go-once – The simulation will only run once, to show how the program works

TypeOfVA – To change the kind of volunteer agent that will appear in the simulation

FullGarbageBin – A monitor that displays the amount of garbage bin that is full

ShortestPathNeeded – A monitor that display the length of shortest path

The output box will display the amount of waste, cost and the number of sequence.

To run the program, set the range of bin and links you want. Then click on setup to display the agents. Finally click on go or go-once to run the program.

Test Report

To test the correctness of the netlogo program, first open the program and select the parameter of the range between bins. Click on go-once to check if it shows the shortest path, click GO so that it runs forever. To collect the data for this project, the program is set to run for three to four hours. There might be times where the netlogo will output an error says the memory is too large. This is because, it has run for too long, thus restarting the program will solve the problem. Finally, the collected data will be exported in a ".csv" format to excel. The five data will be taken and calculate its average by using a nova single factor.

REFERENCES

1. Zanella, A., N. Bui, A. Castellani, L. Vangelista, & M. Zorzi. 2012. Internet of things for smart cities. *IEEE Internet of Things Journal*, 1(1), pp. 22–32.
2. Benjamin, A., & J. Beasley. 2010. Metaheuristics for the waste collection vehicle routing problem with time windows, driver rest period and multiple disposal facilities. *Elseview*, 37(12), pp. 2270–2280.
3. Mamun, M. A., M. A. Hannan, A. Hussain, & H. Basri. 2015. Integrated sensing systems and algorithms for solid waste bin state management automation. *IEEE Sensors Journal*, 15(1), pp. 561–567.
4. Catania, V., & D. Ventura. 2014. An approch for monitoring and smart planning of urban solid waste management using smart-M3 platform. *The 15th Conference of Fruct Association* (pp. 24–31). St. Petersburg: IEEE.
5. Sanjeevi, V., & P. Shahabudeen. 2016. Optimal routing for efficient municipal solid waste transportation by using ArcGIS application in Chennai, India. *Waste Management*, 34(1), pp. 11–21.
6. Hannan, M., M. Arebay, R. Begum, & H. Basri. 2011. Radio frequency identification (RFID) and communication technologies for solid waste bin and truck monitoring system. *Waste Management*, 31(12), pp. 2406–2413.
7. Faccio, M., A. Persona, G. Zanin. 2011. Waste collection multi objective model with real time traceability data. *Waste Management*, 31(12), pp. 2391–2405.
8. Mamun, M. A., M. A. Hannan, A. Hussain, & H. Basri. 2013. Wireless sensor network prototype for solid waste bin monitoring with energy efficient sensing algorithm. *IEEE 16th International Conference on Computational Science and Engineering* (pp. 382–387). IEEE.
9. Azad, S., A. Rahman, A. T. Asyhari, & A.-S. K. Pathan. 2017. Crowd associated network: Exploiting over a smart garbage management system. *IEEE Communication Magazine*, 55(7), pp. 186–192.

Index

Printed in the United States
By Bookmasters